Education in the Moral Domain

Education in the Moral Domain brings together the results of twenty-five years of research on the domain theory of social cognitive development. On the basis of that research – which shows that morality is a domain distinct from other social values – the author provides concrete suggestions for creating a moral class-room climate, dealing with student discipline and integrating moral values within the curriculum.

Among questions addressed are the following: Is morality a set of rules we acquire like any other? Are there universal aspects to morality, or is it culture specific? Is there such a thing as moral character? How best can teachers make use of our knowledge about children's moral and social growth in their every-day classroom practices?

Integrated answers to these questions result in a comprehensive approach that does not reduce moral education to a process of induction or inculcation, but rather harnesses children's intrinsic motivation to comprehend and master their social worlds.

Larry P. Nucci is Professor of Education and Psychology at the University of Illinois at Chicago, where he is also director of the Office for Studies in Moral Development and Character Formation. He is editor of *Moral Development and Character Education: A Dialogue,* and he is coeditor of *Culture, Thought, and Development* (with Geoffrey Saxe and Elliot Turiel).

Education in the Moral Domain

LARRY P. NUCCI

University of Illinois at Chicago

CAMBRIDGE
UNIVERSITY PRESS

PUBLISHED BY THE PRESS SYNDICATE OF THE UNIVERSITY OF CAMBRIDGE
The Pitt Building, Trumpington Street, Cambridge, United Kingdom

CAMBRIDGE UNIVERSITY PRESS
The Edinburgh Building, Cambridge CB2 2RU, UK
40 West 20th Street, New York, NY 10011-4211, USA
10 Stamford Road, Oakleigh, VIC 3166, Australia
Ruiz de Alarcón 13, 28014 Madrid, Spain
Dock House, The Waterfront, Cape Town 8001, South Africa

http://www.cambridge.org

© Cambridge University Press 2001

First published 2001

Printed in the United States of America

Typefaces Palatino 9.75/13 pt. and Optima   *System* QuarkXPress 4.01 [AG]

Library of Congress Cataloging in Publication Data

Nucci, Larry P.
    Education in the moral domain / Larry Nucci.
        p. cm.
    Includes bibliographical references.
    ISBN 0-521-65232-4 – ISBN 0-521-65549-8 (pb)
        1. Moral education. 2. Personality development. 3. Education – Aims and objectives. I.
    Title.
    LC268.N83 2001
    370.11′4–dc21   00-059880

ISBN 0 521 65232 4 hardback
ISBN 0 521 65549 8 paperback

In loving memory of my father,

Salvatore Nucci

Contents

Foreword by Elliot Turiel		*page* ix
Acknowledgments		xv
Introduction		xvii

PART ONE. THE NATURE OF MORALITY AND THE
DEVELOPMENT OF SOCIAL VALUES

1	**Morality and Domains of Social Knowledge**	3
2	**Morality and Religious Rules**	20
3	**Morality and the Personal Domain**	52
4	**Morality in Context: Issues of Development**	76
5	**Morality in Context: Issues of Culture**	94
6	**Morality and Emotion**	107
7	**Reconceptualizing Moral Character**	124

PART TWO. CLASSROOM APPLICATIONS

8	**Creating a Moral Atmosphere**	141
9	**Integrating Values Education into the Curriculum: A Domain Approach**	169
10	**Fostering the Moral Self**	196
	Conclusion: Keeping Things in Perspective	215

Additional Resources		217
References		219
Index of Names		237
Index of Subjects		240

Foreword

Engaging in education in the moral domain is hard to fault. Almost everyone agrees that it should be done, that it must be done. Most everyone wants the children of their society to be, at least, guided in the process of becoming less aggressive, less violent, more altruistic, more fair, more charitable, more civil, and much more. To be sure, some have argued that education in the moral domain is not appropriate for schools because it should be left to the family and/or religious training. Regardless of where it occurs, educating children morally is generally considered good, virtuous, and a necessity.

Beyond the general agreement that children should be educated morally, there has been, and continues to be, a great deal of controversy and debate over how it should be conducted. These debates are often intense and emotional, to the point that it is argued that certain types of moral education should not occur at all because, it is thought, they can do more harm than good. In the early part of the twentieth century, the debate included two very influential social-scientific thinkers, Emile Durkheim and Jean Piaget. Each presented elaborate and well-articulated views representing two sides of the issue.

For Durkheim, an eminent sociologist, moral education occurs most effectively in schools where children can participate in groups more formal and less flexible than the family. Through participation in group life, children form an emotional attachment to society, coming to respect its rules, norms, and authority. Children also form what Durkheim referred to as a spirit of discipline, needed to control behavior and channel it into societal expectations.

For Piaget, an eminent psychologist, Durkheim's approach was lacking in two key ways. One was that he failed to recognize that morality involves respect for persons and judgments of justice and equality. The second was that Durkheim failed to recognize that development involves, through children's social interactions, a progressive construction of ways of understanding the world, and not solely an accommodation to the social environment. The development of morality is best facilitated if children participate in cooperative relationships, especially with their equals (their peers). The educational implications of these approaches were articulated by Piaget (1932, p. 342) in the following way:

> Durkheim regards all morality as imposed by the group upon the individual and by the adult upon the child. Consequently, from the pedagogic point of view, whereas we would be inclined to see in the "Activity" School, "self-government," and in the autonomy of the child the only form of education likely to produce a rational morality, Durkheim upholds a system of education which is based on the traditional model and relies on methods that are fundamentally those of authority, in spite of the tempering features he introduced into it in order to allow for inner liberty of conscience.

This debate, which has been played out through the twentieth century, put briefly and in rather simple terms, is between the idea that the acquisition of morality involves an acceptance of societal standards and norms and the idea that it involves the development of ways of thinking about right and wrong or good and bad. In the latter part of the century, the debate included somewhat different terms and concepts. On the side of the incorporation of societal values are proponents of character development and character education. In that view, moral conduct comes about through the formation of traits of character valued by the society and within its long-standing traditions. Education involves firmly transmitting these virtues and traits through discipline, examples of good acts, and the telling of stories exemplifying traditional values.

One of the best-known and most vocal proponents of the character-education approach is William Bennett, who has compiled stories for the public to narrate for purposes of moral education (Bennett 1993). Bennett also stridently criticizes those who would educate children to judge, examine, and critically evaluate moral matters. In particular, Bennett considers moral-education programs based on the theories and research of Lawrence Kohlberg, who followed and extended Piaget's work, as entailing miseducation because of the emphasis on children's choices, decisions, deliberations, and judgments. Here, too, the debate has been over whether the acquisition of morality involves the transmission of traditions, rooted in society, or the development of ways of relating to others, rooted in understandings of justice, rights, equal consideration of persons, and the welfare of people.

One of the real strengths of Kohlberg's approach to moral education in the schools was that it was grounded in research on moral development and in associated philosophical analyses. In this regard, Kohlberg made a deceptively simple but, I believe, very important point about moral teaching that highlights a crucial shortcoming in most efforts at moral education, including the character-education approach. Kohlberg noted that all too often, psychology is expected to provide only knowledge about methods for moral teaching. He argued, however, that we cannot know about methods or means of teaching and learning in the absence of knowledge about the substance of that which is taught and learned. As he put it (Kohlberg 1970, pp. 57–8):

> If I could not define virtue or the ends of moral education, could I really offer advice as to the means by which virtue could be taught? Could it really be argued that the means for teaching obedience to authority are the same as the means for teaching freedom of moral opinion, that the means for teaching altruism are the same as the means for teaching competitive striving, that the making of a good storm trooper involves the same procedures as the making of the philosopher-king? It appears, then, that either we must be totally silent about moral education or else speak to the nature of virtue.

What Kohlberg meant by speaking to the nature of virtue is that it is necessary to provide substantive definitions and analyses of morality. In part, this is a philosophical enterprise. The nature of morality, then, has a bearing on how it develops, which in turn has a bearing on how it might be taught. Analyses of the philosophical bases of morality also tell us about the ends to which we educate. In too many cases, I would argue, the ends or goals of moral education are to have children "become good," with only vague conceptions held as to what it means to be good. As examples, to be good involves possessing certain traits of character, or acquiring a conscience that incorporates society's standards, or behaving in particular ways, such as avoiding violence, helping, sharing, caring for others, and being unselfish. I believe that Kohlberg was correct in stating that methods of teaching the good are used in ways disconnected to what is being taught. We see, as a consequence, a number of such disembodied recommendations for teaching morality: Read children stories about people who do good, provide them with adults who model good acts, use consistent punishments, be firm in discipline, and so on. If you know the appropriate methods and want to make a good storm trooper, then it is simply a matter of implementing the teaching methods appropriately.

Societies, cultures, social relationships, and personal lives are more complicated than that – in at least two respects. One is that people, including children, do have conceptions of the moral. Kohlberg and Piaget attempted to account for people's conceptions of the moral (and for definitions of the substance of the domain) by basing educational methods on research informative of children's moral judgments and changes in such judgments. However, their theories of development and the moral-educational applications did not account for a second complication in social lives – which is that people make nontrivial social and personal judgments of a nonmoral nature. These, too, must be taken into account, both in explanations of social and moral development and in viable educational applications.

To put it another way, a problem in most efforts at moral education is that the only or main concern is with morality. In this book, Larry Nucci insightfully and deeply discusses the complex and multifaceted issues that need to be taken into account in moral education. Nucci's analyses go well beyond education in the moral domain. His analyses are centrally on moral education, but he is also concerned with education in realms that are in the purview of the personal. People the world over are deeply concerned with moral goals. They are also concerned with the interests and goals of their society. And they are concerned with personal goals and areas of personal jurisdiction. Moral decisions often require considering and coordinating each of these domains of development. Nucci connects the different domains, which are each very important in people's lives, to the education of children.

The scope and depth of Larry Nucci's analyses and recommendations for education make contributions that are new, that further the field significantly, and that can be effective by their very lack of simplicity. It is easier to implement educational recommendations that are simple and straightforward. It is, however, more difficult to be effective in making a difference in children's lives when implementing simple and straightforward recommendations. The research on moral, social, and personal development tells us that the straightforward recommendations are not likely to work very well.

It is not, by the way, that I think that with this book Larry Nucci will quell the controversies and debates about moral education. This is not likely, though it is to be hoped that many will resonate to what he has to say since Nucci takes a clear point of view on morality and its development. Nucci's point of view, in a general sense, is aligned with the side that views morality as entailing the construction of judgments about welfare, justice, and rights. In keeping with the injunction that it is necessary to ground psychological and educational methods of teaching and learning in substantive analyses of the domain of morality, Nucci carefully spells out his positions. As I already noted, an additional feature of his formulations is that it is also necessary to spell out other domains importantly related to moral lives in order to engage in moral education. Nucci carefully, insightfully, and perceptively presents two interrelated stories. One is a theory and research story. (I must note that it is a point of view I share, and about which he and I have collaborated.) The second is an educational story.

The order of presentation of the two parts of the book is not at all arbitrary. Nucci lays out the issues and research findings in great detail in the first part – which provides empirical and theoretical grounding for the second part of the book on classroom applications. As we can see just from the table of contents, the first part of the book is comprehensive. Both parts of the book are also quite comprehensible. This is a book that provides ideas for researchers and is accessible to the educated public (of course, especially teachers). In the first part of the book, Nucci makes an excellent case for the point of view on domains by articulating the theoretical position, supporting it with evidence, and considering key issues. These include the relations of morality to religion, culture, social contexts, and emotions. Moreover, he contrasts the approach with the common view of morality as character.

In the work on domains of development, Larry Nucci has been instrumental in providing rich formulations of the place of the personal – how people think about issues of autonomy, privacy, and choice. These ideas contribute to our knowledge about children's development and add greatly to our thinking about moral education. In his early work, Nucci conducted precise and innovative research showing that children make judgments about areas of activity they consider out of the realm of moral or conventional regulation and within the jurisdiction of individual choice. Children's judgments about the personal realm do not preclude moral judgments. Morality, as well as convention, are domains that coexist in children's thinking.

In later work, including this book, he has extended this line of work to include analyses of the role of the personal in the context of children's interactions and negotiations with parents. He has also provided elaborate formulations of the significance of the personal in psychological development. An arena of personal jurisdiction is part of an individual's social identity and is necessary for adequate psychological development – along with connections to others through participation in the social system and consideration of their welfare and rights. Moreover, the inclusion of the personal domain in people's psyches, in conjunction with their societal and moral attachments, provides a richer and more accurate account of the place of individuals in culture than do stereotypical characterizations of people and cultures as individualistic or collectivistic.

The importance of the idea of a personal domain to our thinking about moral education is that it separates selfishness from the personal and forces us to include personal considerations in the context of teaching about morality. I (or Nucci) do not mean to say that people never act selfishly. Rather, this is to say that there is a legitimate realm of personal jurisdiction that must be taken into account in communicating with young people. It will not do simply to implore them to give up their personal interests for the good of others or society. Perhaps even more importantly, personal freedom is not in opposition to morality. A sense of identity and personal agency contributes to the nature of social relationships, including those of reciprocity and cooperation.

All of this makes for not-so-easy tasks for educators concerned with the welfare of children and their moral development. Larry Nucci, I believe, is well aware that he makes life a little more difficult for the moral educator. Those who are persuaded by his point of view will find the difficulties intellectually enriching and pedagogically informative. In this book, Larry Nucci has combined a rigorous approach to theory and research on social and moral development with great sensitivity to practices in classrooms and schools. This is one of those rare works that intelligently moves between the worlds of research and educational practice.

Elliot Turiel
University of California, Berkeley

Bennett, W. J. 1993. *The book of virtues.* New York: Simon & Schuster.
Kohlberg, L. 1970. Education for justice: A modern statement of the Platonic view. In N. F. Sizer and T. R. Sizer, eds., *Moral education: Five lectures,* pp. 56–83. Cambridge, MA: Harvard University Press.
Piaget, J. 1932. *The moral judgment of the child.* London: Routledge & Kegan Paul.

Acknowledgments

A number of scholars have read and commented on chapters or on drafts of the book as a whole. I wish to thank William Arsenio, Marvin Berkowitz, Melanie Killen, Ann Marie Ryan, Judith Smetana, Cecilia Wainryb, and Elliot Turiel for their comments and suggestions throughout the writing of the book. I wish also to thank Terrance Brown, Daniel Hart, James Leming, Gil Noam, and Theodore Sarbin for providing me with information or materials on selected topics. Students in my undergraduate and graduate courses also read portions, or in some cases, all of the manuscript. I wish to thank them for keeping me grounded and for helping me to make the book accessible to professional educators. I am grateful for the suggestions, information, and advice each of these people has given me. If there are errors or lacunae in the final product, it is only because of my own limitations.

My wife Maria helped to edit the manuscript and provided encouragement as this project moved forward. More importantly, she has been central to the development of many of the ideas that made their way into this book through the exchanges we have had over the past twenty-five years. This book could not have been written without her presence.

Finally, I wish to thank my editor, Julia Hough, for believing in this project and for helping to bring this book to fruition.

Introduction

Few areas of education are as central to the purposes of public schooling as the formation of children's social values. For members of the multicultural democracies, none is more controversial. At the core of current controversies is how we are going to define what we mean by morality. Among the questions we need to answer are the following: Is morality a set of rules we acquire like any other, or does morality constitute a set of understandings that are in some way distinct from other areas of social knowledge? Does morality involve or even rely on cognition, or is it simply an emotion like empathy or guilt that guides our conduct? Are there universal or transcultural aspects to morality, or is morality culture specific? If there are universals in morality, does this mean there are moral absolutes? Does morality rest on religious norms, or are moral and religious concepts distinct from one another? Do moral understandings change over the course of history, or is morality ahistorical and transcendent? Can morality be taught, or does it have to be "caught"? Is there such a thing as moral character? If not, how do we account for and foster the development of people who act in accordance with a set of moral principles? Finally, how best can teachers make use of our knowledge about children's moral and social growth in their everyday classroom practices?

This two-part book addresses those questions by bringing together the basic findings from what has been referred to as the "domain theory" of social development, and the related work that has been done on classroom practice. The discoveries that have emerged from domain theory permit us to do several things essential to moral education within a pluralist democracy. First, as the title of this book suggests, it allows us to define what is meant by the moral domain in a manner that transcends cultural and religious boundaries. The book opens with a discussion of the basic scope and definition of the moral domain. The initial chapter pro-

xvii

vides an overview of the research evidence gathered within the United States and across the globe that accounts for the emergence of morality in early childhood as a domain distinct from matters of social convention or personal preference. With the discussion of the moral domain as a backdrop, the focus moves to research involving devout religious children and adolescents that examines whether their views of moral issues are determined by religious rules or the word of God.

Domain theory also permits us to understand cultural and contextual variations in people's social values. Although the basic underpinnings of all human morality have a common conceptual core, most "real life" social judgments are complex and involve the use of knowledge from more than one conceptual framework. As a result, one cannot reduce contextualized moral issues to a simple formula or set of absolute norms. The paradox, then, is that morality is both based on a set of nonrelative universals and yet ultimately plural in its application.

One issue that seems to divide the world's cultures is the relative degree to which people are accorded personal freedom and privacy. This set of concerns is addressed through a discussion of the personal domain of social values. Evidence is presented that human beings strive to maintain a zone of privacy and personal choice around issues that pertain to their sense of self and unique personal identity. This striving for a personal domain comprises a fundamental element in establishing the dynamic relation between the individual and society. For educators and parents, the issues dealt with touch on central themes of the limits of legitimate social authority, and the interplay between development and parental control over their children. The discussion also begins the analysis of cross-domain interactions through a consideration of how the interplay among morality, societal convention, and the personal result in cultural differences in the definition of personal rights and freedoms. This marks the beginning of an ongoing discussion throughout the book regarding the sources of tension between morality and the normative structures of social systems.

This discussion opens by focusing on the age-related shifts in the structure of knowledge within each domain, and the features of age-typical cross-domain interactions. Teachers are provided with a framework for understanding how to match the level of complexity of sociomoral issues with the developmental levels of their students. The examination of age-related cross-domain interactions also provides for an account of the contradictions that have arisen as a result of research on traditional developmental (i.e., Kohlbergian) accounts of moral psychology. This last contribution provides a new way to look at the developmental aims of moral education so that we can meaningfully engage children at all grade levels in the act of principled moral reflection.

We then move to an examination of the ways in which interactions among morality, the conventions of society, and peoples' culturally based assumptions about the nature of the world generate cultural and historical variations in values. This discussion provides insights into how seemingly incommensurate cultural worldviews can share the same universal moral core. It also provides a basis for understanding how members within a culture can be impervious to the moral contradictions within their own existing social system, and how ethnocentric interpretations of cultural values can mask the principled moral perspectives of other cultural groups. Finally, the resulting analysis provides a basis from which individuals can engage in moral reflection and moral critique of their own cultural practices and social structure.

A comprehensive account of moral psychology entails more than an explanation of the emergence of sociomoral knowledge and reasoning. It must also connect with the affective and motivational bases for moral action. Consequently, we next address the motivational and characterological elements that enter into a person's moral actions. We begin by looking at the role of emotion in selecting and energizing one's actions. The rich emerging literature on children's emotional development eliminates the false dichotomy between emotion and cognition in moral experience. Moral experience is not a matter of either cognition or emotion, but rather an inevitable integration between thought and feelings. This work helps us to understand the nature of moral motivation and some of the sources of moral pathology.

Finally, we take up the issue of moral character. This entails a critique of traditional notions of character currently in vogue in certain educational programs. The argument moves toward a contemporary reconceptualization of the issue in terms of self-construction and self-consistency. The work addressed here draws from narrative views of self that recognize people as multifaceted rather than defined in terms of traits or virtues.

The overview of domain theory and research presented in Part One of the book provides the foundation for Part Two, which offers concrete illustrations of how one might use domain theory as a guide to educational practice. This section deals with three interrelated aspects of sociomoral education: establishing a moral climate or atmosphere (issues of classroom management and structure), integrating values education into the curriculum, and fostering the moral self (personal character).

The educational practices introduced are designed to stimulate students' development into socially competent adults who are able to fit into their sociomoral worlds, but who also take a critical moral perspective toward themselves and the social worlds they inherit. As outlined in Part One of the book, the moral domain forms a universal core set of values around issues of human welfare and justice. It is the development of these moral concepts that anchors sociomoral education. The social world, however, is multifaceted. Issues of right and wrong are determined not only by morality but also by the conventions and factual assumptions shared by the larger society. Enabling students to negotiate the sociomoral world, and to arrive at moral positions in complex situations, involves not only stimulating their moral reasoning but also developing their concepts of convention and personal rights.

The second section of the book provides teachers with tools for how to stimulate conceptual development within the moral, conventional, and personal domains and for how to engage students in critical moral reflection on issues involving overlap between morality and nonmoral social values or norms. Teachers are shown how to analyze the domain-related features of school norms, practices, and curricula. Through the use of actual classroom examples, teachers are provided with suggestions for how to integrate attention to domain into classroom management, classroom climate, student discipline, and uses of the academic curriculum.

Running throughout is the unifying theme that education in the moral domain should challenge the student's sense of what is right and fair, and ask that the student apply those understandings to his or her everyday life. On this account, moral education is not a matter of induction or inculcation, but a process that harnesses children's intrinsic motivation to comprehend and master their social worlds.

PART ONE

The Nature of Morality and the Development of Social Values

CHAPTER ONE

Morality and Domains of Social Knowledge

In my education classes, I often start off by asking students to state what they would consider to be the highest, most moral act. Invariably, students propose risking one's life to save the life of another as the most moral thing a person could do. I then present them with the following scenario and ask whether it is similar to what they had in mind.

A man is waiting at a train station. On his right, about twenty feet away, stands a woman reading a magazine. The man glances to his left to check if a train is coming and sees to his horror that another man, about twenty feet from him, is in a crouched position clearly aiming a gun at the woman. The man is too far away to either push the woman or stop the shooter. So he yells out "duck" as he steps between the shooter and the woman just as the gun is fired. As a result, the bullet intended for the woman strikes him in the arm, saving the woman's life.

Generally, my students accept this scenario as a rather dramatic instance of what they had in mind. I then ask them to consider the following alternative scene.

The same people are on the train platform in the same relative positions as in the first version. However, the man in the middle is in this case unaware of the presence of the gunman. While waiting for the train, he notices that his shoe is untied. Just at the moment that our "hero" bends forward to tie his shoe, the gunman fires at the woman. The bullet hits him in the arm, and the woman's life is saved.

Despite the fact that the behavior of the "hero" (moving in between the shooter and the woman) and outcome (woman is saved) are the same, my students do not consider the second scenario as a depiction of a moral action. This is because there was no element of moral choice involved in the second set of events. The decision to move forward was unrelated to the moral elements of the situation, and the moral outcome (preservation of life) occurred quite by accident. On the basis of this example, my students conclude that moral action as opposed to an accidental or reflexive behavior requires moral judgment.

Now some objections may be raised to the interpretation the students offer with regard to this example. First, it may be argued that the act of saving someone's life is an instance of supererogation (performing beyond the call of duty) and is not an example of action based on moral obligation (e.g., to refrain from harming another). This objection does not, however, negate the importance that the students placed on volition as a necessary element of moral action, and no one would argue that the act of saving someone's life is without moral meaning. A second, and more pointed, objection would be to accept the example as portraying a moral action, but to argue that even in the first instance the person was not acting on the basis of rational choice, but did so out of instinct or emotion. This position makes clear that emotion plays an important role in morality. Moreover, this interpretation reminds us of how many everyday moral actions seem to take place automatically without reflection.

In fact, some recent writers have placed great emphasis on the apparent lack of reflection in everyday moral activity, and have argued that morality is guided by an inherited emotional "moral sense" (Wilson 1993). The role of affect and emotion in the selection and motivation of moral action will be taken up again more thoroughly in a later chapter. For our purposes here, it is enough to recognize that the fact that a judgment is made quickly, and seemingly without reflection, does not necessarily mean that it was made "unthinkingly." It takes little reflection, for example, for an adult to answer the question, "How much is one plus one?" The seeming automaticity of the response does not negate the answer as a product of thought, however quickly done. Similarly, while moral actions may be motivated by emotion, and take place with very little conscious reflection, they always involve an element of thought. This is why we don't consider the "prosocial" behavior of animals (e.g., placing their own lives at risk in order to protect their young) to be truly moral. We attribute such behavior to instinct rather than to the animal's morality. Indeed, if our hero were acting solely out of instinct or automatic emotional processing, my students would not consider his behavior to have had any more "moral" status than that of the man who saved the woman's life by accident.

At the core of what we mean by morality, then, is knowledge of right and wrong. Conduct is moral if it involves selection of particular courses of action that are deemed to be right. In the above example, if we were to shift our focus from the "hero" to the shooter, we would quickly see that the person's moral culpability stems from his choice to harm another person. If it were to turn out that the shooter were delusional and incapable of understanding the meaning of his actions, we would view the events as tragic rather than in moral terms. Thus, while the human experience of morality may contain many things, such as emotions (which may be rooted in our evolutionary history), the defining element of morality is moral cognition. Moreover, our deliberations about right and wrong are not confined simply to those things we do seemingly automatically out of habit, or out of an emotional sense that a course of action is right. Moral issues are among the most engaging things that people think about. It isn't just philosophers who reflect on moral issues. Just about everyone has pondered the morality of various courses of action and reflected upon the moral meaning of personal decisions. This begins very early in life in the context of deciding on issues of fairness among playmates and siblings, and continues into the twilight concerns over death with dignity.

IDENTIFYING THE MORAL DOMAIN

One of the central questions raised by philosophy and psychology is whether morality constitutes a domain or category of understanding distinct from other aspects of our knowledge. The behaviorist theories of learning, which at one time dominated American educational practice, made no distinctions among types or forms of knowledge and saw all learning as simply the acquisition of content or procedures resulting from environmental consequences experienced as reinforcements or punishments (Skinner 1971). From that perspective there was no particular difference between an academic subject like arithmetic and morality, and the issue of moral education became simply the application of educational technology to generate a set of socially defined and desired behaviors. More recently, however, as a consequence of what has been called the "cognitive revolution," there has been a recognition that knowledge is not uniform but is structured within different domains or conceptual frameworks. Verbal and mathematical knowledge, for example, are not reduced to one another, and the teaching of reading and arithmetic call upon different curricula and teaching strategies.

While it may seem fairly obvious that moral cognition is something different from mathematics or text comprehension (reading), it has been less apparent that morality is a domain apart from knowledge of other social values. For the most part, researchers and educators have accepted the everyday usage of the term *morality* (standards of social right and wrong) as defining the field of inquiry or instruction. Moral education, according to this conventional view, involves the socializing of students into socially accepted standards of behavior so that they learn to know "right" from "wrong" (Ryan 1996). This global approach draws no distinctions among very disparate forms of social right and wrong, and it offers no criteria for inclusion or exclusion within the moral category of social norms. Behaviors as different as harm to another person and failure to wear conventional dress are both considered "wrong" and, therefore, subject to moral socialization. Thus, there is no sense in which morality is viewed in this conventional perspective as something apart from knowledge of social norms in general.

Within philosophy, however, attempts have been made to establish criteria for determining what *ought* to count as a moral value. According to formalist ethics[1] (e.g., Dworkin 1977; Frankena 1978; Gewirth 1978; Habermas 1991), this notion of *ought* carries with it two related ideas. One is that what is morally right is not something that is simply subject to individual opinion but carries with it an "objective" prescriptive force. The second, related idea, is that what is morally right, because it is "objectively" prescriptive, holds generally and can be universalized across people. These two criteria, prescriptivity and universality, are linked together in philosophical analyses to issues of human welfare, justice, and rights.[2]

What we have learned through research over the past twenty-five years is that people in general, and not just philosophers, also do not hold global conceptions of social right and wrong, but reason very differently about matters of morality, convention, and personal choice (Nucci 1977, 1996; Turiel 1983). More specifically, these conceptual differences become apparent when people are asked to evaluate different actions in terms of criteria similar to those set out in formalist ethics.

---

[1] Formalist ethics is not the only philosophical system to be concerned with definitions of morality. I bring in formal criteria here as a way of illustrating the basic distinctions that can be made between morality and the conventions of society. These same kinds of distinctions are also made by children and adults in their own natural reasoning about social and moral issues. People also combine formalist with nonformalist ideas in their moral cognition. Some of these nonformalist aspects of everyday morality will be brought into the discussions in later chapters about emotion and moral character.

[2] Carol Gilligan (1982) has made a strong case for care as an alternative moral orientation to a morality of justice. I will take up the issue of care and morality in the Chapter 6 discussion of the role of affect in morality.

Within the domain theory of social development, morality refers to conceptions of human welfare, justice, and rights, which are a function of the inherent features of interpersonal relations (Turiel 1983). As such, prescriptions pertaining to the right and wrong of moral actions are not simply the function of consensus or the views of authority. For example, it is not possible to hit another person with force and not hurt that other person. That is because hurting is an inherent consequence of hitting. A moral judgment about unprovoked harm ("It is wrong to hit.") would not be dependent on the existence of a socially agreed-upon norm or standard but could be generated solely from the intrinsic effects of the act (i.e., hitting hurts). In this example, the prescriptive force of the moral standard "It is wrong to hit." is objective in the sense that the effects of the act are independent of the views of the observer, prescriptive in the sense that the issue of wrong stems from the objective features of the act, and generalizable in the sense that the effects of the act hold across people irrespective of background. Similar analyses could be done regarding a broader range of issues pertaining to human welfare that would extend beyond harm to concerns for what it means to be just, compassionate, and considerate of the rights of others. In studies on reasoning about a broad range of issues, it has been found that moral judgments are structured by the person's understandings of fairness and human welfare (Turiel 1983).

In contrast with issues of morality are matters of social convention. Conventions are the agreed-upon uniformities in social behavior determined by the social system in which they are formed (Turiel 1983). Unlike moral prescriptions, conventions are arbitrary because there are no inherent interpersonal effects of the actions they regulate. For example, among the many conventions children in our society are expected to learn is that certain classes of adults (e.g., teachers, physicians) are addressed by their titles. Since there are no inherently positive or negative effects of forms of address, society could just as easily have set things up differently (e.g., had children refer to their teachers by first names). Through accepted usage, however, these standards serve to coordinate the interactions of individuals participating within a social system by providing them with a set of expectations regarding appropriate behavior. In turn, the matrix of social conventions and customs is an element in the structuring and maintenance of the general social order (Searle 1969).

These two forms of social regulation, morality and convention, are both a part of the social order. Conceptually, however, they are not reducible one to another and are understood within distinct conceptual frameworks or domains. This distinction between morality and convention is nicely illustrated by the following example (collected in the U.S. Virgin Islands during the research for Nucci, Turiel, and Encarnacion-Gawrych 1983) taken from an interview with a 4-year-old girl regarding her perceptions of spontaneously occurring transgressions at her preschool.

MORAL ISSUE: *Did you see what happened?* Yes. They were playing and John hit him too hard. *Is that something you are supposed to do or not supposed to do?* Not so hard to hurt. *Is there a rule about that?* Yes. *What is the rule?* You're not to hit hard. *What if there were no rule about hitting hard, would it be all right to do then?* No. *Why not?* Because he could get hurt and start to cry.

CONVENTIONAL ISSUE: *Did you see what just happened?* Yes. They were noisy. *Is that something you are supposed to or not supposed to do?* Not do. *Is there a rule about that?* Yes. We have to be quiet. *What if there were no rule, would it be all right to do then?* Yes. *Why?* Because there is no rule.

As I stated earlier, the distinction between morality and nonmoral norms of social regulation, such as convention, has not been generally made in values education. Traditional values educators, such as Kevin Ryan (1996) and Edward Wynne (1989), hold that moral values are established by society. They treat all values including morality as matters of custom and convention to be inculcated in children as a part of what they refer to as character education. The kind of distinction drawn here is also at variance with accounts that have had the greatest impact on developmental approaches to moral education. In contrast with behaviorism and traditional approaches to moral education, the accounts of moral development offered by Piaget (1932) and Kohlberg (1984) were informed by and included philosophical distinctions between morality and convention. However, while differing in their interpretations of the ages at which such changes take place, both Piaget (1932) and Kohlberg (1984) maintained that only at the highest stages of moral development can morality be differentiated from and displace convention as the basis for moral judgments.

Over the past twenty-five years, however, more than sixty published articles have reported research demonstrating that morality and convention emerge as distinct conceptual frameworks at very early ages and undergo distinct patterns of age-related developmental changes. This research is reviewed in detail in Helwig, Tisak and Turiel 1990; Smetana 1995a; Tisak 1995; and Turiel 1998a. Three main forms of evidence have been offered in support of the contention that morality is a conceptual system distinct from understandings of nonmoral social norms. The first consists of studies examining whether or not individuals make conceptual distinctions between moral and nonmoral social issues on the basis of a number of formal criteria. The second form of research consists of observational studies of children's social interactions to determine if the pattern of social interactions associated with moral issues is different from the form of social interactions around nonmoral issues. The third form of research has examined the age-related changes in the ways in which people reason about moral and nonmoral concerns. Most of the attention of each of these three forms of research has been upon the distinction between matters of morality and social convention. Other work has looked at the development of understandings of personal prerogative and issues of self-harm (prudence). Those latter issues will be dealt with in detail in chapter 3. What follows is an overview of the research on the moral–conventional distinction.

RESEARCH ON THE MORAL AND CONVENTIONAL DOMAINS

Studies of the Moral–Conventional Distinction

The way in which researchers have determined whether or not people make a conceptual distinction between morality and convention has been by asking people to evaluate various actions in terms of one or more of the following criteria:

> *Rule contingency:* Does the wrongness of a given action depend upon the existence of a governing rule or social norm? (The reader will recognize this criterion from the interview with the 4-year-old child described above.)
>
> *Rule alterability:* Is it wrong or all right to remove or alter the existing norm or standard?
>
> *Rule generalizability:* Is it wrong or all right for members of another society or culture not to have a given rule or norm?
>
> *Act generalizability:* Is it wrong or all right for a member of another society or culture to engage in the act if that society/culture does not have a rule about the act?
>
> *Act severity:* How wrong (usually on a 5-point scale) is a given action?

For the most part, these criteria map onto the formal criteria for morality presented by formalist ethics. Rule contingency and rule alterability both refer to the philosophical criterion that a moral norm be prescriptive. Rule and act generalizability both refer to the philosophical criterion that the moral norm apply universally to all persons.

In addition to being asked to make criterion judgments, people are also asked to provide justifications for the answers they give. These justifications allow researchers to determine which substantive bases people employ to make their criterion judgments. In the example presented earlier, the young girl responded to the rule contingency question about hitting by responding that it would be wrong to hit, whether or not a governing rule were in effect. The substantive justification for judging hitting as wrong was that hitting has harmful effects on another person.

In order to gain clear-cut answers to whether or not people make distinctions between morality and convention, researchers have asked people to make judgments that would constitute prototypical examples of moral or conventional issues. Issues have been presented in contexts in which the acts in question are generally not in conflict with other types of goals or events. More complex issues involving conflict and overlap have also been studied, and I will discuss that work in Chapters 4 and 5. In studies which have involved observations of children's interactions, children have been asked to evaluate real situations they had just witnessed (as in the previous example). In most cases, however, issues have been presented in story or pictorial form. The types of issues used as moral stimuli have had to do with welfare and physical harm (for instance, pushing, shoving, hitting, and killing), psychological harm (such as teasing, hurting feelings, ridiculing, or name calling), fairness and rights (such things as stealing, breaking a promise, not sharing a toy, or destroying others' property), and positive behaviors (things like helping another in need, sharing, or donating to charity).

Consistent with the assumptions of domain theory, children and adults distinguish between morality and convention on the basis of these criteria. Moral issues are viewed to be independent of the existence of social norms and generalizable across contexts, societies, and cultures. Social conventions, on the other hand, are rule dependent, and their normative force holds only within the social system within which the rule was formed. Justifications people give for their criterion judgments are also in line with the distinctions that have been drawn between the moral and conventional domains. Judgments of moral issues are justified in terms of the harm or unfairness that actions would cause, while judgments of conventions are justified in terms of norms and the expectations of authority.

There are, as one would expect, age and experience effects on the ability of people to make these domain distinctions. The youngest age at which children have been reported to differentiate consistently between morality and convention is 2 1/2 years (Smetana and Braeges 1990). The toddlers in the Smetana and Braeges (1990) study were more likely to generalize moral issues across contexts (view such issues as unprovoked hitting of another child as wrong both at home and at another day-care setting) than they were to generalize conventions (putting toys away). They did not, however, make distinctions based on any of the other dimensions used in that study. By about age 3 1/2, however, children treated moral and conventional issues differently on the basis of several criteria, including seriousness and rule contingency, as well as generalizability.

The same study demonstrated that children are capable of making rudimentary distinctions between issues of morality and convention during the third year of life. This study and other work (Nucci and Turiel 1978; Smetana 1981) have demonstrated that by age 4, children have developed fairly consistent and firm differentiations between familiar moral and conventional issues encountered in home or preschool settings. As children become older, their understandings of moral and conventional issues are extended beyond events with which the children have had direct personal experience to include the broad range of issues, familiar and unfamiliar alike, which constitute moral and conventional forms of social events (Davidson, Turiel, and Black 1983). Moreover, as children develop, they become better able to apply more abstract criteria, such as cross-cultural generalizability, to differentiate between issues within the two domains.

Studies that examine whether children differentiate between morality and convention have not been limited to the United States or Western contexts, but have been conducted across a wide range of the world's cultures. Such studies have been conducted with children and adolescents in northeastern Brazil; preschool children in St. Croix, the Virgin Islands; Christian and Moslem children in Indonesia; urban and kibbutz Jewish children and traditional village Arab children in Israel; children and adults in India; children and adolescents in Korea; Ijo children in Nigeria; and children in Zambia. (For a complete listing of these studies see Smetana 1995a or Turiel 1998a.) With some variations in specific findings regarding convention, the distinction between morality and convention has been reported in each of the cultures examined. Only one study (Shweder et al. 1987) has claimed to have obtained data indicating that individuals within a non-Western culture (members of a temple village in India) make no distinction between morality and convention, and that result has been disputed by findings from a subsequent study (Madden

1992). In all cases, children and adolescents have been found to treat moral issues entailing harm and injustice in much the same way. Children across cultural groups and social classes have been found to treat moral transgressions, such as unprovoked harm, as wrong regardless of the presence or absence of rules, and have viewed the wrongness of such moral transgressions as holding universally for children in other cultures or settings, and not just for their own group. This is a rather remarkable set of findings, and has to stand as one of the more robust phenomena to have been uncovered by psychological research.

Some cultural differences have been reported, however, in findings regarding children's treatment of social conventions. In some respects, this has been due to differences in methods employed by researchers from different investigative groups in framing questions posed to children. For example, in a study conducted in northeastern Brazil (Haidt, Koller, and Dias 1994), children were presented with descriptions of rules from two cultures. In each case, one culture had a rule just like the child's own culture, and the other did not. Children were asked to indicate whether one of the cultures was doing the better thing. Overwhelmingly, children indicated that the culture whose rule was like their own was doing the better thing. This form of question, however, does not differentiate between what children view as universally obligatory from what they view as preferred. The fact that children in the study preferred their own rules to other ones may or may not mean that they saw it as wrong for other cultures to do things differently. Indeed, when children from the same area of Brazil were directly asked to evaluate whether it would be wrong or all right for people of another culture to engage in a given act if the other culture had no rule about the act, children universalized moral prescriptions (e.g., it would be wrong to hit). They did not, however, tend to universalize their own conventions (e.g., eat chicken with a fork instead of with one's hands) (Nucci et al. 1996).

Failure to employ methods that directly and clearly assess criteria people use to evaluate moral and conventional acts accounts for studies failing to observe distinctions between morality and convention (Haidt et al. 1994; Shweder et al. 1987). When such methodological issues are taken into account, however, some cultural differences in treatment of social conventions still remain. For instance, Korean children and adolescents made much greater use of justifications pertaining to social status, social roles, appropriate behavior, and courtesy than is commonly observed in American children's reasoning about conventions (Song et al. 1987). Ijo children and adolescents in Nigeria (Hollos et al. 1986), Arab children in

Israel (Nisan 1987), and lower class children in northeastern Brazil (Nucci et al. 1996) affirmed the importance of customs and tradition to a greater degree than did American children. In each of these latter studies, however, issues of culture were confounded with social class. A general finding is that middle-class children worldwide appear to be more willing than lower-class children to view conventions as alterable and culture or context specific. Untangling what aspect of observed cross-country differences in children's treatment of convention is due to culture, and what is due to cross-cultural effects of social-class hierarchy, is an issue for future research.

In sum, the overwhelming body of research evidence is consistent with the proposal that morality is conceptualized differently from convention. As I noted earlier, this finding has been used by some writers on moral development (viz., Wilson 1993) to sustain the view that morality is based on an innate moral sense. That is not the view being presented here. On the contrary, the observed emergence of morality and convention as distinct conceptual systems is to be accounted for in terms of the qualitatively differing forms of social interaction children experience in the context of these two forms of social regulation. Let's turn, then, to an overview of the research that has looked at those patterns of social interaction.

Origins of the Child's Construction of Morality and Convention

Morality and convention may both be thought of as rule-governed behaviors. What distinguishes them, according to domain theory, is that in the case of morality, the source of the rule is reflection upon the effects of the act, whereas in the case of convention, the status of the act is a function of the presence or absence of a governing rule. We should expect, then, that social experiences and interactions associated with moral transgressions would revolve around the effects of acts upon the self and others as victims. On the other hand, given the arbitrary nature and consensual basis of conventions, we would expect social experiences concerning conventions to come in the form of external social messages focusing on normative expectations, rules, and efforts to achieve social conformity.

A good way to get a sense of whether morality and convention are associated with different patterns of social interaction is to observe what takes place in the context of transgressions. Morality and convention both define social right and wrong. By observing breaches of social norms, it is possible to learn whether or not an officially stated norm is actually responded to as such. In a study of children's social interactions in free-play settings, for example, we discovered that middle-class suburban children almost never respond to another child's use of profanity (Nucci and Nucci 1982a). Within the context of that peer culture, adult-generated norms regulating profanity were simply not in play. When transgressions are responded to, the social give-and-take both indicates the responsibilities of participants and affords a way to discern whether patterns of exchange are associated with particular kinds of acts. Such interactions have been characterized as entailing a kind of social grammar in which children negotiate, test, employ, and clarify social norms (Much and Shweder 1978). Children's responses to one another's transgressions have also been viewed as efforts to repair the social fabric (Sedlak and Walton 1982) and to negotiate social responsibility. A number of studies, therefore, have looked at patterns of interaction in the context of moral and conventional transgressions.

The patterns of peer interactions surrounding moral and conventional transgressions are illustrated in the following events observed in a study of children in free-play settings (Nucci and Nucci 1982a). In each case, the transgression is italicized.

Social Convention

1. *A boy and a girl are sitting together on the grass, away from the other children,* tying their shoes. Another boy (2) sings out to them, "Bobby and Alison sittin' in a tree, K-I-S-S-I-N-G," etc.
2. A girl (1) *is sucking on a piece of grass.* Girl (2) says to girl (3), "That's what she does, she sucks on weeds and spits them out." Girl (3) says, "Gross!" Girl (2) says, "That's disgusting!" Girl (1) then places the piece of grass down and ceases placing grass in her mouth.

Moral

1. *Two boys (1 and 2) are throwing sand at a smaller boy (3).* Boy 3 says, "Dammit – you got it in my eyes. It hurts like hell. Next time I'm gonna kick your heads in." Boy (1) says to boy (2), "Hey, did you hear that? Next time he's gonna kick our heads in." They both laugh and throw more sand in the face of boy (3). Boy (3) then spits at boy (1) and runs away.
2. *Two boys have forcibly taken a sled away from a younger boy and are playing with it.* A girl who was watching says to the boys, "Hey, give it back, a – – holes. That's really even odds, the two of you against one little

kid." The girl then pulls the sled away from one of the older boys, pushes him to the ground, and hands the sled back to the younger boy. He takes the sled and the incident ends.

As can be seen in these examples, the social experiences of children differ by domain. In the case of moral events, children experience such issues as victims as well as perpetrators or third-person observers. The transgression (such as hitting, stealing, or damaging property) is followed by peer reactions focusing on the intrinsic effects of the act (that is, by statements of injury or loss, or by evaluations of the act as unjust or hurtful). Generally, these reactions have a high degree of emotion. In the case of very young children, the reaction may consist solely of crying. In addition, children tend to avenge moral transgressions or avert further actions through attempts at retaliation or, in the case of young children, by involving adults. Peer reactions are, in turn, generally followed by transgressor responses. For the most part, these reactions either attempt to repair social relations (a) through direct apology for the act, (b) by efforts at restitution, or (c) by simple cessation of the behavior; or they attempt to explain or excuse the act by (a) claiming that it was justifiable retribution for a prior harm ("You hit me first."), (b) claiming that no harm was intended, or (c) claiming that no substantial harm or injustice resulted from the act ("Oh, you're all right. I just tapped you."). Transgressor reactions in a minority of cases (see moral example 1) also include derision of the respondent and/or continued engagement in the transgression. This last form of reaction, however, is more common in the context of conventional events.

In contrast to the pattern of interactions observed in moral events, peer interactions involving breaches of convention tend to arouse relatively little emotion and focus on the normative status of the acts. The transgression (such as engaging in sex-role counterbehavior, violating dress norms, or using an improper form of greeting) is followed by peer responses focusing on social norms and social expectations. Respondents state governing rules, evaluate the acts as odd or disruptive, and attempt to achieve conformity through ridicule (see conventional example 1). Transgressor reactions to these peer responses include attempts to conform through compliance with the norm or defense of their conduct through challenges of the rule ("We don't have to do that. Who made up that dumb rule?"). Finally, because conventions achieve their force through social consensus and/or imposition by authority, transgressors sometimes react to peer respondents by challenging their authority to uphold the norm ("You're not my mother.") or by ignoring the respondent and continuing to engage in the behavior.

These patterns of child response to transgression have been observed in emergent form among toddlers (Dunn and Munn 1985, 1987; Dunn and Slomkowski 1992; Smetana 1984, 1989) and preschool children in home and school contexts (Much and Shweder 1978; Nucci and Turiel 1978; Nucci and Weber 1985; Ross 1996). Beginning in toddlerhood, children respond to violations of moral transgressions generally as victims. Their responses indicate that they have experienced such acts as hurtful. In turn, their reactions provide information to peer transgressors about the hurtful effects of the actions. Very young children generally do not respond to violations of conventions. This finding is not surprising in that conventional acts are not in themselves prescriptive. By preschool, however, children begin to respond to peer violations of generally held conventions, such as dresses for girls and not boys, but do not as yet respond to peer violations of conventions particular to the school setting (e.g., norms regarding classroom cleanup), which are left to the adults to worry about (Nucci et al. 1983).

The pattern of adult responses to children's transgressions is also different by domain. Adult responses to moral transgressions complement those of children and often follow them in time (Smetana 1984). Mothers of toddlers provide social messages focusing on the hurtful effects of moral transgressions, and also attempt to persuade children to engage in prosocial behaviors and share or "be nice" (Gralinski and Kopp 1993). As children grow older, these adult responses become more elaborated as children are provided more explicit social messages regarding the harmful impact of their actions and are asked by teachers and parents to consider the perspective of the other person ("Mary, how do you feel when people lie to you?"), as well as to reflect on their own motivations for acting as they did ("Why did you do that?"). Adult responses to convention also complement those of children. Mothers' responses to toddlers' violations of convention generally focus on commands to cease the behavior, and less frequently include statements that address the conventional features of the acts (e.g., the underlying rules or the disorder caused by the action)(Smetana, 1984). As children develop, mothers and teachers provide more comprehensive statements regarding the underlying social rules and social expectations.

By elementary school, adult feedback about violations of convention take the form of direct rule statements or reminders of rules and expectations ("Raise your hand before talking."), as well as statements labeling the transgressions as unruly; disorderly ("It's getting too noisy in here."); unmannerly ("Chew with your mouth closed. Where are your manners?"); inappropriate for the context ("Dan, those ripped jeans are okay for play, but not for school."); and generally inconsistent with conventional expectations ("That's not the way for a Hawthorne student to act." "Susan, act your age.").

In early adolescence, as children begin to struggle with the functions and meaning of conventions within the larger social order, adult messages to children sometimes contain explanations of these more abstract connections. As will be outlined later in the book, the effectiveness of these more abstract messages is a function of the developmental level of the child.

In sum, the pattern of adult responses to moral and conventional events complements those of children. It is interesting to note however, that the relative proportion of child transgressions involving adult or child respondents differs by domain. Adults respond less often to children's moral transgressions than do other children. Conversely, adults are more likely than children to respond to violations of conventions. For example, a study of 2- and 3-year-old children's social interactions (Smetana 1989) reported that conflicts with peers occurred primarily over issues of possessions, rights, taking turns, aggression, and unkindness (all moral issues), whereas children's conflicts with mothers occurred primarily over manners and politeness, rules of the house, and cultural norms (all conventional issues). Similar findings were reported for somewhat older (3- and 4-year-old) children in a study looking at naturally occurring events in the home (Nucci and Weber 1995). This study found that the majority of children's moral events took place in free-play settings and involved feedback from children more often than from the mothers. Violations of convention, on the other hand, were more generally responded to by mothers than by young children.

These patterns also carry over to school settings. Children are more likely than teachers to respond to other children's moral transgressions, whereas teachers are the primary respondents to violations of school convention (Nucci and Nucci 1982b; Nucci and Turiel 1978). These findings are consistent with the view that children's moral understandings develop primarily out of peer interactions (Damon 1977; Piaget 1932).

Part of the explanation of the differences in rate of responding to moral transgressions is due to the fact that moral transgressions often take place and are resolved out of the view of parents or teachers. This factor alone, however, does not account for the rate with which parents and teachers engage in responses to children's moral transgressions. It also seems that adults and children both appear to prefer to allow children to resolve their own moral disputes, a trend that increases as children get older. For example, one study reported that while parental responses to children's moral events increase during toddlerhood, adult intervention appears to decrease from preschool years to middle childhood (Gralinski and Kopp 1993). Similarly, it has been found that the rate of teacher responses to children's moral transgressions at school gradually decreases from grades three to five, and by grade seven is so infrequent that the researchers were unable to apply statistical analyses to the patterns of adult response (Nucci and Nucci 1982b). For their part, preschool-age children would rather work out conflicts on their own without adult intervention as the preferred means of resolving moral disputes (Killen and Turiel 1991), and beginning in middle childhood, children gradually ask for less help from adults in resolving moral conflicts (Nucci and Nucci 1982a, b).

These trends say nothing about the importance or effectiveness of adult as opposed to peer responses to moral issues. However, these findings are consistent with the characterization of morality as emerging out of intrinsic features of social interactions, features that are accessible even to young children. These findings sit in contrast with traditional views of children as the passive recipients of adult morality. The arbitrary nature and relative opaqueness of conventions, on the other hand, may help to explain why children are less likely than adults to respond to social convention. While young children do respond to violations of peer conventions of dress, speech, and play patterns (Corsaro 1985; Killen 1989; Nucci and Nucci 1982a; Nucci, Turiel, and Gawrych 1983), it is not until middle childhood that children respond to peer breaches of the norms of adult-structured institutions, such as school (Nucci and Nucci 1982b). The emergence of such peer responses with age may be related to developmental changes in children's conceptions of the social organizational functions of convention. I will take up these developmental issues in Chapter 4 when we look at how moral and social judgments are made in context. For now, the important point is to recognize that children's constructions of their notions of morality and of the conventions of society are emerging out of different aspects of their social experiences. It is the qualitatively different nature of moral and conventional events and interactions children experience that accounts for the fact that children think about morality and convention in such different ways.

CONCLUSIONS

In this chapter we have seen that a core component of moral action is moral judgment. We have also seen that contemporary research on children's moral and social judgments indicates that morality constitutes a domain of understandings and judgments distinct from other social norms and values, such as social conventions or personal preferences and tastes. Perhaps the most powerful and important part of these research findings for educators in pluralist democracies is that the domain of morality is structured around issues that are universal and nonarbitrary. The core of human morality is a concern for fairness and human welfare. Thus, there is a basic core of morality around which educators can construct their educational practices without imposing arbitrary standards or retreating into value relativism.

The origins of moral knowledge can be traced to the early exchanges children have around actions that affect the rights or well-being of themselves or other people. Young children are not simply learning the rules of adult society but are coming to conclusions about the ways in which particular kinds of (moral) actions affect the very ability of people to get along with one another. This is not to say that morality and children's moral judgments are not affected by other social norms and values. Morality coexists with other domains and dimensions of values and assumptions that people maintain about the nature of the world and people's place within it. Thus, educators need to be cognizant of the ways in which children construct their understandings of these other normative frames, and the ways in which moral and nonmoral values interact as children generate actions in their everyday lives. In the chapters that follow I will take up some of those relations to other values in more detail. The first issue I want to address is the relation between morality and religious norms. I take that up in Chapter 2.

CHAPTER TWO

Morality and Religious Rules

Conventionality is not morality. Self-righteousness is not religion. To attack the first is not to assail the last (Charlotte Brontë, 1977, 1847, p. 3).

One question frequently asked by those concerned with moral or character education is whether morality can be addressed independently of religious values. Responding to that question is timely and relevant to teachers and parents alike. The current plea for God and prayer to be put back into the classroom derives from an old and enduring belief that morality and religion are inseparable. This belief extends beyond the parochial scope of specific religious groups. The problem this point of view presents to teachers and administrators of any pluralist democracy, however, is that it forces school personnel to choose among the values of differing religious groups. For schools in the United States this issue presents teachers and administrators with the particular legal dilemma of teaching about morality without, at the same time, violating First Amendment freedoms and constitutional provisions regarding the separation of church and state. In the 1970s, many schools dealt with this issue by retreating into the value relativism of values-clarification programs (Simon, Howe, and Kirschenbaum 1972). Other schools and districts have simply attempted to avoid the issue entirely by not engaging in any purposeful effort at moral or character education. From the perspective of fundamentalist and nonreligious parents alike, the promotion of value relativism and the purposeful avoidance of moral teaching in public schools is a cause for alarm. Moreover, assumptions about the inseparability of religion and morality raise concerns among fundamentalists that the teaching of values within public schools without Bible study and prayer will undermine the moral beliefs of their children. In the 1980s and 1990s, parents of fundamentalist children in the United States have responded to such concerns by withdrawing their children from public schools and, in increasing numbers, engaging in the practice of home schooling (Lyman 1998).

For civil society in the United States or any other pluralist democracy, the ramifications of a failure to resolve such educational concerns satisfactorily are self-evident. One index of the complexity of questions regarding the relation between morality and religion is the fact that this has been an enduring area of controversy debated by philosophers since Plato's time (Crittenden 1990). At least one aspect of these issues, however, has been resolved by research that has examined whether children and adolescents make a distinction between the rules and practices specific to their religion, and those moral issues that ought to be common to religions other than their own and to secular society as well. In that research, we applied the distinction we have drawn between moral and nonmoral areas of social regulation to examine how Christian and Jewish children conceptualize the rules of their respective religions.

MORALITY AND RELIGIOUS NORMS AS SEEN BY CATHOLICS

The first of these studies focused on traditional Roman Catholics for two main reasons: (1) Catholicism has a clearly designated authority and procedure for interpreting and determining what constitutes sinful behavior (i.e., the pope, usually after consultation with other bishops, has the ultimate authority to interpret and hence determine matters of doctrine), and (2) Catholicism, as one of the world's largest and oldest organized religions, has become an integral part of many sociocultural systems.

In the study (Nucci 1985), Catholic adolescents and young adults were asked to make a number of judgments about actions considered sins by the Catholic Church. Some of the actions, such as stealing, killing, rape, slander, and so forth, entailed harm or injustice toward another and were classified by us as matters of morality. Other actions, such as failure to attend religious services on Easter or Christmas, fasting prior to communion, the use of contraceptives, masturbation, premarital sex between consenting adults, divorce, and ordaining women, entailed violations of worship patterns or social behavior prescribed by Catholicism as an institution. These actions were classified as nonmoral and akin to matters of social convention. Items were presented in questionnaire form and all were randomized to control for response bias. The items used in the study are listed in Table 2.1 (one item, homosexuality, is not listed since it was the focus of a subsequent study to be discussed in Chapter 5). It should be pointed out that nonmoral religious prescriptions are not, strictly speaking, conventions, since they are presumably derived from scripture and are not considered by the devout to be the products of social consensus. With Catholicism this issue is complicated by the existence of church authorities (i.e., the pope and the bishops) who are empowered to determine such issues for members of the Catholic faith. It was yet our view that such issues would not be treated as matters of morality by Catholics.

Participants in the study were asked to make three kinds of judgments. First, they were asked to rate the seriousness of each transgression using a 4-point scale on which 1 = not wrong at all and 4 = very seriously wrong. The remaining two judgments required subjects to employ criteria for identifying the moral (i.e., prescriptivity, universality) as set out in domain theory. Judgments of the prescriptivity of various actions was evoked by asking (1) whether it would be wrong or all right for the pope in conjunction with the bishops to remove the attendant moral and conventional rules, and (2) if it would be wrong or all right for a Catholic to engage in a given behavior once the rule was removed. Judgments of the universality of acts as constituting wrongful behavior were evoked by asking whether it would be all right or wrong for members of another religion to engage in the behavior if the other religion had no rules or standards regarding the acts.

Participants in the study were 100 sophomores attending religion classes at two Chicago Catholic high schools and equal numbers of undergraduates attending a Chicago-area university. A preliminary set of questions determined that both groups were devout, practicing churchgoers (92% of the university Catholics and 95.3% of the high school students received communion at least monthly). In addition, nearly all of the participants in both groups adhered to the traditional Catholic beliefs that Mary remained a virgin at the time of Christ's conception, that Christ is God and rose from the dead, and that Peter was the first head of the church.

With regard to subjects' judgments of the seriousness of transgressions, we found that both the high school and college-age Catholics rated the moral transgressions as more serious than violations of Catholic conventions. This finding occurred despite the fact that according to church dogma, engagement in a number of the prohibited conventional behaviors entail the same severe penalty (i.e., damnation) as engagement in the prohibited moral acts. These data are consistent with findings from other research in secular settings indicating that children and adolescents tend to rate moral transgressions as more serious than violations of convention (Tisak and Turiel, 1988), and indicate that the Catholic adolescents and young adults in our study based their judgments of the greater seriousness of moral transgressions on criteria other than the punishments assumed by Catholic dogma. It is our view that these Catholics judged the moral transgressions to be more serious because of the intrinsic effects such actions as hitting, stealing, slander and rape have on the recipient of the act.

Findings for the high school and college-age Catholics' responses to questions regarding the removal of Church rules are presented in the table. As can be seen there, the overwhelming majority of the participants (on average 91.6% high school, 98% university) viewed it as wrong for church authorities to remove rules governing moral transgressions, such as hitting and stealing. In contrast, on average, less than half of the high school (40.8%) and university (32.7%) Catholics viewed it as wrong for the pope to remove the church rules regarding nonmoral (conventional) behaviors, such as fasting prior to communion, the ordination of women, the use of contraceptives, or engaging in premarital sex. Responses to questions regarding whether or not it would be wrong to engage in the various actions once religious prohibitions were removed essentially paralleled the findings regarding the removal of the rules themselves. It would appear that to the extent that devout American Catholics grant the pope and other religious leaders the authority to alter the standards for "good" or "right" Catholic conduct, this authority extends only to actions in the nonmoral (conventional) domain.

One possible explanation for this finding is that the majority of American Catholics, contrary to Church dogma, do not view the pope as infallible in matters of faith. Our own data would tend to bear that out. Only 23% of our university sample and 28% of our high school participants adhered to the belief in papal infallibility. These findings are in line with other surveys of American Catholic attitudes dating back to the 1970s (cf. NBC News Poll 122, 1979). For the remaining quarter of our subjects, who professed a belief in papal infallibility, our findings may reflect an incredulity on their part that the pope would make the error of removing church rules governing moral actions. In either case, these results are in line with the view that people may generate ideas about the prescriptivity of moral actions independent of the rules or pronouncements of religious authorities.

With respect to relativity questions (i.e., questions about other religions), we found that Catholics tended to universalize only the moral is-

TABLE 2.1. Percentages of High School and University Catholics
Responding "It Would Be Wrong" to Questions Regarding Religious Rules

Type of Rule	Would it be wrong or all right for the pope and cardinals to drop the rule about the act?		Suppose that another religion, religion B, has no rule or law about the act. Would it be wrong or all right for a member of religion B to do the act?	
	High School	University	High School	University
Moral				
Hitting and hurting	93	100	92	98
Rape	98	100	98	100
Murder	98	100	98	98
Kidnap and ransom	97	100	94	98
Stealing	98	100	92	100
Damaging another's home	90	100	94	98
Sell dangerous defective car to unsuspecting buyer	79	96	83	94
Slander	90	98	82	98
Betray another's personal secrets	90	96	92	94
Racial discrimination in hiring	72	89	75	84
Ridiculing a cripple	97	100	90	98
Allowing another to be punished for one's own misdeeds	97	100	96	98
Church convention				
Not attending services on Sunday	46	42	39	12
Eating 15 minutes before communion	38	34	19	12
Receiving communion without confession	50	47	45	35
Year without communion	57	38	36	14
Not attend mass on Easter or Christmas	62	54	48	31
Ordaining women	39	16	29	08

Type of Rule	Would it be wrong or all right for the pope and cardinals to drop the rule about the act?		Suppose that another religion, religion B, has no rule or law about the act. Would it be wrong or all right for a member of religion B to do the act?	
	High School	University	High School	University
Sexual conventions				
Premarital sex	29	32	17	12
Masturbation	43	18	25	14
Birth control (the "pill")	22	16	27	08
Divorce	18	31	22	27
Marital sex for pleasure	21	12	25	06

sues. The findings are also summarized in Table 2.1. On average, 91% of the high school participants and 97% of the university students viewed it as wrong for members of another religion to engage in acts that were moral transgressions (e.g., stealing, harm to another) even if the other religion had no rules regarding the acts. In contrast to moral issues, fewer than half of the Catholics (on average 33.8% high school, 18.2% university) were willing to universalize Catholic conventions and treat as wrong engagement in such conventional actions by members of religions that do not regulate those behaviors. The tendency of the participants in the study to acknowledge the relativism of their church's conventions is highlighted by findings that the percentages of participants viewing acts as wrong for members of another religion were significantly less than the percentages of participants who viewed it as wrong for Catholics themselves to engage in the behaviors if the pope removed the governing rules. In sum, these findings indicate that Catholics distinguish between church conventions, which serve to organize and regulate the behaviors of persons who define themselves as Catholics, and those moral acts that have an intrinsic effect upon the rights and well-being of others, Catholic and non-Catholic alike.

Our study of Catholics provided very strong support for our hypotheses regarding morality and religion. It must be said, however, that Catholicism, because of its organizational structure, seems ideally suited for the type of question we posed. Catholics, particularly since Vatican II, have become accustomed to the notion that church regulations may be altered by the hierarchy, and therefore relative to the historical period. As our research has shown, Catholics extend this relativity only to church regulations that refer to matters of convention. Nonetheless, one might ask whether members of fundamentalist or orthodox groups, which eschew the notion of a temporal Church hierarchy and presumably derive their rules directly from scripture, would react in a similar fashion when asked about the alterability or universality of their religious conventions. To address these issues we conducted subsequent studies with Amish/Mennonite and Dutch Reform Calvinist Christian, and with Conservative and Orthodox Jewish children and adolescents.

MORALITY AND RELIGIOUS NORMS AS SEEN BY FUNDAMENTALIST CHRISTIANS AND JEWS

The findings I will be discussing came from several different studies (Nucci 1985; Nucci and Turiel 1993). The results from these studies, however, present a fairly consistent picture, and so to keep from being repetitive, I will talk about them together. We modified our methods from the study with Catholics and employed extensive interviews rather than questionnaires. This allowed us to get a better sense of the reasons children had for the responses they gave to individual questions. Before I get into the details of our methods, let me say something about the backgrounds of the children and adolescents who participated in the research.

Christian participants. The Christian children who participated in the research were conservative Mennonites from a rural area of Indiana and a subgroup of Amish/Mennonite children from the same area. The Mennonites constitute a religious denomination within the larger Anabaptist community, which had its origins in the Swiss reformation. Historically, the Amish are an offshoot of the Mennonite community, which itself has branches that are relatively "liberal" in comparison with the group that participated in our study. Within the particular Indiana locale where we conducted our research, the Amish and Conservative Mennonites shared the same parochial school overseen by congregational pastors and administered by an Amish principal. The beliefs and lifestyle of the Conservative Mennonites and Amish in this population were essentially the same, with very minor differences in the dress of women within each group.

The group as a whole is distinguished by their isolation from much of contemporary society and their rejection of most aspects of modern technology. With regard to the latter, the lifestyle of this population was a bit less restrictive than the lifestyle adopted by their relatives in Pennsylvania (e.g., families within this community were permitted to own cars, most homes had electricity, and the school was very proud of its one Apple computer). These accommodations to modernity were justified as serving the ability of the community to effectively conduct their work. As explained by the Amish school principal, the group remained committed, despite these accommodations, to serving as a witness to Christ by remaining outside the mainstream of American customs and maintaining themselves as a "queer people." One of the children humorously quipped to me regarding their lifestyle, "If you think we're weird you ought to go to Pennsylvania." Among the beliefs and practices held by these children and their families were a number common to other Anabaptist groups, such as the rejection of infant baptism and papal authority. In addition, they adhered to a prohibition against radio or television in the home and to a prescribed plain mode of dress, the latter being more marked among the women than the men. Women, for example, were all required to wear a prescribed head covering following baptism, and were prohibited from wearing trousers. In most cases, the girls in the study wore solid-color, calf-length homemade dresses patterned after those of their seventeenth-century ancestors. A total of 64 Amish/Mennonite children participated in the study. Half of the children were girls and half boys distributed across four age groups (10 to 11, 12 to 13, 14 to 15, and 16 to 17 years of age).

Jewish participants. To expand our investigation within the Judeo-Christian tradition, we followed our study with the Amish/Mennonites with one focusing on Jewish children. Two groups of Jewish children from the Chicago metropolitan area participated in our interviews. The first group was 64 Conservative Jewish children, with equal numbers of boys and girls at ages 10 to 11, 12 to 13, 14 to 15, and 16 to 17 years. These children (and their families) were all active members of Conservative synagogues and attended parochial, private religious schools. The second group was 32 Orthodox Jewish children, with equal numbers of boys and girls at ages 14 to 15, and 16 to 17 years. The Orthodox children attended an Orthodox Jewish academy (high school) and followed Jewish dietary laws, dress customs, and holiday rituals. Many of the Conservative children followed these same practices, but with less consistency than did the

Orthodox. For example, the Orthodox boys wore head coverings at all times, while most of the Conservative boys wore theirs only at school or during prayer. In addition, the Conservative children tended to observe few of the dietary laws (such as prohibitions against eating pork) prescribed by Orthodox Judaism, and came from homes that purchased foods from nonkosher producers. We chose to interview children from these two groups because they were representative of the two branches of traditional Judaism. None of the Orthodox children, for example, was part of a fundamentalist sect, such as the Hassidic.

The schism between the Orthodox and Conservatives had its historical origins in the Enlightenment as a response to Spinoza's critiques of traditional Judaic teachings. The Orthodox rejected Spinoza and the Enlightenment out of hand. Others, however, were deeply influenced by Spinoza, and later Hegel, to formulate the philosophy of the Reform movement. The Conservatives took a middle position between the Reform movement and the Orthodox. Like the Reform movement, they accepted the idea that aspects of Jewish scripture were to be understood as historical products, rather than solely a record of divine revelation. Like the Orthodox, however, they found the Reform movement's rejection of traditional ritual unacceptable. The Conservatives view rituals and religious norms as fundamental connections to historical Jewish experience (Borowitz 1968).

The Interview

Each of the Christian and Jewish children was individually interviewed for approximately ninety minutes (spread over several sessions) regarding his or her conceptions of moral and nonmoral religious prescriptions. Amish–Mennonite children were asked about four moral issues (stealing, hitting, slander, damaging another's personal property) and seven nonmoral religious issues (day of worship, work on the Sabbath, baptism, women wearing head coverings, women preaching, interfaith marriage, premarital sex between consenting adults). The premarital sex questions were only asked of children 14 years of age and older. The interview used with Jewish children included the same moral issues (stealing, hitting, slander, and damage to personal property) that were used with the Amish/Mennonites. The nonmoral religious issues discussed with Jewish children matched those we had used with the Christians, but were modified to make them appropriate for Jewish subjects. The nonmoral issues were day of worship, work on the Sabbath, men wearing head coverings, male circumcision, women reading from the Torah, interfaith marriage, maintaining kosher dietary laws, and premarital sex between consenting adults. Three issues (dietary laws, interfaith marriage, and premarital sex between consenting adults) were presented only to children above the age of 13.

Interviews for both sets of children asked three main sets of questions. Each question set was designed to generate a specific criterion judgment and corresponding justification. The first dealt with the alterability of religious rules. The children were asked: "Suppose all the members of the congregation and the ministers(rabbis) agreed to [alter/eliminate] the rule about [the act], would it be wrong or all right for them to do that?" "Why/why not?" The second question dealt with the children's views of the universality of the status of the acts as transgressions. The issue here was not whether children believed that an act was universally considered to be wrong, but whether in their minds the acts *should* be considered wrong. Children were asked: "Suppose that in another religion they don't have a rule about [the act], would it be wrong or all right for them to [engage in the act] in that case?" "Why/why not?" Inasmuch as the groups in these studies, unlike the Catholics in our initial research, do not acknowledge a final earthly authority (i.e., the pope and bishops) over scriptural interpretation, we included a third set of questions aimed at determining whether the status of acts as transgressions was contingent on God's word as recorded in scripture. Each child was asked: "Suppose Jesus[God] had not given us a law about the act, the Bible [Torah] didn't say anything one way or another about [the act]. Would it be wrong or all right for a Christian [Jew] to do [the act] in that case?" "Why/why not?"

Interview outcomes

Let us begin discussion of the results of those interviews by considering the findings presented on Table 2.2 regarding children's (alterability) judgments of whether it would be wrong or all right for religious authorities to remove or alter the rules governing various actions. As shown in the table, all three groups of children consistently stated that it would be wrong for the authorities or the collective membership of the congregation to remove rules prohibiting actions in the moral domain. These findings are in line with what we would predict on the basis of domain theory, and are consistent with what we found with Catholics. The children's responses to the same question with respect to what we had considered nonmoral issues, however, were not consistent with a distinction between

TABLE 2.2. Percentages of Amish/Mennonite (A), Conservative Jewish (C), and Orthodox Jewish (O) Children Responding "It Would Be Wrong" to Criterion Judgment Questions

Issue	Alterability			Generalizability			God's Word		
	A	C	O	A	C	O	A	C	O
Nonmoral									
Day of worship	42	86	94	20	1	0	0	0	0
Work on Sabbath	92	80	100	50	0	0	0	0	0
Baptism/ Circumcision	77	81	81	31	0	6	0	0	2
Wearing head coverings	67	48	69	16	0	6	0	0	0
Women preaching/ reading from the Torah	56	41	63	19	0	0	6	0	0
Interfaith marriage	42	42	88	19	14	25	0	14	9
Keeping kosher	—	20	91	—	0	09	—	0	2
Premarital sex	41	23	81	34	11	47	12	06	38
Nonmoral average	60	53	83	27	03	12	03	03	06
Moral									
Stealing	92	94	94	100	92	91	84	94	97
Hitting	94	88	91	91	92	94	88	97	100
Slander	92	94	88	97	97	91	84	91	100
Property damage	95	95	97	89	98	97	91	97	97
	93	93	93	94	95	93	87	93	98

morality and nonmoral issues, and were clearly different from the pattern of answers provided by Catholics. For example, nearly as many Amish/Mennonite children said it would be wrong for religious authorities or the congregation to alter the prohibition against work on Sunday as said it would be wrong to remove the rules against moral transgressions, such as hitting and hurting others or damaging another's personal property. Orthodox Jewish children were even more reluctant than the Amish/Mennonites or Conservative Jews to grant their religious authorities power to alter or remove nonmoral religious rules. There was no statistical difference between the overall percentages of alterability judgments that Orthodox Jewish children made of moral and nonmoral issues.

These outcomes appear to embody the assumptions shared by fundamentalist Christians and Conservative or Orthodox Jews that religious norms are established through scripture, rather than by earthly authority. For the Amish, this is consistent with their historical rejection of papal authority and their reliance on literal interpretations of the Bible for guidance in their daily lives. The justifications children from each of these three denominations provided in explaining their judgments about the nonmoral issues tended to bear that out. The most common reason given for objecting to the notion of religious authorities altering such rules was that the rules were a part of "God's law." In the case of the Amish/Mennonites and Orthodox, this justification was given 80% of the time in support of judgments that it would be wrong to alter such rules.

Looking at the complete set of justifications, however, indicated to us that a "revealed truth" orientation was not all that was operating in the alterability judgments of these Christian and Jewish children. Between 30% and 40% of the justifications Jewish children gave for their judgments regarding the alterability of nonmoral religious norms focused on the organizational, historical, or symbolic functions such norms provided in terms of structuring the religion as a social system. In the case of Amish/Mennonites and Conservative Jews, such reasons were generally given in support of the notion that religious authorities could, in fact, alter or remove some religious rules. However, such judgments were also offered in support of the notion that it would be wrong to change existing rules. This was particularly the case with Jewish children who were keen on the notion of maintaining such rules to sustain links with the past. With respect to moral issues, it was apparent that children had reasons beyond "God's law" to object to alterations in the governing rules. Approximately 40% of the justifications provided by Amish/Mennonites and 75% of the justifications provided by Jewish children for objecting to alterations in the rules governing moral actions focused on the intrinsic features of the acts as hurtful or unjust.

If we turn from the alterability results to a consideration of our findings with respect to the children's responses to generalizabilty questions, we find an increased differentiation between moral and nonmoral issues. As can be seen in Table 2.2, actions that entail moral transgressions were judged by over 90% of the children to be wrong even for members of another religion that had no rules governing the acts. There were no denominational differences in these findings; Christians and Jews treated these issues in the same way. In contrast, far fewer children from any of the three denominations we examined responded that it would be wrong for members of another religion to engage in actions we had identified as nonmoral, if the other religion had no rules governing the acts. It would appear then that, as in the case with Catholics, the Amish/Mennonite and Jewish children we interviewed universalized moral issues, but viewed as relative to their religious prescriptions many nonmoral actions.

There were denominational differences associated with these judgments, with the Amish somewhat more willing than Jewish children to universalize the nonmoral rules of their religion, and Orthodox Jews more willing to universalize Jewish norms than were Conservative Jews. This observed difference between Christians and Jews is not surprising, given the proselytizing nature of Christianity sustained by the belief that Christ came to save mankind and that each Christian should serve as a witness to this and spread the "good news." While both Judaism and Christianity contain natural-law perspectives within their religious traditions that would support generalizing moral rules, Jews make an explicit differentiation between moral laws that any human being should be able to construct from direct experience, and those rules that can only be known through God. The latter set of rules are thought to constitute a special set of obligations for Jews. In effect, one can be a good person without being Jewish, but one cannot be a good Jew without adhering to this second (nonmoral) set of rules (Danon 1972).

The justifications children provided across the denominations help to explain their generalizability judgments. Across denominations, there was a tendency for children to contextualize nonmoral religious rules as relative to particular religious systems. This is somewhat surprising with respect to the Amish/Mennonites, given the "God's law" justification provided for their alterability judgments and the requirement to bear witness to Christ. The Amish, however, bear witness in a much less intrusive way than is done by many other Christian sects. It is through their lifestyle itself that they bear witness. Through their distinctiveness, they hope to draw attention to the Christian gospel, as well as protect themselves from the temptations of the "world." The reasons provided by Amish/Mennonite children for not generalizing their nonmoral rules include an assumption that such rules are subject to interpretation, and that members of other religions might simply be ignorant of God's law. Both justifications are concordant with two other values held by this denomination: (1) One should not sit in judgment of others, and (2) one can make a distinction between those who are "saved" (chosen) and those who are not. Thus, the ignorant may be excused and the deviant tolerated, but they are nonetheless not part of the community (i.e., Mennonites) closest to God.

In this latter attitude, the Amish/Mennonites and the Jewish children we studied would seem to be of similar minds. What is interesting in this context is that in contrast to the relative tolerance shown regarding non-moral issues, the Amish/Mennonite and Conservative and Orthodox Jews we interviewed, like the Catholics in our questionnaire study, viewed it as wrong for members of other religions to engage in actions (e.g., slander) constituting transgressions in the moral domain. Instead of evoking God's law as a basis for such judgments, the majority of our Amish/Mennonite and Jewish subjects were expecting even the nonbeliever to view such actions as wrong because of their intrinsic effects upon the rights and welfare of others.

The last set of questions in this part of the interview was intended to examine directly whether or not the children viewed morality as dependent on God's word. Children's responses to the "God's word" questions are summarized in Table 2.2. As can be seen there, few children at any age and of any denomination felt it would be wrong to engage in any of the nonmoral behaviors if God (as indicated in scripture) had not provided any prescription or statement governing the act. These judgments were mirrored in the justifications they provided. In nearly all cases, the children explained that such actions would be all right essentially because there was no longer any law from God regulating the acts. The only exceptions to this predominant trend were in relation to sexual and gender-based issues in which some prudential (personal safety/risk) and natural-order justifications (e.g., women are not suited by nature to lead a congregation) were provided. Prudence and natural-order reasons were also offered by some Orthodox children as a basis for maintaining kosher dietary laws.

In contrast, between 80% and 100% of children across denominations stated that engagement in any of the acts entailing a moral transgression would continue to be wrong even if there were no biblical prescription or statement by God concerning the act. The justifications children provided in support of such judgments all dealt with the intrinsic features of the acts as hurtful or unjust. This last set of findings suggests that even for deeply religious children from fundamentalist or orthodox backgrounds, morality stems from criteria independent of God's word.

The following excerpts (edited for length) from our interviews with Amish/Conservative Mennonite and Conservative and Orthodox Jewish children illustrate the thinking of these children regarding the relationship between religious prescription and the regulation of moral and nonmoral(conventional) behavior. The first is from an interview with an

11-year-old Amish boy, Sam (a pseudonym). The first portion of the interview deals with the Amish convention that women wear head coverings. The biblical source of this convention is Paul's Letter to the Corinthians (I:11). The boy's responses are given in the context of a story that tells of a Conservative Mennonite girl who attends a local public junior high school where none of the other girls wears a head covering. In order not to be different, the Mennonite girl, Mary, decides not to wear her head covering to school.

The second excerpt presents this same child's responses to questions regarding a moral issue, stealing. The excerpts are as follows:

SAM, Conservative Mennonite boy (11 years, 11 months)

Religious Convention: Women wearing head coverings.

I: Was Mary right or wrong not to wear a head covering at school?

S: Wrong, because the Bible says you should, the women should have their hair long and have it covered with a covering and the men should have their hair short.

I: Do you think it really matters whether or not a Mennonite girl wears a head covering?

S: It depends on if you are baptized or not. If you are baptized, you should.

I: How come?

S: Because that's the way God wants it.

I: Can that rule about head coverings be changed?

S: Yes, I suppose it could.

I: Would it be all right for the ministers to remove the rule about women wearing head coverings?

S: No.

I: Why not?

S: Because God said that's how He wants it, and that's how He wants it.

I: If the ministers did remove the rule about head coverings, then would it be all right for girls not to wear the head coverings?

S: If they were obeying the minister and not God, it would be, but if they were obeying God and not the ministers, then it wouldn't.

I: Suppose it wasn't written in the Bible that women are supposed to wear head coverings, God hadn't said anything about head coverings one way or the other. Would it be all right for women not to wear head coverings then?

S: Yeah, it would be okay then, because if God didn't say so, it wouldn't matter.

I: The other girls at Mary's school belong to religions that don't have the rule about head coverings. Is it okay that those religions don't have the rule?

S: It's all right if that's the way their church believes.
I: Well, then is it okay for those girls not to wear head coverings?
S: Yeah.
I: Why is it okay for them but not for Mary?
S: Because she goes to a Mennonite Christian church, she should obey the Mennonite Christian laws.
I: Could a woman still be a good Christian and not wear a head covering?
S: It depends on her, it depends on if she is really a good Christian and has accepted Christ.
I: Well, then, why wear a head covering?
S: Because if you are around people more often, like if one person doesn't have one and the other one does and they are both good Christians, and they are both walking and a guy comes up and says, man, I can tell which one's a Christian out of them. This one over here has a covering and I can tell she is, but over here I don't know for sure because she doesn't wear one. I would have to do some questioning before I know for sure.

Moral Issue: Stealing

I: Is it okay to steal?
S: No.
I: Why not?
S: Because that is one of the Ten Commandments that God put in the law and gave to Moses and He expects us to obey these laws and if we don't obey these laws, we can know for sure that we will not go to heaven, we will absolutely go to hell.
I: What's wrong with stealing?
S: Having something that does not belong to us and taking it from someone else, it would just irritate you. Like, one time my sister stole my radio batteries. I didn't know that they were and then I found out that she had them in her tape recorder and I thought that these were the exact ones so I took them back. Actually, she had them in her drawer and she saw these were missing so she came back four hours later while I was in bed sleeping and she just grabbed them right out of there and put mine back in. By this time, she had worn mine down and they weren't working so I thought for sure that she had just wore hers out and so I went and stole mine back which were really hers. My conscience just bothered me until I returned them and took the other ones and I found out that these were the correct ones to be having anyway.
I: Should the rule about stealing be followed?
S: Yes, or else we will go to hell. And all of those will know, and those who are on earth already know that hell is a bad place. There's fire and brimstone and you could die down there! And everybody that goes there, they know that they are a sinful person.

I: Suppose all the ministers decided to drop the rule about stealing so that there was no rule about stealing. would that be all right?

S: No.

I: Why not?

S: Because God said that it wouldn't be expected of us and he expects us to obey him.

I: Would it be all right for a Christian to steal if the ministers dropped the rule?

S: No, because you still wouldn't be able to go to heaven, you'd have to go to hell.

I: Suppose the people of another religion don't have a rule about stealing. Is that all right?

S: No.

I: Why not?

S: Because if they have their Bible, then they know about the law.

I: Suppose they don't use our Bible, they have a different religion and it doesn't have a rule about stealing. Is that all right?

S: No, because God said that thou shalt not steal and that goes for everybody.

I: If they didn't know about the rule, would it be okay for them to steal?

S: No, because it would still make everybody unhappy.

I: If God hadn't said anything about stealing one way or the other, would it be okay to steal then?

S: No.

I: Why Not?

S: Because if people would steal, then the world wouldn't be very happy.

I: Could you say more about that?

S: Like when my sister stole my batteries, it really irritated me. If everybody's stuff kept getting stolen, everyone would be mad and say, "Hey, where's my stuff?" It would be terrible; nobody could keep anything that was theirs. I wouldn't like it.

As we have seen, Sam makes a distinction between issues of morality (i.e., stealing) and matters of religious convention. Now, let's place Sam's interview into context with the following excerpts from an interview with a 9-year-old Conservative Jewish girl we will call Marsha. Marsha was also interviewed about stealing and the Jewish norm that requires boys to wear head coverings (kippot).

MARSHA, Conservative Jewish girl (9 years, 7 months)

Religious Convention: Men wearing head coverings.

I: Was Jonathan right or wrong not to wear his kippah to the public school?

M: It was wrong because he's not showing his, uh, his, like his religion. You should always show how good your religion is, and you should always keep the mitzvah. And also, he's probably disobeying his parents.

I: Okay. Do you think it matters whether or not Jewish boys wear kippot?

M: I think it matters. For one thing, you can never tell if it's a Jewish man or not a Jewish man and you could say, "Can I, uh, can I have, can you give charity to the people, to the poor people?" And they would say, "No, I'm not Jewish." How would I know? Like you'd get really embarrassed, because you don't really know, and also like, when you are trying to do something really good and you find out he's not wearing a kippah and also it shows that he doesn't, like, go in the laws of HaShem[God].

I: But why do Jewish boys dress differently? Why do they wear kippot?

M: Because it's a law of HaShem, and they're just supposed to.

I: Suppose that the rabbis got together and removed the rule about wearing kippot. Would that be all right?

M: No.

I: Why not?

M: Because it's been that way and that's a rule.

I: Well, if they did agree and removed the rule, then would it be all right for Jewish boys not to wear kippot?

M: No.

I: Why not?

M: Because the rule is there and it was meant to stay there.

I: The Christians don't require boys to wear kippot, is that all right?

M: Yeah.

I: Why?

M: Because, well, because that's not one of their rules. They don't respect God in the same way.

I: Is it okay that they respect god in a different way?

M: Yes. The religion is different. What they do is not our business, and if they want to do that they can.

I: Suppose that it never said in the Talmud or anywhere else in scripture anything about wearing kippot, then would it be all right for Jewish boys to read the Torah or pray without wearing a kippah?

M: Yeah. I mean why would anybody need to do it if it wasn't there? How would anybody know?

Moral Issue: Stealing.

I: Is it okay to steal?

M: No, because its a law in the Torah, and it's also one of the Ten Commandments.

I: Does that rule have to be followed?

M: Yeah.

I: Why?

M: Because HaShem said so in the Torah, and, uh, you should follow all the mitzvahs of HaShem. The Torah has 613 mitzvahs.

I: Suppose all the rabbis got together and decided not to have a rule about stealing. Would that be okay?

M: No.

I: Why?

M: Because like I said before in some of the other questions, it's a rule of HaShem. They can't like change it 'cause like once when Moishe was walking, his sons wanted, there was a law and they wanted to change it, and they changed it and their punishment was to die.

I: Suppose that people of another religion do not have a rule about stealing. Is that all right?

M: Probably yes – but no. So, it's like half yes and half no.

I: Could you explain that to me?

M: Well, like if they don't have a rule they might think that it's okay to steal, and no because it still wouldn't be.

I: Why would it still be wrong?

M: Because you're taking something from another person. And the other person – let's say it was a real gold pen or something and you really love it, like it was a present or something from your bar mitzvah or something, or bat mitzvah, and it would be really wrong for the other people. Because it's like a treasure to them. Like on a Peanuts show, Linus can't live without his blanket. It's like a beautiful present to him and he really needs it. It's like a treasure. Without it he probably can't live. And another thing is because, say there's one person and he steals from another person who steals from the first person who stole things. Well, he would feel, both, like one that got stealed from would get real angry and the one that already stole with the first stealer also would get angry because his stuff was stolen. That he already stole, probably.

I: Suppose that there was never a law in the Torah. God never made it one of the Ten Commandments or one of the 613. He just didn't say anything about stealing. Would it be okay to steal then?

M: No. Still I don't think it's right because you're taking something from somebody else. But to some people probably yes, because they think it's fair because, well, they might say, "Finders keepers, losers weepers."

I: I see. Is it right to say that?

M: No, because they really took it and they didn't just find it, and the other people didn't lose it. It's not fair. And besides, it's also a lie. So there are two wrong things in that then.

What is evident in the excerpts of both of these Christian and Jewish children is that they acknowledge that the rule about head coverings is based on the word of authority (God), that it is relative to a particular interpretation or view of that authority's norms, and that it serves the concrete, social, organizational function of distinguishing girls from boys and members of their particular religious community from others. In contrast with their views about head coverings, both children treated stealing as universally wrong, and wrong even if God did not have a rule about it. The wrongness of stealing, according to both children, is that it leads to hurtful and unjust consequences. According to both children, engagement in such actions has a tendency to generate acts of retaliation, which themselves tend to evolve into a vicious circle of self-perpetuating harm and injustice. Each child employed evidence from his and her own personal experience as a touchstone from which to evaluate these moral transgressions. As I suggested in Chapter 1, children construct their initial understandings of morality out of their experiences as victims, observers, or perpetrators of unjust or hurtful actions. Those experiences provide children with an understanding of the intrinsic elements of morality, elements that exist as a part of human relations apart from the particulars of their religious faith.

A few of the Jewish children made an effort in their interviews to articulate the connection between these inherent, rational features of morality and the distinction drawn in Jewish theology between the norms that express particular obligations for Jews and moral obligations that hold for all people. In the following excerpt, David, a 14-year-old Orthodox Jewish boy, employs the distinction made in Judaism between the laws between man and man and those between man and God in order to address the distinction he made between breaking the rules of the Sabbath and engaging in slander.

DAVID, Orthodox Jewish boy (14 years, 6 months)

I: David, is it okay to slander someone?
D: No.
I: Why not?
D: The definition of slander means that you are damaging someone else's reputation. That's probably one of the worst things that you can do.
I: Suppose that the rabbis got together and agreed that there should be no rule about slander, would that be all right?
D: No. That's like saying what's wrong with ruining this man's life?
I: Is it like breaking the Sabbath?
D: No. It's not like breaking the Sabbath. Sabbath is a law between man and God, and this is a law between man and man. It would be more like stealing. Okay – It is a law clearly stated in the Torah – and besides that, I mean, just because of what it does to other people.

I: Suppose nothing was written in the Torah about slander, God hadn't said anything about it. Would it be right to slander in that case?

D: Well, I suppose some people might do it then, but I wouldn't. It still wouldn't be right. All the laws between man and man are rules that are just necessary for society to exist. If you know what an act does to other people then you wouldn't do that.

I: You wouldn't or shouldn't?

D: Shouldn't.

I: So, you differentiate between laws between God and man, and man and man?

D: Yes. When you ask the questions if God hadn't said anything about it, then would it be all right. The way I answered that was if it was a commandment between God and man, then if He had not said anything it would be fine. Because, uh, the only purpose of it was because God said so. Well, He might've had some ulterior motive, but we don't know what it is. But, between man and man, those are rules that, um, that you need to live a healthy life and not run around anything like wild animals.

I: So, now with the laws between man and man, do you think that they are wrong because they were forbidden by God, or were they forbidden, because they are wrong?

D: I guess both are true. I mean having it forbidden makes it officially wrong, but being morally wrong was the cause for the prohibition.

In David's interview, he made a distinction between actions in the moral domain that have an inherent moral basis and rules established by religious authority that appear to be arbitrary. As children become older, their understandings of the purposes of the nonmoral norms of their religion deepens as they are better able to comprehend the symbolic or organizational functions of such norms. We can see some of these changes within the following excerpt from an interview with a 17-year-old Amish youth whom I will refer to as Joseph. He is responding to the same vignette regarding head coverings as the previous children.

JOSEPH, Amish (17 years, 10 months)
Religious Convention: Women wearing head coverings

I: Was Mary right or wrong not to wear a head covering at school?

J: She was wrong.

I: How come?

J: Because a head covering, usually, symbolizes that she is a member of the church and she is to wear it all the time.

I: Do you think it really matters whether or not Mennonite girls wear head coverings?

J: I think it matters.

I: And why is that?

J: I guess it is a symbol of what God has done for them and they are then under submission. I guess, to be honest, as a boy, I don't know about that in detail, but I know one thing, that it is a sign of submission.

I: Why does a head covering mean that?

J: Well, in the Bible it says that the woman is supposed to keep her head covered and I think that if a girl is going by the standards of the Bible, then she should wear it.

I: What do you mean by submission in this case?

J: For a married lady, it means that she is under submission to her husband and to God. For a girl, I guess it would be under her parents' submission and to God also.

[At another point in the interview, Joseph had this to say.]

I: When you say identifying with the world, what do you mean?

J: Well, like, you want to look like them, you don't want to be different.

I: Why should a Mennonite look different?

J: I don't know that she would have to, she is really considered different. And, she would dress different, of course.

I: Why should they dress different?

J: So that people can see that they are not associated with the world. It is a witness to the power of God, rather than identifying with the world.

In this excerpt from the interview with Joseph, we can see that many of the nonmoral norms prescribed by religion serve similar functions in terms of structuring worship patterns and community that secular conventions do. This suggests that a part of children's religious development rests upon their developing conceptions of convention, custom, and tradition. In Joseph's interview regarding women's head coverings, he goes well beyond the concrete understanding that head coverings distinguish members of one's own group from others, evidenced in the interviews with Sarah and Sam, to explain how such rules regarding head coverings function as a symbol of the hierarchical, sex-typed order of Amish and Conservative Mennonite society, and the subordinate relationship of that society to God. Joseph extends his interpretation of head coverings to the more general symbolic function of Amish dress in order to express the fundamental perspective of his religious community and this particular way of discharging its obligation to serve witness to God's authority and majesty. What became clear from these interviews, however, was that children and adolescents do not base their interpretation of the importance of such religious norms on the same criteria as their views about morality. The force of such nonmoral norms rests ultimately in their connection to religious authority, whereas the force of moral norms derives from their connection to the impact that moral transgressions have upon human welfare.

Morality and God's word. The relation between morality and religious authority as understood by Jewish and Christian children was made even more clear in answers to a subsequent set of questions, which looked more specifically at the role of God's commands in determining the person's moral concepts. Our use of these questions emerged serendipitously out of an interview done early on in our conversations with Jewish children. The event occurred in the context of an interview with an 11-year-old Conservative Jewish émigré from the then–Soviet Union, whom we referred to as Michael. In responding to questions regarding whether it would be all right for Jews to hit and hurt others if God had no rule regarding such behavior, Michael spontaneously brought up the biblical story of Abraham and Isaac. In Michael's version of the biblical account, an angel of God conveyed a message to Abraham that he should kill his son, Isaac. Abraham, recognizing the command as a test of his faith, reluctantly prepared to sacrifice his son. As Abraham was about to slay Isaac, an angel of the Lord took hold of Abraham's arm to prevent him from cutting his son's throat. When asked what he thought about this, Michael's reply was "Had to." When asked what he meant, Michael explained, "Look, God is perfect, He couldn't allow Abraham to kill his son. Killing is wrong. It was only a test." At this point, the interviewer began to pursue further the general issue of the relation between God's commands and morality:

I: Michael, how do we know that what is written in the Torah is really the right thing to do?

M: He doesn't harm us, do bad for us. We believe in God. We think God wrote the Torah, and we think God likes us if we do those things and we think we are giving presents to God, by praying and by following His rules.

I: Okay, but how can we be sure that what God is telling us is really the right thing?

M: We've tried it. We've tried every rule in the Torah and we know.

I: Suppose God had written in the Torah that Jews should steal, would it then be right for Jews to steal?

M: No.

I: Why not?

M: Even if God says it, we know He can't mean it, because we know it is a very bad thing to steal. We know He can't mean it. Maybe it's a test, but we just know He can't mean it.

I: Why wouldn't God mean it?
M: Because we think of God as very good – absolutely perfect person.
I: And because He's perfect, He wouldn't say to steal? Why not?
M: Well, because we people are not perfect, but we still understand. We are
not dumb either. We still understand that stealing is a bad thing.

Michael's spontaneous comments captured features of a centuries-old
philosophical debate. Beginning with Plato's account of Socrates' dialogue with Euthyphro, philosophical arguments suggesting that God's
commands in and of themselves cannot determine what is moral have
turned on what is known as the "open question." Put simply, the open
question asks the following: "God commands X, but is X right?" To answer, one must invoke criteria for the good that are independent of God's
word. In Nielsen's (1973) treatment of this issue, the case is made that in
order for God's commands to be moral, it must at least be the case that
God is good. From this premise, Nielsen argues that Judeo-Christian conceptions of God presuppose prior, independent conceptions of goodness
that serve as criteria for differentiating God from Satan or other preter-
natural forces.

Though it was not our purpose to analyze or test those philosophical
positions, our research on religious conceptions of the relations between
morality and God's word were informed by such discussions of the open
question. Michael's interview had suggested to us that such questions
were ones that children would find interesting and well within their conceptual abilities. Following our interview with Michael, we added a section of questions in which children were asked whether God's commands
could make right something that most children treated as morally wrong.
These questions were asked of all of the Jewish participants in the research. The Amish religious authorities, however, found these questions
to be ones which they thought might cause their children to question their
faith. Therefore, we asked these questions of a second group of 32 Christian children who were members of the Dutch Reform Calvinist community in the Chicago metropolitan area.

These children all attended a parochial school that emphasized religious teaching. This group, like the Amish and Mennonites, has its origins
in the Swiss reformation. Unlike the Amish and Conservative Mennonites, the Dutch Reform Calvinists do not take a literal view of the Bible and
have an organized church structure and theology to help guide their interpretation of scripture. Like the Amish and Conservative Mennonites,
however, the Dutch Reform Calvinist community, from which our study

participants were drawn, hold the word of God to be compelling. We chose to interview children from this community because of their strong belief in the compelling nature of God's commands, stemming from an acceptance of God's perfection and omniscience, which extends to a belief in predestination.

Children were asked: "Suppose God had commanded (written in the Bible) that Christians/Jews *should* steal. Would it then be right for a Christian/Jew to steal?" We also asked children whether they thought God would make such a command, and if so, why or why not? It was our hypothesis, informed by Michael's' interview and results from our other questions, that children's answers would reflect their efforts to coordinate conceptions of moral issues in terms of the intrinsic effects of such actions on others with their conceptions of God as omniscient, omnipotent, and perfect. In particular, we expected that children would (1) reject the notion that God's command to steal would make stealing morally right and (2) reject the notion that God would command Christians or Jews to steal as a normative behavior.

Our analyses of the children's responses revealed that the majority of children from each denomination and at each age rejected the notion that God's command to steal would make it right to steal: 75% of the Dutch Reform Calvinists, 86% of the Conservative Jewish, and 84% of the Orthodox Jewish children responded this way. The apparent overall difference between the Christian and Jewish groups was due to the responses of younger children within the Christian community: 69% of Dutch Reform Calvinist children under the age of 13 rejected the notion that God's command would make it right to steal, while 81% of the children above age 13 responded that way.

The following excerpts from an interview with a 15-year-old Dutch Reform Calvinist girl (Margaret) and from an interview with a 9-year-old Conservative Jewish girl (Marsha) are typical of responses provided by children who rejected the notion that God's command to steal would make stealing right:

MARGARET, Dutch Reform Calvinist female (15 years, 7 months)

I: Suppose that God had written in the Bible that Christians should steal. Would it then be right for Christians to steal?

M: Probably, I think people would maybe do it. Because if it was written in the Bible and that's what God said that we should do, then people would probably do it. I mean more often. 'Cause that's what God said, and it's easier to do than to go against God.

I: So, if God said it, people would do it. But would they be right to do it?

M: No. It still wouldn't be right.

I: Why not?

M: 'Cause you're taking from somebody else, and it still wouldn't be right. After all, who would want this to happen to them?

I: Do you think God would command us to steal?

M: No.

I: Why not?

M: Because it's not the right thing to do, and He's perfect, and if He's stealing, He can't be perfect.

MARSHA, Conservative Jewish female (9 years, 7 months)

I: When we were talking before, you said that God had provided 613 rules in the Torah, but I have a question. How do we know that what is written in the Torah is really the right thing to do?

M: Because HaShem [God] chooses the right things.

I: How do you know that HaShem chooses the right things for us to do?

M: That's a hard question. I guess I trust Him. I'm afraid of Him, that means I trust Him, probably. Probably 'cause He helps me. He helps me do my stuff. I mean like He takes care of me sort of. Whenever I should deserve a punishment, He gives it to me.

I: Suppose that God had written in the Torah that Jews should steal; God commanded all Jews to steal. Would it be okay then for Jews to steal?

M: No.

I: Why not?

M: Because they know, they have a brain. They know it's really bothering the person they take it from.

I: Do you think God would ever command us to steal?

M: No.

I: Why not?

M: Because He's good. Like He's strict as a teacher, and He's nice as a, what's the nicest person in the world? I don't know what the nicest person in the world is. He's as nice as the nicest person in the world, or animal.

In the responses of these two children, we see that although there is both fear and awe of God's power, neither child accepts the notion that God's command to steal would make it right to do so. According to both children, such action would continue to be morally wrong because of its effects upon the victim. The Conservative Jewish girl, Marsha, like her counterpart, Michael, points to the irrationality of such a norm, and the assumption that rational beings "Because they know, they have a brain" would recognize a norm condoning theft as inherently counter to the needs and interests of people. Furthermore, in a manner matching Michael's' responses to similar questions, both girls coordinated their moral positions with an assumption of God's goodness. In the case of the 15-year-old Dutch Reform Calvinist girl, Margaret, this extends to the conclusion that if God were to make such a command, it would negate his status as a perfect being. In the following excerpts, we see evidence that such thinking for some of the children we interviewed constitutes the very criteria for worshipping God:

MARK, Dutch Reform Calvinist male (15 years, 4 months)

I: Do you think God would say that we should steal?

M: No.

I: Why not?

M: Because He's good in every way, and He wouldn't encourage people to do wrong.

I: But if God said to steal, would it make it right?

M: Well I'd still have doubts about it. If you knew it was from God, then you might think it was right. But, I really – I probably wouldn't – ah – worship God – if He said – if He encouraged us to do bad things.

I: How do we know that what is written in the Bible is the word of God and not the word of the devil?

M: Well, because we realize that many parts of the Bible are just good common sense, and that they are things that we would normally think. Like the Ten Commandments, that's right to you even before you understand the Ten Commandments. So, if a person told you to do what was right, you'd realize that this was a person who was good.

I: I see, and does God have to be good?

M: Well, yes. Because worshipping an evil being would not be a very intelligent thing to do.

NORM, Dutch Reform Calvinist male (16 years, 6 months)

I: Suppose that God had written in the Bible that Christians should steal. would it then be right for Christians to steal?)

N: No, then He wouldn't be a just God. And there are, I'm sure there are people who would go against Him, then, if He were an unjust God, even though He had absolute power.

We see in the thinking of these two adolescents a rejection of the Nietzschean dictum that might makes right, as well as Euthyphro's position that morality is determined by God's commands. Instead, what appears to be evidenced in these interviews is an attempt by children to coordinate their notion of the just Judeo-Christian God with what they *know to be morally right*.

While such was the case among the majority of children, a significant minority (between 15% and 20%) stated that God's command to steal *would* make stealing morally right. Such responses were of two types. The first type, provided by three of the Christian and three Conservative Jewish children under the age of 13, reflected a failure to coordinate conceptions of God's perfection with conceptions of God as omnipotent. The following set of excerpts from a Dutch Reform Calvinist girl, Cathy, serves as an illustrative example:

CATHY, Dutch Reform Calvinist female (10 years, 8 months)

I: How do we know that what the Bible tells us to do is really the right thing?
C: You have to believe.
I: Suppose God had made a commandment that we should steal. Would it then be morally right to steal?
C: Yes.
I: So, who would be the better people then, the ones who stole or the ones who didn't steal?
C: The ones who stole.
I: Why would they be the better people?
C: Because they were obeying God's law.
I: Why should people obey God's law?
C: Because God is the only God. He made us, and He made the world, and He rules the world, and we are supposed to do what He says.

In this first portion of the interview, Cathy focused on God's power and authority as the criterion for her judgment of the right or wrong of stealing. In the very next section of the interview, however, her focus shifted to God's goodness and an evaluation of moral actions in terms of their consequences:

I: Do you think that God would tell us to steal?
C: No.
I: Why not?
C: Because God is – He's supposed to be good.
I: Is stealing good?
C: No.
I: Why not?
C: 'Cause – it's bad. It's not right. You're taking another person's stuff and they would probably get upset. I don't want my stuff stolen.

In this transcript we see two seemingly contradictory positions coexisting in the thinking of this 10-year-old girl. One the one hand, she evaluated the wrongness of stealing on the basis of its effects on the victim and
coordinated that evaluation with her expectation that God would not con-
done stealing since God is good. On the other hand, she evaluated the
right or wrong of stealing in terms of God's commands. She did not con-
join her notion of God's goodness with his omnipotence, but simply focused on the latter criterion to the exclusion of the former when evaluating the morality of actions commanded by God. This mode of thinking
was continued in the remaining portion of her interview:

I: Do you think it would be right if the children at school hit and hurt each
other?
C: No.
I: Why not?
C: Because hitting hurts!
I: Suppose that God said that children should hit one another. Do you think
it would be right then for children to do that?
C: Yes.
I: How come?
C: Because God said.
I: But wouldn't it still hurt to hit?
C: Yes.
I: Then would it be right or wrong to hit?
C: It would be right.
I: How come?
C: Like I told you, because God said.

The thinking of this 10-year-old girl was not seen in the interviews of
any of our participants over age 13. However, since only three Christian
and three Conservative Jewish children provided responses of the form
just described, we cannot conclude whether such reasoning is a function
of developmental level or if it simply reflects an alternative mode of conceptualizing the relationship between morality and God's word.

A second, and more sophisticated, type of reasoning provided by adolescents who felt that God's command to steal would make stealing
morally right resulted from efforts to coordinate notions of God's perfection with conceptions of God's omniscience. In this form of reasoning, the
assumption is maintained that God is good, and that his command to steal
(or to engage in some other apparently hurtful or unjust act) would reflect
good intentions and an ultimately good outcome. Since God is all-know-

ing, only He can anticipate and comprehend an outcome that may simply be beyond the grasp of temporal consciousness. In reasoning of this type, one sustains faith in the goodness of God without requiring that His ends be comprehensible to the faithful. Such thinking is provided in the following excerpt from an interview with a 17-year-old Dutch Reform Calvinist girl we refer to as Faith:

FAITH, Dutch Reform Calvinist female (17 years, 6 months)

I: Faith, how do we know that what is in the Bible is really the right thing to do?

F: I believe that the Bible is the word of God and that God knows everything and God made us, so what He said must be true.

I: It may be true, but how do we know that what God is saying is really morally right, if He says act a certain way that that's the morally right way to act?

F: He created us, so He knows what's best for us, so whatever He says must be the best thing to do.

I: Suppose that God had written in the Bible that Christians should steal. Would it then be right for Christians to steal?

F: If God said so, I guess it would be, yes.

I: How come? What would make it right?

F: Because God is the author of everything and He's holy, and whatever He would say has to be right.

I: Suppose God had said that Christians should murder. Would it then be right for Christians to murder?

F: It would be the same as with stealing. If He said it, it would be all right because He's God and He knows everything. He knows the end of everything, and if He said that it was all right [Faith sighs and laughs nervously], I guess it would be.

I: You seem a little bit conflicted.

F: Well, I mean, I know it would be hard for me to be able to handle it, because there's things in His word that I already don't understand. But, you just have to take it by faith and believe that He is God and He knows what He is saying.

Faith's thinking nicely illustrates how a deep conviction and faith in God's goodness, coordinated with a belief in God's omniscience, can lead a person to accept conclusions about the moral rectitude of actions commanded by God that run counter to the person's own intuitions about the actions. The reasoning of such individuals, however, is not structured by an unreflective acceptance of God's authority. On the contrary, the notions of God's moral authority, held by the participants in this study, stemmed from their assumptions about the inherent goodness of the Judeo-Christian God. Should that assumption be challenged, then God's authority in moral matters would be called into question. This reasoning is reflected in the remainder of Faith's interview:

FAITH (continued)

I: How do we know that when we are "hearing the word of God" that we are hearing God's word and not the devil?

F: Well, the Bible is the only test you could give it, and the Holy Spirit inside you.

I: What do you mean, the Holy Spirit inside you? How does that help?

F: I believe the Holy Spirit leads me and convicts me. If I don't believe something is – goes along with, or is part of God's character, then I'll check it out in the Bible and pray about it, and ask for guidance.

I: Do you think murder is part of God's character?

F: No, but if it said in His word that it was all right to kill, then God must be a different kind of God.

I: So, if He were a different kind of God, would it be all right to do it – to kill?

F: Well, I don't know. That changes the whole thing. So, I don't know.

In summary, there was clear evidence in this study that Christian and Jewish children evaluate moral issues on the basis of criteria independent of the word of God. Consonant with research done in secular contexts, the children's concepts of morality focused on the intrinsic justice and welfare outcomes of actions. On the basis of such "objective" criteria, the children established a moral position from which they apprehended the moral aspect of the just and compassionate Judeo-Christian God. In each of the interviews (with the exception of six with young children), we saw evidence that religiously engaged children attempted to bring together their notions of God as perfect with their own conceptions of the morally good. Thus, for these children, concepts of God, the word of God, and morality are not one and the same thing.

CONCLUSIONS

The studies described in this chapter indicate that children's moral understandings are independent of specific religious rules, and that morality is conceptually distinct from one's religious concepts. These studies also mean that morality for the secular child, as well as for the devout Christian or Jew, focuses on the same set of interpersonal issues: those pertaining to justice, human welfare and compassion. While we did not report specifically on the beliefs of children from other religions, findings from cross-cultural studies discussed in Chapter 2 are consistent with the assumption that such basic moral concerns are shared across the range of human societies and groups. For the public schools, this means that there can be moral education compatible with, and yet independent from, religious moral doctrine. There is, then, considerable common ground on which deeply religious people from different religious perspectives, along with nonreligious people, can come to terms regarding the central concerns of their children's moral development. That common ground, however, requires a more constrained use of moral language to refer to the domain of issues that pertain to the inherent and universal features of human social interaction. By focusing on this moral core, public schools can forthrightly meet their obligations, rather than hide behind a smoke screen of value relativism.

At the same time, these findings point to the wisdom of keeping the teaching of particular doctrinal values out of the hands of public schools, and keeping it in the families, churches, synagogues, mosques, and temples where the particularistic values of different faiths can be celebrated without conflict. It was clear that in the minds of the religious children we interviewed, those particularistic values (e.g., day of worship, women leading worship services) stem from their relation to religious rather than temporal authority. Their connection to a particular faith community means that such values and norms are likely to be incommensurate across faiths. This is a source of tension that exists within all pluralist societies. As such, an attitude of tolerance based on the moral principles of mutual respect and fairness must prevail. Those principles of fairness, mutual respect, and concern for the welfare of others are the content of the moral domain and, as such, should be the core values fostered through moral education.

CHAPTER THREE

Morality and the Personal Domain

I do not like broccoli. And I haven't liked it since I was a little kid and my mother made me eat it. I'm President of the United States, and I am not going to eat any more broccoli (George Bush, April, 1990).

Autonomy . . . appears only with reciprocity, when mutual respect is strong enough to make the individual feel from within the desire to treat others as he himself would wish to be treated (Jean Piaget, *The Moral Judgment of the Child*).

Up to this point we have been focusing on the ways in which people conceptualize morality and nonmoral (conventional and religious) norms. In order to have a complete picture of the nature of morality and moral development, we also need to consider whether and in what ways people bracket off some areas of their behavior as matters of privacy and personal choice. The relationship between morality and personal freedom is a complex one that has been the subject of sometimes heated debate within philosophy and the social sciences, as well as at the level of public policy.

Morality and personal freedom are often thought of as being in opposition. Some philosophers (e.g., Augustine 401/1963; Kant 1785/1959) and psychologists (e.g., Freud 1923/1960, 1930/1961) have viewed morality as the struggle between the egoistic and selfish desires of the self and the rational and legitimate concerns for the treatment of others. From these views, morality is the achievement of the suppression of the passions and destructive impulses of the self-interested individual. This dichotomy between personal freedom and morality has a counterpart in the writings of some contemporary students of culture who tend to classify the morality of various societies on a continuum, from the individualistic/permissive to the collectivistic/traditional (Miller and Bersoff 1992;

Shweder 1990). According to this analysis, there are basically two kinds of moral cultures: one (Western culture), which is based on rights, and another (primarily non-Western cultures), based on duties (Shweder, Mahapatra, and Miller 1987). This oppositional view of personal freedom and autonomy on the one hand and morality on the other has also been employed by some contemporary American social scientists (e.g., Bellah et al. 1985; Sampson 1977) and commentators (Bennett 1992; Etzioni 1993; Kirkpatrick 1992) as a basis from which to critique the moral status of contemporary American society. According to these analyses, contemporary American culture is characterized by self-contained individualism (Sampson 1977), an overemphasis on rights (Etzioni 1993), and too little attention to collective norms and traditions (Bennett 1992; Kirkpatrick 1992; Wynne 1986). These views of culture have been criticized, however, as overly simplistic (Wainryb and Turiel 1995), and the related judgments of the contemporary American scene found to be biased and historically inaccurate (Turiel, 1998b).

Leaving characterizations of the morality of American society to the side, let us turn toward an alternative way of looking at things in which personal freedom, morality, and social norms interact in the social development of children. The position that will be explored is that morality and personal autonomy are interrelated, coexisting aspects of social life among individuals in all cultures. People are simultaneously individualistic and other directed, autonomous and interdependent.

THE PERSONAL DOMAIN AND FORMATION OF THE INDIVIDUAL

As a way of introducing the research we are about to discuss, let me ask you, the reader, to consider the following questions:

1. Who should be able to determine who your best friends are?
2. If you keep a personal diary, who should be able to read it, and who should be the person who makes that determination?
3. Who should decide how you style your hair?

   In terms of the previous questions, why did you answer the way that you did? Or, to put it another way, why does it matter who determines or decides such things for you?

When I have asked these things of my undergraduates, they have invariably answered that they, and they alone, should be the ones to determine or decide such things for themselves. In our work on values formation and social reasoning, we have labeled such issues as content for what we refer to as the *personal* domain.

The personal refers to the set of actions that the individual considers to pertain primarily to oneself and, therefore, to be outside the area of justifiable social regulation. These actions are not matters of right and wrong but of preference and choice (Nucci 1995). While there is considerable cultural variation in the specific things that are considered personal, allowance for some area of personal choice appears to be culturally universal. These cultural issues are discussed in more detail later in this chapter. Examples of personal issues within American culture include the content of one's correspondence and self-expressive creative works, one's recreational activities, one's choice of friends or intimates, and actions that focus on the state of one's own body (Nucci 1981; Nucci, Guerra, and Lee 1991; Smetana 1982; Smetana, Bridgeman, and Turiel 1983).

By their very nature, personal issues are a circumscribed set of actions that define the boundaries of individual authority. If you responded in ways similar to my students, then you justified claims to control over the issues presented in my questions by asserting their importance to your ability to maintain personal integrity, agency, and individuality. Identifying and controlling what is personal serves to establish the social border between the self and the group. Making choices about personal things allows us to create what is socially individual or unique about ourselves. This is something different from the unique features due to our biological inheritance, such as our fingerprints or facial image. Identical twins, for example, who share the same DNA will nonetheless have a unique sense of self because of the choices that they make within the personal domain. It is control over the personal that serves to confirm a person's sense of himself or herself as having agency instead of being a martinet scripted by socially inherited roles and contexts. In sum, the personal represents the set of social actions that permit the person to construct both a sense of the self as a unique social being, what the classical American psychologist William James (1899) called the "me," and the subjective sense of agency and authorship, or what James referred to as the "I."

This view of the personal is compatible with psychological theories offered by writers of diverse perspectives who also see a close link between personal autonomy and the formation of the individual (Baldwin 1897, 1906; Damon and Hart 1988; Erikson 1963, 1968; Kohut 1978; Mahler 1979; Selman 1980), and the work of researchers and clinicians who see strivings for control over a personal sphere of actions present in early childhood and perhaps even in infancy (Mahler 1979; Stern 1985). As I noted in the introduction to this chapter, however, the view of the self as autonomous has been criticized as reflecting a particular Western cultural construction, in which the self as individual is decontextualized from the social, cultural milieu (Cushman 1991; Sampson 1985; Shweder and Bourne 1984). These critiques are justified as a counterpoint to idyllic characterizations of the individual as an entirely self-generated and self-contained system. After all, none of us determines our own parentage, or the historical and cultural settings of our childhoods. On the other hand, such critiques are themselves oversimplifications, which run the risk of stereotyping by dividing cultures into those that recognize autonomous selves and those that do not (Greenfield and Cocking 1994; Turiel 1994).

For one thing, it is not the case that conceptions of self as autonomous are restricted to Western culture. Although notions of "self," like beliefs about the personal, are highly variable, all observed cultures contain some differentiated view of self, and people in all cultures appear to hold idiosyncratic, individual views of themselves as distinct persons with particular interests (Spiro 1993). In addition, there is reason to believe that establishment of a personal domain of privacy and behavioral discretion is itself a psychological necessity (Nucci 1995). A wealth of clinical data has demonstrated that disruption in the formation of personal boundaries damages individual psychological health (Kernberg 1975; Kohut 1978; Mahler 1979; Masterson 1981), and suggests that there are basic psychological limits to the extent that others (including society) can impinge on the private lives of individuals.

EMERGENCE OF THE PERSONAL IN CHILDHOOD

The view of the individual being presented here is consistent with characterizations of self as heterogeneous rather than simply individualistic. The personal that is constructed is always situated and in dialogue with others, with social norms and cultural metaphors (Hermans, Kempen, and van Loon 1992; Sarbin 1986). Thus, the particular expression of the personal will be a function of the historical and cultural context. With regard to individual development, this is not simply a process of society shaping and molding the person, nor is it simply a matter of the child reconstructing at an individual level the social messages provided by society or socializing agents, such as parents or teachers. The child establishes personal borders through a process of interpersonal negotiation. The

child is active not only in the sense of interpreting input but also of seeking to establish areas of choice and personal control within which to operate as an individual. The child's exercise of choice, however, often takes
place in the context of relationships that are inherently asymmetrical.
Since children are dependent on adult protection, nurturance, and teaching, a child's freedom of action is almost always at the mercy of adults.
This is especially the case in relations between children and parents,
where issues of adult authority and responsibility are intertwined with
parental tendencies to invest their own familial and personal identities in
their children. A number of studies have examined these issues within the
family context, and it is to those studies that we will turn next.

Family Interactions and Children's Personal Domain

The emergence of children's autonomy involves two interrelated factors.
One is the development of the child's competencies, and the other is the
child's establishment of boundaries between what is within the child's
area of privacy and personal discretion and what falls within the purview
of adult authority and social norms. With regard to the former, it is easy
to see how newfound competencies, such as the ability to walk, provide
the toddler with greater possibilities for autonomy than exist for the infant. Erikson (1963) was one of the first theorists to connect the emergence
of competencies in early childhood with the child's assertion of personal
authority over the self. The prevalence of children's noncompliance to
parental authority within the "terrible twos," as Gesell (1928) referred to
this period in development, was explained by Erikson (1963) as an expression of the child's efforts to establish bounded control over the self.
This becomes paramount for the 2-year-old as an extension of the child's
emerging abilities, especially the ability to communicate his or her desires
through speech.

   The key aspect of this period for Erikson (1963) was the child's negotiation of authority with the parent. According to Erikson (1963), failure to
establish a balance between the child's areas of discretion and the parent's
enforcement of social regulation resulted in problems of psychological adjustment with far-reaching significance. Erikson's (1963) observations
predated more recent descriptions of the strivings for control over a personal sphere of actions as evident in early infancy (Mahler 1973; Stern
1985). It also preceded other work characterizing early- and middle-childhood noncompliance as evidence of a continuing exchange between children and adult authority regarding children's assertions of control over

their own lives (Brehm and Brehm 1981; Crockenberg and Litman 1990; Stipek, Gralinski, and Kopp 1993).

Running through all of this research and theory is a depiction of negotiation between children and adults while children are striving to establish themselves as autonomous individuals. Yet, what is being negotiated is left unspecified in these accounts of individuation and the development of children's autonomy. From our point of view, we would expect parents of young children to exert considerable control over children's moral behavior, their conventional conduct, and actions that put the child at risk of personal harm. It would be in the process of establishing the child's area of personal discretion that we would expect to see most parent–child negotiation.

These issues were initially explored in an observational study (Nucci and Weber 1995) of the at-home interactions between 20 middle-class suburban mothers and their 3- or 4-year-old children. The parenting styles of the mothers fell within what Baumrind (1971) described as authoritative parenting. These mothers had a set of firmly established behavioral expectations, but were flexible in their disciplining of children.

Pairs of mothers and children were observed during four activity periods over a span of three days. Among the things that we discovered was that mothers almost never negotiated with children regarding moral, conventional, or prudential forms of conduct. On the other hand, nearly one-quarter of the observed interactions around personal issues involved negotiation and concession on the part of the mothers. What is also interesting is the degree to which negotiations took place in the context of mixed events. A mixed event is one in which there is overlap among the domain characteristics of the action. Over 90 percent of the observed mixed events involved overlap between conventions or prudential concerns about the child's safety and the personal domain. Mothers engaged in negotiation with their children about such mixed events about half of the time. This type of interaction over a mixed issue is illustrated in the following:

Mother: Evan, it's your last day of nursery school. Why don't you wear your nursery sweatshirt?
Child: I don't want to wear that one.
Mother: This is the last day of nursery school, that's why we wear it. You want to wear that one?
Child: Another one.
Mother: Are you going to get it, or should I?
Child: I will. First I got to get a shirt.

Mother: [Goes to the child's dresser and starts picking out shirts.] This one? This one? Do you know which one you have in mind? Here, this is a new one.

Child: No, it's too big.

Mother: Oh, Evan, just wear one, and when you get home, you can pick whatever you want, and I won't even help you. [Child puts on shirt.]

This case presents a conflict between a dress convention (wearing a particular shirt on the last day of school) and the child's view that dress is a personal choice. The mother acknowledges the child's resistance and attempts to negotiate, finally offering the child a free choice once school is over. This example illustrates several things. For one, the mother provided direct information to the child about the convention in question: "This is the last day of nursery school, that's why we wear it." At the same time, she displayed an interest in fostering the child's autonomy and decision making around the issue. The child's resistance conveyed that his personal interest was not simply cut off but was guided by the mother, who linked it to his autonomy: "Are you going to get it, or should I?" . . . "you can pick whatever you want, and I *won't even help you.*" In the end, there is compromise. The child got to choose, but within a more general, conventional demand (enforced by the mother) that he wear a shirt.

The verbal dance engaged in by the mother and child in this example illustrates that the mothers in this study acted in ways that indicated an understanding that children should have areas of discretion and personal control. The excerpt also illustrates ways in which children, through their resistances, provided mothers with information about the *child's* desires and needs for personal choice. Analyses of the children's responses showed that assertions of prerogative and personal choice did not occur to the same degree across all forms of social interaction, but were disproportionately associated with events involving personal issues. Assertions of prerogative and choice comprised 88% of children's responses in the context of mixed events and 98% of their responses in the case of predominantly personal events. In contrast, such responses comprised less than 10% of children's statements in the context of moral or prudential events and about 25% of their responses to conventional events. These behavioral measures indicate that middle-class preschool-age children are able to distinguish the personal from matters of social regulation. Interviews conducted with the children revealed that they viewed personal, but not moral or conventional, behaviors as ones that should be up to the "self" and not the mother to decide.

This (Nucci and Weber 1995) observational study also provided evidence that middle-class mothers provide children areas of personal choice without requiring a process of negotiation. Mothers generally do not explicitly tell young children that a particular behavior is something that is a matter of the child's personal choice. When they do give such explicit statements, they resemble the following discussion between a mother and her daughter over the girl's hair style:

> *Mother:* If you want, we can get your hair cut. *It's your choice.*
> *Child:* I only want it that long – down to here. [Child points to where she wants her hair cut.]

More typically, the social messages mothers directed to children about personal issues were in the indirect form of offered choices, such as illustrated in the following exchange:

> *Mother:* You need to decide what you want to wear to school today.
> *Child:* [Opens a drawer.] Pants. Pants. Pants.
> *Mother:* Have you decided what to wear today?
> *Child:* I wear these.
> *Mother:* Okay, that's a good choice. How would you like your hair today?
> *Child:* Down. [Child stands by the bed, and her mother carefully combs her hair.]

In the latter interaction, the mother, through a set of offered choices, conveys the idea that dress and hairstyle are matters for the child to decide. The child might then infer that such behavior is personal. Through both the direct and indirect forms of communication, mothers show a willingness to provide children areas of personal discretion. The fact that mothers are more likely to tell children what to do in the context of moral, conventional, and prudential behaviors than in the context of personal ones is in itself an indication that mothers view the former as issues in which the child needs to accommodate to specific, external, social demands and meanings, while the personal issues are for the child to interpret and control.

In sum, mothers displayed systematic differences in their responses to children when the issues in question were ones within the child's personal domain. The study also provided evidence that children play an active role in relation to their mothers, and provide feedback in the form of requests and resistances to their mothers that afford mothers information regarding the child's claims to areas of personal control. This feedback is not simply a generalized resistance to adult authority (Brehm and Brehm 1981; Kuczinski et al. 1987), but is a limited set of claims to choice over a personal sphere. This is most evident in cases of mixed events, and it suggests that mothers open to their children's feedback have direct access to information about their own children's needs for a personal domain. Smetana's (1989b) work on adolescent–parent conflicts indicates that similar child resistance to adult control over personal issues continues and increases as children grow up. We will take up these issues of adolescent development at later points in this chapter.

As already stated, the child's construction of the personal is not accomplished solely at the individual level, nor determined by the culture, but through reciprocal interaction between the child and members of society. For this to occur, there must also be some understanding on the part of adults that children should be accorded an area of personal discretion. We have already seen evidence of this in the observations of mother–child interactions. This issue was examined directly in an interview study with middle- and working-class mothers of young children conducted within the same community and a neighboring suburb (Nucci and Smetana 1996).

The interview focused on the mothers' views of whether and around what sorts of issues children should be given decision-making authority, and around which issues mothers should exert their authority. They were asked to explain how they determined which behaviors to leave up to their children, and why they allowed or encouraged children to determine those things for themselves. Mothers were also asked about their sense of the kinds of issues that generated conflicts between themselves and their children, how these conflicts were resolved, and what role they saw themselves playing in those mother–child exchanges.

All of the mothers interviewed in this study supported the notion that children 4 to 7 years of age should be allowed choice over some things and that children should be allowed to hold their own opinions. Mothers justified allowing children to exercise choice on the grounds that decision making fostered competence and that allowing children to hold opinions of their own fostered the development of the child's agency and self-esteem. Thus, these mothers appeared to value permitting their children areas of freedom in order to foster their personal development and autonomy. Mothers placed boundaries, however, around those actions that they left up to children to determine. Mothers stated that their children were allowed to exercise choice over such personal issues as play activities, playmates, amount and type of food, and choice of clothes. On the other hand, mothers stated that they placed limits on children's actions when they went counter to family or societal conventions and when they posed risks to the child or others.

In addition to limiting children's activities when they conflicted with conventional, moral, or prudential considerations, mothers stated that they occasionally limited their children's activities in the very areas they had stated they allowed children to determine or control. As we had seen in the observational study (Nucci and Weber 1995), mother–child conflicts over these personal issues often resulted in compromise by the mother. In their interviews (Nucci and Smetana 1996), mothers expressed a willingness to compromise over such issues in order to support the child's agency, self-esteem, and competence. Mothers viewed themselves as acting rationally and pragmatically in response to their perceptions of the child's personal competence and the risks a given act posed to the child. In the context of mother–child disagreements, mothers tended to see themselves primarily as educators, and less often as controllers or nurturers.

When placed together with the results of at-home observations (Nucci and Weber 1995), these interviews with mothers provide an integrated portrait of how mothers and preschool-age children establish and foster the emergence of the child's autonomy and sense of a personal domain of privacy and choice. The picture that emerges is not one of across-the-board struggle and conflict, but rather of a shared and differentiated worldview in which autonomy and choice coexist with obedience and conformity to common norms and rational moral and prudential constraints. Those conflicts that do arise are not random in nature, but generally fall within the range of issues at the edge of the child's personal domain and what the mother views as matters of social convention or the child's safety.

CULTURE AND CLASS EFFECTS ON CHILDREN'S AND MOTHERS' BELIEFS ABOUT THE PERSONAL

The fact that both of the studies in the previous section were conducted in the United States limits their generality. Research across cultures and social classes must be conducted before we can make definitive statements about children's early experiences in the development of their understandings of the personal realm. Recent work that has begun to examine the social judgments of children and mothers from different social class and cultural backgrounds has provided evidence that concerns for the provision of an area of personal choice and privacy is not exclusive to the Western middle class.

Before examining that research, however, let us take a moment to review some of the issues pertaining to assumptions about the relations among culture, class, and parental authority. Research on parental authority prior to the 1980s tended to frame the issue as a question of degree along a single dimension. For example, the most influential system for looking at parental tendencies to control children's actions has been Baumrind's (1971) division of parenting types into the *permissive, authoritative,* and *authoritarian,* in which permissive and authoritarian represent the polar extremes of parental control. Applications of this typology to groups that differ from the U.S. white middle class have proven to be riddled with bias and misunderstanding.

Baumrind (1972), however, was herself one of the first to caution against simplistic applications of her typology. In a study examining the child-rearing practices of African American parents, Baumrind discovered that parental actions that fit in the authoritarian pattern within white families did not result in an authoritarian "syndrome" among African American girls. Instead, the apparently authoritarian parental practices were ones that fostered toughness and self-sufficiency in the girls and were perceived by the daughters as "nurturant care-taking" (Baumrind 1972, pp. 266). In line with Baumrind's interpretation, Bartz and Levine (1978) found that African Americans, relative to whites, expected children to overcome childhood dependency as soon as possible. This held true with educational level of parents controlled for. African Americans and whites in the Bartz and Levine (1978) study did not differ, however, in their tendencies to emphasize children's general rights and their right to have input into family decisions.

The mismatch between white American views of parental authoritarianism and views of parenting in other cultures was perhaps best captured by Chao (1993), who argued that depictions of parental behaviors as authoritarian, controlling, and restrictive have been ethnocentric and misleading. Asian families, for example, have been found to obtain among the highest scores of unquestioning obedience to parents on the Baumrind measure. Labeling such tendencies as authoritarian, according to Chao, is to misread as authoritarian those behaviors that are based on Confucian conceptions of respect for elders. According to Chao, parental concern and love are equated in Asian cultures with firm control and governance. In related research, Rohner and Pettengill (1985) reported that Korean children's perceptions of parental warmth tend to increase as overall parental control increases. According to Rohner and Pettengill, this reflects a more general cultural view of the individual as a "fractional part" of the family. Consequently, decisions that are usually considered to be "individual matters" in the United States are often the subject of family scrutiny and approval in Korea.

Just as it is an error to apply a unidimensional American conception of parental authority on others, it is an oversimplification to accept unidimensional descriptions of parental authority generated by members of other cultures as descriptive of themselves. In a study of Chinese adolescents, Lau and Ping (1987), for example, found that the positive relation between parental control and children's self-esteem and perceptions of parental warmth held only for parental behaviors that served organizational needs and not simply parental efforts to dominate or restrict the child. According to Lau and Ping (1987), it is important to distinguish organizational from dominance or power-assertion forms of control. Jung and Turiel (1994) found that Korean children do not hold an uncritical view of parental authority, but instead evaluate authority in terms of their independent judgments of the act and the context. For example, Korean children were found to reject the legitimacy of a parental command to commit harm. Similarly, Yau and Smetana (1995) reported that Chinese adolescent–parent relations were not without conflict (although less so than in the United States), and that conflicts were over the same types of issues as their American counterparts. Most interesting for our purposes here is that the adolescents in their study positioned their arguments in terms of exercising personal jurisdiction.

In sum, cross-cultural studies of parental authority provide a complex picture that mitigates against the assignment of simple global labels, such as authoritarian or permissive, individualistic or collectivistic, to the parenting practices of cultures or groups. Parenting practices that appear on the surface to be authoritarian or permissive from the perspective of an outsider may have a very different meaning to members within a cultural group. In addition, there is little evidence that the parenting practices of the majority of members of a culture fit within any single typology. As the Lau and Ping (1987) research on Chinese families demonstrated, there are variations in parental behavior even within what on the surface appeared to be a single dimension of restrictive parenting. What is more, the Yau and Smetana (1995) findings argue against simplistic views of parent–child relations within so-called collectivistic societies as "harmonious" or conflict free (Baumrind 1973). Given the complex picture of parenting and parent–child relations, it is clear that caution needs to be exercised in any effort to extend research about mothers' beliefs about children's areas of personal choice to members of non-Western or traditional cultures. In taking these cultural factors into account, however, it is important to resist tendencies to view cultures as homogeneous and to assume that personhood and the individual are concepts of concern only to what are referred to as individualistic cultures.

With these cautionary thoughts in mind, we turn now to research that has begun a direct investigation of culture and class effects on children's and mothers' beliefs about the personal in children. I will report on two studies, both of which we conducted in Brazil.

The first of these studies (Nucci, Camino, and Sapiro 1996) was conducted in the northeastern coastal city of Joao Pessoa. This region of Brazil has been characterized as a collectivistic culture in comparison with the United States and Europe (Triandis et al. 1988). In the study, we interviewed children and adolescents from two social classes about which matters children should be able to control themselves, and which should be regulated by parents or the social group. The items used in the study were selected by the Brazilian researchers in the project as ones that fit the theoretical definitions of the moral, conventional, and personal categories. These items were presented in a brief scenario in which the child's behavioral choice was objected to by authority. Following the reading of the scenario, the child was asked whether it would be all right for the child to do the act in question, and why or why not. For example: "Carolina likes to write her secrets in a diary which she keeps hidden from other people. Imagine that one day Carolina's mother has discovered that she has this diary, and tells Carolina to show her what she has written. In this case, do you think it is wrong or all right for the mother to read her daughter's secret diary? Should it be all right or not for Carolina to keep her diary secret from her mother? Why/why not?"

We found that Brazilian children treated moral, conventional, and personal issues differently. However, we also found social-class differences in the age at which the majority of children consistently identified a set of issues as personal. Middle-class children tended to treat personal issues as up to them to decide at an earlier age than did lower-class children. By adolescence (age 14 to 16), however, there were no social-class differences in children's judgments of items as ones that should be up to the children to control. Nor were there class differences in the reasons given for why an action should be up to the child to decide. By adolescence, across social classes, the majority of subjects justified control over personal issues

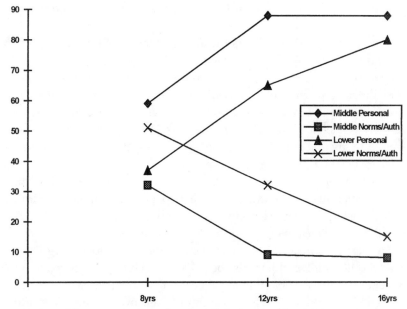

FIGURE 3.1. Mean proportion of personal and norms/authority responses by middle-class and lower-class subjects as a function of age.

in terms of personal rights and the need for personal privacy. These developmental shifts are illustrated in Figure 3.1.

In a second study (Nucci and Milnitsky Sapiro 1995), we interviewed Brazilian mothers about their views of such issues. Half of the mothers were from northeastern Brazil, and the other half were from a large industrial city in the southern region of the country that is culturally similar in many respects to the United States and western Europe. In their interviews, Brazilian mothers from both regions of the country and from both social classes tended to treat personal items as matters that should be left up to children. Compliance with moral and conventional norms, on the other hand, were seen as matters that the mother should not simply leave up to the child. Thus, the Brazilian mothers, like their U.S. counterparts, acknowledged an area of personal behavioral choice for their children. The Brazilian findings, however, also revealed regional and class differences within these broad overall trends. Mothers from southern Brazil and middle-class mothers from both regions were less likely to treat things as up to the parent, and more likely to treat them as negotiable, than were mothers from northeastern Brazil or lower-class mothers from either region. That is to say that the northeastern and lower-class mothers seemed somewhat more authoritarian than the southern and middle-class mothers.

Conversations with mothers during the interviews helped to explain these differences. When asked whether there were some things that children should be allowed to make decisions about, the majority of lower-class Brazilian mothers of *adolescents* and middle-class mothers of *children as well as adolescents* responded affirmatively. When they were asked to give reasons for their responses, lower-class Brazilian mothers of *young children* tended to say that they felt it would be either too dangerous or impractical to give young children decision-making authority over their actions. In contrast, lower-class mothers of *adolescents* gave reasons supporting their child's emerging autonomy, agency, and personal competence. Similar statements supporting autonomy, agency, and competence were offered by Brazilian middle-class mothers of *children as well as adolescents.*

Similarly, the majority of lower-class mothers of 6- to 8-year-old children did not think that parents should allow a child that age to have his or her own opinion about things, while a majority of all other mothers felt that children were entitled to opinions of their own. In the view of the lower-class mothers of young children, their youngsters had not matured sufficiently to have the reasoning capacity to form opinions.

Brazilian mothers who thought that children should have choice about some things spontaneously listed activities or issues similar to those listed by U.S. mothers. The list of things that mothers left up to the child increased as children got older to include some things that mothers had previously viewed as matters of safety. In adolescence, mothers extended the child's personal areas of choice to include academic and occupational decisions, places where the child is permitted to be without seeking parental permission, and staying up late at night. The criteria mothers used to decide whether an issue should be left up to the child were the same across region and social class. These criteria included concerns for the child's safety, their contribution to the child's competence, their appropriateness developmentally, and matters of the child's private or personal domain.

It is interesting to note that Brazilian mothers from all of the groups, including lower-class mothers of young children, responded affirmatively to the question of whether it was important for a child to develop a sense of individuality. Indeed, during the interviews, language referring to individual autonomy was spontaneously employed by the Brazilian mothers irrespective of region or class. They regarded the fostering of individuality as important for the establishment of their child's uniqueness, autonomy, competence, and agency. In other words, the Brazilian mothers expressed essentially the same concerns in this regard as did the mothers we had interviewed in the United States (Nucci and Smetana 1996).

This (Nucci and Milnitsky Sapiro 1995) study with Brazilian mothers demonstrated that beliefs about children's personal choice are not confined to mothers from individualistic cultures. Across social classes and geographic regions, the Brazilian mothers expressed beliefs that children require areas of choice for their personal growth. The manner in which these beliefs were expressed, however, varied as a function of the mothers' underlying assumptions about the nature of their children's needs and capacities. Middle-class mothers, particularly from the southern "modern" region of the country, held views of young children essentially like those of mothers of the U.S. middle class. According to their view, children are to be treated as individuals from infancy and given opportunities to exercise choice to enhance their individual talents and personalities. That middle-class view was different from that of the more traditional lower-class mothers, who thought that the limited cognitive capacity of infants and young children meant that they were not yet ready to make choices or hold opinions of their own. Nonetheless, even these traditional mothers valued the eventual emergence of individuality and agency in adolescence, and they distinguished the adolescent's rights to personal behavioral control from those moral or conventional zones of behavior that are the shared responsibility of parents and others.

In sum, the findings from these two Brazilian studies demonstrate that children raised outside of the United States or European society develop a sense of what is personal, and that parental beliefs about children's personal choice are not confined to mothers from "individualistic" cultures. Across social classes and geographic regions, the Brazilian mothers expressed beliefs that children require areas of personal discretion for their personal growth. These studies also show that there are culture and class differences in the age at which the personal is fully accorded to children. These differences appear to stem from cultural assumptions about the nature of children's needs and capacities. As demonstrated in other research (Wainryb 1991), the assumptions that parents have about the nature of children, such as whether children benefit from corporal punishment, have a powerful impact on the ways parents treat their children. Nevertheless, we found in our study of Brazilian mothers that even the mothers from the more traditional regions of Brazil valued the eventual emergence of individuality and agency in adolescence.

THE PERSONAL AND VALUES CONFLICTS IN ADOLESCENCE

The trends toward an increase in claims of personal discretion and privacy that were observed among Brazilian adolescents point to a general feature of development. As children grow up, they seek greater autonomy and independence from parents. That move toward autonomy requires shifts in the relations between children and adults as young people begin to lay claim to decisions and areas of activity that had been determined by parents or other adults. The revealing quotation from former President George Bush, at the opening of this chapter, illustrates how long such seemingly minor issues of control linger with us even if, as in the case of George Bush, we assume considerable stature and power. The quotation also illustrates another facet of such parent–child issues, namely, that parents generally attempt to exert control and authority in the interests of their children. One can almost hear Mrs. Bush explaining to her son the nutritional value of broccoli and the need for a growing boy to eat his green vegetables.

One of the more interesting and fruitful lines of recent research on children's value formation has examined the pattern of changes that take place in terms of the types of issues and zones of behavior children appropriate as personal matters as they move into adolescence. The work by Judith Smetana and her colleagues at the University of Rochester has helped us to understand the appropriate role of adult authority and the sources of much of what transpires in the form of adolescent–parent conflict.

As we had observed in Brazil, the shift toward greater autonomy for adolescents is not simply the result of actions taken by children. It is due to a series of reciprocal adult–child exchanges. The shifts that do take place are not across the board, however, but are linked to the identification of actions as personal matters. In general, adolescents view adults as retaining authority over moral issues (Smetana 1989b; Smetana, Braeges, and Yau 1991; Smetana et al. 1991). Moreover, adolescents view parents as having a duty or obligation to regulate moral behavior, and see themselves as obliged to obey parental moral rules (Smetana, Killen, and Turiel 1991). Accordingly, the Smetana group has found that moral issues are an infrequent source of conflict in adolescent–parent relationships. Adolescents also typically hold the view that parents have a duty or obligation to regulate the conventions within the family (Smetana and Asquith 1994). However, the endorsement of obedience to convention appears to decline with age. A similar pattern appears to hold for prudential matters that touch on issues of the adolescent's health or safety. Younger adolescents (under the age of 15) generally maintain that parents have the authority, and even the obligation, to regulate behaviors that impinge on the adolescent's safety or well-being (Tisak 1986). As they grow older, however, adolescents tend to view such issues of personal welfare as falling within their own sphere of responsibility and personal jurisdiction (Smetana and Asquith 1994).

As you might expect, adolescent–parent conflicts generally arise in the context of these areas of change. Conflicts tend to occur over issues parents perceive as important to the conventions that serve to organize and structure family and household organization, and which adolescents see as interfering in their personal lives. The kinds of issues that generate most conflicts in American households are such things as preferences for television programs or music, spending decisions (e.g., whether to spend allowance money on games), appearance (dress, makeup), activities (time spent talking on the phone), schedules (bedtimes, curfews), and places the adolescent is permitted to go without seeking specific parental permission (Smetana and Asquith 1994). Parents justify their perspective by appealing to family or cultural norms, parental authority, the adolescent's role-related responsibilities in the family (e.g., cleaning up their room, mowing the lawn, etc.), the need for politeness and manners, and the perceived social cost of adolescent nonconformity (e.g., the parents' embarrassment, concern about others' misperceptions of the child). Adolescents, in turn, understand but reject their parents' social-conventional interpretations of disputes and appeal instead to the exercise or maintenance of personal jurisdiction (Smetana 1989b; Smetana, Brages, and Yau 1991).

Far fewer family disputes arise over issues that concern risks to the adolescent's health or safety. This is because such prudential issues have an objective quality to them that is obvious to both parties. Nevertheless, the tendency of adolescents to engage in risk taking, and to believe in their own invulnerability, is a potential source of aggravation and alarm to parents. In the case of prudential issues, there is a self-evident overlap between the parents' role as nurturer and protector and the adolescent's position as "master of his(her) own house." Matters of personal safety are by definition self-referential, and parents of adolescents often find themselves in the position of shaking their heads as they watch their offspring engage in relatively harmless but foolish actions (e.g., going to school without headgear in subzero winter weather) that are emblematic of their children's desire to take control of their own lives. For the most part, such issues are conflict free, owing to the fact that most adolescents do not engage in high-risk behaviors. In other cases, however, adolescents do make foolish choices with long-term negative consequences.

One measure of personal maturity is the degree to which one can make intelligent cost–benefit analyses of behaviors, such as drug use, that may bring momentary pleasure but long-term damage to the user. Studies of adolescent concepts of drug use have reported a strong relationship between self-reported drug use and the tendency to see the behavior as simply a matter of personal choice (Nucci, Guerra, and Lee 1991). Adolescents who are not involved in drug use tend to see such behavior as wrong because of the potential harm such behavior can cause to oneself. In addition, high drug users are much more likely than low drug users to endorse themselves, rather than parents or others, as having legitimate authority over decisions to engage in drug use (Nucci et al. 1991). However, even when adolescents view prudential issues, such as drug and alcohol use, as legitimately regulated by parents or teachers, adolescents view parents as having significantly less authority over these issues than their parents do (Smetana and Asquith 1994).

The general pattern that emerges from this work on adolescent–parent relations is that there is a gradual increase in the range of issues that adolescents assume as matters of personal choice, rather than remain subject to parental authority. Parents generally lag behind in their recognition of areas within which adolescents should have decision making, but nonetheless give adolescents a wider degree of freedom than they give to younger children (Nucci et al. 1996; Smetana and Asquith 1994). This shift is also accompanied by a degree of adolescent–parent conflict. Smetana (1995b) has recently pooled the data from her series of studies on adolescent–parent conflict to examine the overall patterns that emerge within normal families. Her analysis looked at more than 300 families, and it included findings from her work with Chinese adolescents and parents in Hong Kong. In her report, Smetana (1995b) notes that in addition to her own findings of prototypical and, in some cases, intense adolescent–parent conflicts within her Hong Kong families, anthropological accounts of adolescent–parent conflicts in 160 cultures provide evidence that such conflicts are widespread (Schlegel and Barry 1991). Smetana's work included observations of family interactions, as well as interviews with individual family members.

On the basis of a statistical procedure called cluster analysis, Smetana identified three basic patterns of dealing with adolescent–parent conflict. The most prevalent pattern, labeled *frequent squabblers,* is one in which adolescents and parents engage in frequent, low-intensity conflicts over everyday details of family life. A second, smaller group comprised the *placid* families, who reported rare conflicts, and whose conflicts were of low or moderate intensity. The third group, labeled *tumultuous* families, had frequent conflicts (though fewer than squabblers), which were very intense.

In terms of parenting patterns, these three family patterns did not differ in their rate of regulation of moral, conventional, or prudential issues. The differences that emerged were over the regulation of multifaceted and personal issues. *Tumultuous* and *squabbling* families had more rules than placid families over multifaceted issues. Parents from *tumultuous* families were more likely to be divorced or remarried, and were lower Social Economic Status (SES) than other parents. Parents in *tumultuous* families were more authoritarian, had more rules, were more restrictive of their adolescents' personal jurisdiction, and less likely to engage in compromise or negotiation than either of the other two family types. In these families, parents felt more of an obligation to regulate personal issues, and were less likely to view personal issues as within the adolescents' jurisdiction. Smetana (1995b, 1996) concluded that these families appeared to intrude more deeply than is developmentally or culturally appropriate in their adolescents' personal domains. In other work, we have found that parental overintrusion into adolescents' personal area is associated with symptoms of depression and hostility in the children (Nucci, Hasebe, and Nucci 1999).

Placid families reported fewer conflicts but were not conflict free. These tended to be higher SES families in which parents were professionally employed. They engaged in more joint decision making than did other parents, were less restrictive, and were rated by their children as higher in warmth.

Squabbling families were in many ways similar to *placid* families in their willingness to engage in negotiation and compromise with their adolescent children. Like the *placid* families, they displayed more warmth than the parents in *tumultuous* families. Relative to *placid* families, however, *frequent squabblers* tended to use a greater number of social-conventional rationales.

These findings indicate that a certain degree of adolescent–parent conflict is to be expected, and that it most likely reflects the normal process of realignment between parents and children as children move toward adult status. What is important and of interest is that this realignment is not in the form of an across-the-board negotiation of all moral and societal values, but the very specific adjustment of locus of responsibility for decision making in the personal domain. This shift is not an invention of liberal parenting, or of Western democratic culture, but is a basic part of human development.

THE ROLE OF THE PERSONAL IN THE FORMATION
OF MORAL CONCEPTS OF RIGHTS

As we have seen, the establishment of a personal sphere is essential to the formation of a sense of personal agency and identity. Throughout development, children try to carve out a set of actions that are personal and *outside* of the context of moral and conventional regulation. Thus, it would appear that the personal sits in conflict or at least apart from morality. As was noted at the beginning of the chapter, that dichotomous view of individual interests and moral sentiment is one that is held by a number of writers, including some who bemoan the rise of individualism and the supposed decline of moral standards within American society. What such hand-wringing and dichotomous thinking downplays, however, is the essential role that personal autonomy plays in the moral functioning of people, as well as in the content of morality itself.

While it is true that morality is "other" directed in the sense that morality is concerned with the impact of actions on others, moral sentiments and moral judgments are themselves the products of agency. Formation of the social individual is necessary for the person to engage in the very acts of reciprocity and cooperation that comprise human morality. The *interpersonal* requires a *personal*. As Piaget (1932) put it, in his sole reference to the role of individuality in moral development: "It is only by knowing our individual nature with its limitations as well as its resources that we grow capable of coming out of ourselves and collaborating with other individual natures" (p. 393). As has been documented in this chapter, the construction of such individual boundaries is not a proprietary accomplishment of the Western Enlightenment, but a manifestation of fundamental human psychological needs.

In addition to providing the "breathing room" within which people construct their sense of agency and distinctiveness, the personal contributes to a person's morality by providing the experiential basis from which to construct a moral conception of rights (Nucci 1996). While moral structures of reciprocity require that rights and protections granted oneself be extended to others, moral conceptions of justice and beneficence do not in and of themselves provide us with a way to identify personal rights and freedoms. The linking of personal concepts with rights claims is consistent with philosophical perspectives that ground the notion of rights in the establishment and maintenance of personal agency (Dworkin 1977; Gewirth 1978, 1982). For example, Gewirth argues that "agents value their freedom or voluntariness as a necessary good as long as the possibility remains of purposive action – that is, of action that is able to fulfill and maintain at least those purposes required for the continuation of agency" (1978, p. 53). Later he adds: "Since the agent regards as necessary goods the freedom and well-being that constitute the generic features of his successful action, he logically must also hold that he has rights to these generic features, and he implicitly makes a corresponding rights claim" (p. 63).

Personal concepts serve to identify freedom as a necessary good for maintaining agency and uniqueness. The content of the personal domain is the content of the individual's identified freedoms. This specific content will be influenced by cultural norms and reflect individual idiosyncrasies. Thus, no claim may be made for a universal collection of specific personal rights. In addition, many of the specific actions people consider personal are trivial in nature and would not in and of themselves comprise core values. For example, one can hardly imagine anyone claiming a moral right to have green hair. However, these specifics can be seen as manifestations of broader core requirements for establishing personal boundaries for the self and for fulfilling related needs for personal agency, continuity, and uniqueness (Damon and Hart 1988). These basic elements are one's body and the claims to freedom of expression, communication, and association. These generic claims are obviously influenced by culture, and variations in the degree and form that these freedoms take in turn establish the observed cultural variations in moral content.

The function of the personal, then, is to provide the source and the conceptual justification for the individual's claims to freedom. Such claims to personal liberty do not in and of themselves constitute a moral conception of rights. The function of such personal concepts is to provide the basic information (i.e., the psychological necessity of the personal sphere) needed to extend the moral conceptions of justice and beneficence to include a moral conception of rights.

The formation of the personal and the individual's claims to freedom are necessary for the individual to engage as an *individual* in the discourse (both public and internal) that leads to moral reciprocity, mutual respect, and cooperation. Moral discourse transforms individual claims to freedom into mutually shared moral obligations. Without such mutuality, as

Piaget (1932) correctly pointed out in his discussion of the relation between egocentrism and heteronomous morality, personal claims to freedom can also serve as the source of narcissistic or exploitative orientations. On the other hand, in the absence of claims to freedom emerging
from the personal, there can be no moral conception of rights. Thus,
morality and personal freedom are interdependent rather than oppositional features of human development.

It should be self-evident from what was just stated that beyond the
most abstract categories, we cannot, however, anticipate the content of
such discourse. Nor can we anticipate with certainty whether the claims
of individuals will be viewed as touching upon mutual transpersonal concerns. It is the historically situated generation of individual claims to freedom reflecting ahistorical basic psychological needs that both stimulates
moral discourse and provides the potential for critique of the status quo.
Thus, moral development from this perspective is to be seen as universal
yet plural, individual yet social. Ultimately, it also recognizes that while
individual moral understandings reflect inherent and unavoidable features of human interaction and individual psychological requirements,
the morality of human rights in its most mature and principled forms will
always be the product of collective efforts.

EDUCATION AND THE PERSONAL DOMAIN

Education, like parenting, sits at the crossroads of the child's construction
of areas of personal choice in relation to societal convention and morality.
Schools, even more than individual families, carry the institutional bur-
den of socializing the young into the broader norms of the culture
(Durkheim 1925/1961; Ryan 1989). In addition, schools are being increasingly called upon to educate children in areas of personal behavior, such
as drug use and sexuality, that have individual prudential as well as societal ramifications. For the teacher and school administrator, these issues
bring up a host of concerns regarding appropriate school structure and
approaches and methods of discipline, as well as curricular issues. It is little wonder, then, that critics of public schools, whether of the political left
(Illich 1971) or right (Bennett 1992; Wynne 1986), focus so heavily on the
ways in which schools approach issues of personal freedom and societal
authority. As is evident from the information presented in this chapter, the
balance between what is personal as opposed to societal is a complex and
interwoven mixture of societal values (which are themselves heterogeneous and contradictory) and the course of individual development.

Up to this point, however, the focus of this book has been on domain distinctions and the forms of reasoning associated with each domain. In order to understand the ways in which morality, convention, and the personal overlap and interact, we need to look more closely at how people reason about such issues in a variety of contexts. We take up such issues of overlap and mixture in Chapters 4 and 5.

CHAPTER FOUR

Morality in Context: Issues of Development

In the preceding chapters we reviewed the three main conceptual frameworks or domains in which people structure their ways of thinking about social values. The existence of distinct knowledge systems does not, however, preclude their conjoining or interaction in context (Piaget 1980, 1985). On the contrary, we often make use of knowledge from more than one conceptual system when dealing with issues in the context of everyday events. For example, deciding the best way to divide ten dollars among four people is simultaneously a moral problem, involving the fair distribution of goods, and a mathematical problem, entailing the calculation of proportions, fractions, and sums. Few ethicists or mathematicians would reduce these areas of knowledge to one another. Yet, in this example, we see an instance where mathematics and morality are interwoven, and where an adequate resolution of the problem requires coordination of knowledge from both domains.

Similar situations arise with regard to the three domains of social knowledge discussed in this book. Such overlap is inevitable given that all social interactions take place within societal systems framed by conventions. Thus, although many everyday issues are straightforward instances of either morality, convention, or personal choice, many others contain aspects from more than one domain. In such cases, people may differ from one another in terms of the information they may bring to a situation, the weight they may give to one or another feature of a given issue, and their level of development within each relevant conceptual domain. Understanding the nature of such interactions is crucial to any account of individual and cultural differences in value orientations, as well as to explanations of the inconsistencies in moral judgments people seem to display across varying situations. From an educational standpoint, understanding the nature of potential overlaps and interactions between morality and other social values is central to the construction of curricula and educational practices.

INTERACTIONS BETWEEN MORALITY AND CONVENTION

Two basic forms of overlap occur between morality and convention. In one form, called *domain mixture,* conventional norms sustaining a particular organizational structure are either in harmony or conflict with what would objectively be seen as concerns for fairness or rights. For example, most Americans have stood in line to buy movie tickets. This behavior is clearly a social convention in that one can well imagine an alternative arrangement that would meet the same purposes. On the other hand, anyone who has lined up only to have someone cut in recognizes that queuing, by establishing a procedure for turn taking, serves the moral function of distributive justice. A second example of domain mixture is provided by gender norms, which differentially define the roles which men and women can assume within the social system. In general, such norms serve important organizational functions, such as structuring family systems, but sometimes in such a way as to accord members of one gender (usually men, Okin 1996) greater authority and privilege than the other.

The second type of morality/convention overlap, labeled *second order moral events,* occurs when the violation of a strongly held convention is seen as causing psychological harm (insult, distress) to persons maintaining the convention. In our culture, for example, attending a funeral in a bathing suit would generally be seen as disrespectful of the deceased and insensitive toward the grieving family, and not merely an instance of unconventional conduct.

There are three basic ways in which such instances of domain interaction and overlap may be dealt with (Smetana 1982; Turiel and Smetana 1984). In one form there is a predominant emphasis on one domain, with subordination of the other. For example, in the recent controversy over the role of women in Catholic worship services, some women have framed the issue as a moral matter of fairness and rights. Pope John Paul II, however, argued in the late 1970s that the ordination of women was not an issue of justice or human rights, but rather one of custom and tradition.

A second response to instances of domain interaction or overlap is characterized by conflict regarding how best to conceptualize a particular issue, with inconsistencies and the absence of resolution or reconciliation among components. An illustrative example is provided in Smetana's (1982) research on women's reasoning about abortion, in which she describes the agonizing cases of pregnant women contemplating abortion, who shift between viewing abortion as a matter of personal discretion, privacy, and choice, and viewing the act of abortion as the immoral taking of another person's life.

A third way of responding to instances of domain overlap involves the coordination of the various domain components, so that each is taken into account in the solution of the problem. A commonplace illustrative example of such domain coordination would be the resolution of gender-based inequities resulting from outdated norms for the assignment of household tasks. This has entailed restructuring family norms for how child care and other domestic responsibilities are distributed among family members so that both the husband and wife can fulfill career obligations while also maintaining an orderly and functioning household.

FACTORS INFLUENCING MORAL AND SOCIAL
REASONING IN CONTEXT

There are several factors that affect which form domain interactions will take, and the outcomes that will result from the person's moral and social judgments. Two of these factors, emotion and personal character, will be discussed in separate chapters that conclude Part One of the book. At this point, and in Chapter 5, I will take up a discussion of the other major factors influencing contextualized social and moral judgments. These factors are the person's level of development, the cultural setting, and the person's assumptions about the facts of the situation.

Domain Interactions and Moral Development

A central factor influencing people's responses to the moral and nonmoral components of social situations is development. It is self-evident that a child's moral and social judgments will be different from those of an adult. Because all people, regardless of gender, culture, or social class background, develop with age, development has been viewed as an important route through which to focus moral education curricula (Kohlberg 1984; Lapsley 1996). In fact, a great deal of optimism was generated in the late 1960s and 1970s around the role that development could play in educational programs aimed at rearing "moral children." While there is no question that development plays an important role in an individual's moral reasoning, the weight accorded to developmental factors was overstated. As we will see, this misplaced optimism stemmed in large part from the incorrect assumption that development alone could account for the ways in which people weigh moral and nonmoral concerns (especially the laws and conventions of society) in generating decisions about a morally right course of action. This assumption stemmed from an account of development in which the relations between morality and convention were determined by progression within a single developmental system (Kohlberg 1984).

What we have learned from more recent work is that differences in social judgments, attributable to development, can be seen in the age-related changes that occur in the understandings people have about issues within each domain. Development within the moral domain entails shifts in the ways in which people conceptualize what it means to be fair, along with attendant changes in conceptions of the obligations that follow from moral concerns for the welfare of others. Development in the personal domain involves shifts in concepts of the function that control over personal choice and privacy has for developing and maintaining individuality and personal integrity. Finally, development of concepts of convention follows an oscillating pattern of affirmations and negations tied to shifts in understandings of the role that conventional norms play in structuring predictable patterns of conduct among members of a social group.

When individuals reason about issues that require them to draw knowledge from more than one domain, the resulting judgments will be affected not only by the degree to which aspects from given domains achieve salience, but also by the level of conceptual development the individual has reached within each domain. A little-researched issue is the extent to which natural development within the moral, personal, and conventional domains occurs in synchrony. To the extent that development occurs at roughly the same rate across domains, we can describe within very broad limits the structure of age-related shifts in reasoning corresponding to prototypical cross-domain interactions. As I will discuss in greater detail in this chapter, this appears to be what has been captured by Kohlberg's (1984) description of stages of moral development. There is however, experimental evidence that demonstrates that development within the moral and conventional domains can occur separately and at different rates.

As part of an educational intervention within the context of an eighth-grade American history class (Nucci and Weber 1991), we set up conditions so that students either focused the content of their group discussions around moral issues of fairness and harm to others, or matters of social convention and social organization. At the end of the four-week instructional unit, we assessed both groups for their levels of reasoning in both the moral and conventional domains. As one might expect, the group that focused on moral issues had higher levels of moral judgment than the group that focused on matters of convention. Conversely, the group that focused discussions around convention had attained higher levels of understanding in the conventional domain. This relatively short-term intervention demonstrated that differential social experiences can result in different rates of development in these two domains, and provides additional evidence that morality and convention comprise distinct conceptual and developmental systems.

The likelihood of developmental asynchrony adds to the factors that would help explain individual variations in contextualized moral judgments. An individual who is at Level 1 in Domain A and Level 1 in Domain B will exhibit a different pattern of reasoning in the context of multidomain issues than will a person who reasons at Level 2 in Domain A and Level 1 in Domain B, and so forth. Given the rates of change that take place in intellectual and physical growth during childhood and adolescence, we would expect asynchrony to be fairly common in the moral and social judgments of school-age children. Analyses of the sociomoral reasoning of children and adolescents have provided findings that age-related changes in the elements of sociomoral judgment assessed by the Kohlberg interview do not occur in synchrony. Instead, the evidence provided by this global measure indicates that a mixture of elements from different phases of development, rather than synchronous shifts, characterizes sociomoral development throughout childhood (Colby, et al. 1983; Turiel 1975). Developmental lags and advances in one area relative to another are part of the normal pattern teachers observe in student progress. Such asynchronies in the development of social judgments may help explain how two students with seemingly similar levels of understanding of the function of social norms can appear so different in terms of their sense of fairness or moral obligation.

With respect to social growth, cross-domain interactions may serve as an important source of input for stimulation of change in the concepts maintained in related conceptual systems. Development of moral conceptions of rights, for example, may be stimulated by preceding advances in the child's conceptions in the personal domain regarding the nature of personhood and the importance of personal choice (Nucci 1996). Similarly, the emergence of principled moral positions may be stimulated in early adulthood by the prior construction in the conventional domain of a relativistic negation of convention as simply the arbitrarily established norms of a particular society. This moral equation of societies as conventional systems may stimulate a search for moral moorings independent of one's particular cultural frame. On the other hand, it may also simply allow for the adoption of a relativistic political ideology in which such moral questions are left unresolved. The possibility of cross-domain interaction, thus, does not imply a deterministic set of developmental outcomes.

Having gotten a flavor of how development might impact the form of interdomain interactions associated with moral growth, let us turn to a more detailed description of age-related changes in concepts of morality and convention, and the age-typical patterns of interaction that emerge between these two domains. We will do so with reference to Kohlberg's stages of moral development. This will allow us to get an overview of the major age-related changes that occur within each domain, and also to account for the basic findings and observed contradictions that have arisen in research employing the Kohlberg stages. The Kohlberg sequence is the most widely researched description of moral development available. It has also served as the basis for a number of influential educational innovations (DeVries 1995; Power, Higgins, and Kohlberg 1989a). Despite this widespread influence, Kohlberg's (1984) standard account of stages of moral development does not represent the full range of sociomoral decision-making patterns that individuals present (Rest et al. 1999). For one thing, there is considerable within-person variation in the moral reasoning patterns that individuals exhibit across contexts (Bandura 1991). This variation is inconsistent with the assumption that the Kohlberg stages capture the structure of a person's moral reasoning.

In the process of conducting their careful and extensive research aimed at standardizing moral-stage scoring, the Kohlberg group (Colby and Kohlberg 1987; Colby et al. 1983) discovered that individuals at all points in development may respond to Kohlberg's moral dilemmas by reasoning from a perspective of either rules and authority (Type A reasoning) or justice and human welfare (Type B reasoning). In addition, individuals at all ages and levels may present what the Kohlberg group has referred to as a "relativistic metaethical orientation." From the vantage point of our current understanding of the domain-related heterogeneity in people's social cognition, such within-stage variation can be accounted for by recognizing that the Kohlberg tasks generate reasoning employing knowledge from more than one conceptual system.

This variation occurred because the methods Kohlberg (1984) employed to study moral judgment used stimulus materials that combined the presentation of moral dilemmas with moral conflicts. A moral dilemma pits one moral consideration (e.g., stealing) against another (e.g., harm to persons). A moral conflict pits a moral consideration (e.g., stealing) against a nonmoral factor or norm, such as obedience toward authority or the law. The moral "dilemmas" that comprise the primary assessment tool for measuring moral stage as defined by Lawrence Kohlberg's (1984) influential theory combine both dilemmatic and conflictual elements. Kohlberg (1958) set out in his original research to study whether there was a developmental progression in the ways in which people at various ages weigh the needs of persons against the conventions and norms of society. His purpose was to uncover whether development led to the kinds of principled moral positions posited by rationalist philosophers, such as Kant, and suggested by the developmental research of Piaget (1932).

As was alluded to in Chapter 2, Kohlberg's (1984) standard account describes moral development as moving from early stages in which moral understandings of fairness are intertwined with prudential self-interest and concrete concerns for social authority, to conventional moral understandings in which morality (fairness) is intertwined with concerns for maintaining social organization defined by normative regulation. Finally, at the highest, principled stages of morality attained by a minority of the general population, morality as fairness is fully differentiated from nonmoral prudential or conventional considerations, and morality serves as the basis from which the individual not only guides personal actions but also is able to evaluate the morality of the conventional normative system of society.

Kohlberg (1984) appears to have described the sequence of age-related changes in the ways in which moral and nonmoral (especially conventional) concerns are typically integrated in overlapping contexts. For example, Stage 4 (conventional) moral reasoning, as described in the Kohlberg system, reflects the emergence in middle to late adolescence of understandings in the *conventional* domain that social norms are constituent elements of social systems (Turiel 1983). This reinterpretation of the Kohlberg stage progression is set out in Table 4.1. It presents the major age-related changes (levels) in people's thinking within the moral and conventional domains, alongside the age-typical stage described by Kohlberg's (1984) theory. The descriptions of moral development are provided in the left-hand column of the table. The sequence of changes in concepts of social convention (Turiel 1983) is presented in the middle column. The Kohlberg stage sequence is presented in the right-hand column. The

TABLE 4.1. Levels of Moral and Conventional Development in Relation to Kohlberg's Stages

Approximate Ages	Moral Domain	Conventional Domain	Kohlberg Stage
		Conceptual Framework	
5–7 years	Recognition of prima facie obligations (e.g., not to hit and hurt others). However, beyond those basic requirements, fairness is prioritized in terms of self-interest. *member of society*	Conventions are "reified" as descriptions of empirical regularities (e.g., women are supposed to wear dresses because women wear dresses and men don't).	*Stage 1* Rules are to be obeyed. One should avoid physical damage to persons and property. Inability to coordinate perspectives of self and others; thus, favoring the self is seen as right.
8–10 years	Fairness is now coordinated with conceptions of "just" reciprocity defined primarily in terms of strict equality, with some beginning concerns for equity.	Negation of the conception of conventions as empirical regularities. Exceptions to conventions (e.g., some women wear pants) taken as evidence that conventions are arbitrary. The mere existence of a norm not a sufficient basis for compliance.	*Stage 2* Morality as instrumental exchange – "You scratch my back, I'll scratch yours"; Act to meet one's own interests and needs and let others do the same. Rules followed only when in someone's interest.
10–12 years	Fairness seen as requiring more than strict equality. Concerns for equity (taking into account the special needs, situations, or contributions	Concrete understanding that conventional rules maintain order (e.g., prevent people from running in the halls). Top-down conception of social authority and	*Stage 3* Being good means living up to what is expected by people around you, and by one's role (e.g., good brother/sister). Fair-

(continued)

TABLE 4.1 (continued)

	Conceptual Framework		
Approximate Ages	Moral Domain	Conventional Domain	Kohlberg Stage
	of others) are now coordinated with reciprocity in structuring moral decisions.	rules. People in charge make rules that preserve order. Rules may be changed and vary by context.	ness is the golden rule. One should be caring of others.
12–14 years	Consolidation of the relations between equity and equality in conceptions of what is fair and caring in social relations.	Conventions are now viewed as "nothing but" social expectations. The arbitrary nature of convention is viewed as undercutting the force of a rule. Acts are evaluated independent of rules.	*Stage 3B (Pseudo Stage 6)* Moral decisions based on the fairness or harmful impact of actions independent of governing rules, or role expectations. Morality prioritized over convention. No evidence of a "prior to society" orientation.
14–17 years	Continuation of consolidation.	Emergence of systematic concepts of social structure. conventions as normative and binding within a social system of fixed roles and static hierarchical organization. *There's a system*	*Stage 4* Morality as codified in the laws of the governing system. Adherence to law provides an objective basis for what is right. Maintaining social-system basis for moral order and equal protection from harm. Notions of equity and equality same as in Stage 3.

17–20 years	Transition to adult morality.	Negation of view that uniform norms serve to maintain social systems. Conventions are "nothing but" societal standards that have become codified through habitual use. Systems of norms are arbitrary.	*Stage 4½* Morality is relative to systems of laws and norms. No system may lay claim to moral superiority. What is right is a function of what seems most right for the person in his/her situation.
Adulthood	*(Moral Domain Extrapolation)* Application of conceptions of fairness and beneficence to reasoning about one's social system. Morality understood to be independent of norms of particular systems. Coordination of universal and prescriptive features of morality with incommensurate/intrinsic worth of all persons. Logical extension of moral obligations to treatment of humankind.	Conventions as uniformities that are functional in coordinating social interactions. Shared knowledge of conventions among members of social groups facilitate interaction and operation of the system.	*Stage 5* "Prior to society" perspective: What is moral are values and rights that exist prior to social attachments and contracts. Such values and rights are those which any rational being would want to see reflected in a moral society.

ages presented at the far left hand side of the table are approximations and are intended as markers of development, rather than as fixed points of maturation.

Age 5 to 7 Years

As was described in Chapter 2, morality begins in early childhood with a focus upon issues of harm to the self and others. Preschool-aged children are very concerned with their own safety, and understand that it is objectively wrong to hurt others. Three-year-olds, for example, understand that it is wrong to hit and hurt someone, even in the absence of a rule against hitting, because "When you get hit, it hurts, and you start to cry." In research on age-related changes within the moral domain, Davidson, Turiel, and Black (1983) found that up to about age 7, moral judgment is primarily regulated by concerns for maintaining welfare and avoiding harm and is limited to directly accessible acts. Young children's morality, however, is not yet structured by understandings of fairness as reciprocity. Fairness for the young child is often expressed in terms of personal needs and the sense that one isn't getting one's just desserts. "It's not fair" often means "I didn't get what I want," or that someone's actions caused the child to experience harm.

While young children's conceptions of morality can be drawn from direct experience with the effects of moral actions, their conceptions of social convention need to be constructed out of their experiences with the norms or expectations that regulate such acts, rather than from any features of the acts themselves. In attempting to make sense out of this con- ventional aspect of their social world, children search for patterns or regularities that would allow them to predict the right course of action. For children approximately 5 to 7 years of age, the regularities and patterns they observe combine with the explicit information they are told (e.g., parent or teacher statements of rules or expectations) to form a conception of conventions as upholding a set of empirical regularities. For example, children observe that women and not men generally wear dresses. From this empirical regularity, children construct a straightforward set of conclusions: Men don't wear dresses because men aren't women; therefore, only women should wear dresses. For a man to wear a dress would be to violate this empirically established regularity of the social world.

As can be seen in Table 4.1, Stage 1 of the Kohlberg scheme contains elements from the rule-following orientation of young children's conventional domain understandings and from the concerns for concrete effects of actions on others that characterize young children's moral concepts. Although this mixture of convention and morality maps onto occasions when young children refer to rules and social expectations when considering a moral course of action ("Ooh, you're going to get in trouble."), it does not account for the content of reasoning exhibited when young children spontaneously share with others or object to the actions of a bully. In such cases, the child's morality is operating independent of the conventional norms of the setting, focusing instead on the salient moral features of the situation.

Age 8 to 10 Years

The moral intuitions of early childhood allow children to consider the impact of actions on others. In settings where the child's own interests are not importantly at stake, young children can be touchingly generous and benevolent (Eisenberg 1986; Staub 1971). At the same time, however, young children have difficulty balancing the needs of more than one person at a time. In the absence of some clear procedure for resolving competing moral needs, young children appear to use arbitrary standards for assigning value to persons (e.g., age, gender), and have particular difficulty in weighing the needs of others against their own desires (Damon 1975, 1977). Thus, we witness the contradiction of the generosity and openness of young children, and an arbitrariness and selfishness charac- teristic of the age. Resolving these contradictions involves changes in the child's conceptions of persons, in their understandings of what is required to maintain interpersonal relations, and in their general intellectual capacity to comprehend the logical implications for the self of one's actions on others. This is a tall order. And, these issues are revisited throughout the course of moral development.

The great accomplishment of early-childhood moral development is the construction of notions of moral action tied to structures of "just" reciprocity (Damon 1975, 1977; Turiel and Davidson 1986;). The web of reciprocal interpersonal interactions takes the child beyond the minimal moral requirements of concerns about prima facie harm to what Piaget (1932) referred to as the social logic of justice. By approximately 6 to 8 years of age, children begin to construct a set of moral understandings that compellingly tie the actions of one person to the reactions or responses of the other. By age 10, these notions of reciprocity are generally consolidated into notions of moral "necessity" resulting from a moral logic that requires equal treatment of persons. This "strict" reading of equal treatment, however, may allow for a kind of tit-for-tat morality in which moral obligation extends only to those from whom one can expect something in return, and only to the extent that actions maintain a balanced "moral ledger."

With regard to convention, development shifts the ways in which children interpret instances in which people deviate from typical patterns of conventionally regulated behavior. At the earliest level, children treat such exceptions from observed regularities as error. By age 8 to 10 years, children view such exceptions to empirical regularities as evidence that conventions don't really have much normative force and don't matter. For example, 5- to 7-year-old children generally respond that it would be wrong for a man to accept a job as an infant nurse because nurses are women (Turiel 1983). Their knowledge of counterexamples of sex-typed behavior, such as women serving in the armed forces, are not seen as evidence that their position is an overgeneralization. In contrast, 8 to 10 year olds employ counter-examples, such as girls playing on baseball teams, as evidence that all gender-related conventions (and by extension all conventions) may be ignored.

Kohlberg's Stage 2 captures the morality of direct reciprocity typical of this age group. According to the Kohlberg account, morality at this stage is characterized by instrumental exchange. Individuals act on the basis of meeting their own interests and letting others do the same. The negation of convention typical of this age is associated in the Kohlberg account with an instrumental approach to rules, such that rules are followed only when they are in someone's self-interest (e.g., to stay out of trouble).

Age 10 to 12 Years

Beginning around age 8, children show signs of an awareness that differences in the capacities and needs of individuals should be met with special considerations. For example, children will generally adjust their physical play when interacting with physically handicapped peers. These intuitions are coordinated between the ages of 10 and 12 years into a notion of fairness as requiring more than strict equality. Concerns for equity (taking into account the special needs, situations, or contributions of others) are now coordinated with reciprocity in structuring moral decisions (Damon 1975, 1977). Treating others fairly may mean treating people unequally in the sense that equity requires adjustments that bring people into more comparable statuses. In concrete terms, children begin to realize, for instance, the fairness inherent in the "unequal" treatment that par-

ents provide to siblings who are at different ages when it comes to privileges and responsibilities.

This expansion of morality frees the child from considering what is fair
solely in terms of direct reciprocal exchange, and it allows for extensions of
moral (fair) treatment to those from whom one has no expected repayment
and to those who have even been ungracious or unfair to the self. With respect to this latter point, it allows the child to go beyond a tit-for-tat morality of retribution to deal with transgressors without resorting to the same
kinds of hurtful acts employed by the transgressor (Lapsley 1996).

In terms of convention, the negations of the previous level are replaced
by a concrete affirmation of the functional value of conventions as serving to maintain social order. Children recognize that conventions vary by
context and that exceptions exist within contexts. However, they also
maintain that things work "better" when there is some organization established by rules. For example, rules are needed in order to keep everyone from running in the school hallways and creating chaos. Along with
this concrete conception of social order is a concrete notion of social hierarchy. People in charge make the rules, which others are expected to follow. There is, however, no understanding of societies as systems and,
thus, no way of justifying particular social norms beyond very obvious
concrete givens. For example, children at this level do not understand the
functional significance of titles (e.g., Mr., Mrs., Dr.) in forms of address as
reflecting hierarchical social position. Children often state that one should
use titles as a sign of respect for the person being addressed. When asked
why use of the title is more respectful than use of a first name, the children are unable to answer, other than to say that the authorities who have
organized things favor the rule.

Within the Kohlberg typology, the overlap between these age-typical
forms of moral and conventional thinking are combined to form the Stage
3 "good boy/girl" form of conventional morality. At Stage 3 within the
Kohlberg system, being good means living up to what is expected by people around you and by one's conventionally defined role (e.g., good
brother/sister). Fairness is no longer the instrumental reciprocity of Stage
2, but rather an equitable rendering of the golden rule. Fairness means going beyond raw justice toward a view that one should be caring of others.

Age 12 to 14 Years (Stage 3 B)

During early adolescence, there is further consolidation of the relations
between equity and equality constructed in late childhood. Efforts to

bring these two aspects of fairness into relation, combined with the prescriptive and universalizable elements of morality, open adolescents to consideration of the moral meaning of their relations with others beyond their own group.

With respect to conventions, adolescent reflection on their earlier concrete understandings of norms leads to a negation of their earlier position in which norms are justified in terms of their relation to social authority. The adolescent stands this childhood conception on its head, and conventions are negated as being nothing but the dictates of authority (Turiel 1983). Since the acts being governed by convention are arbitrary, the rules have no meaning. Thus, the issue of whether or not titles are more respectful than first names is answered in the negative. First names and titles have equal moral value. Whether to call a teacher by Mr. or Mrs. rather than his/her first name is therefore a matter of (a) prudence (i.e., violation of the rule about titles could have sanctions), (b) moral consideration (i.e., some teachers feel strongly about the rule and are "hurt" when addressed by first name), or (c) personal preference.

The Kohlberg system has no stage that would correspond to these descriptions of moral and conventional thought. However, the descriptions do help to take into account some of the anomalous findings with adolescent subjects reported within the Kohlberg literature. In Kohlberg's (1958, 1963) original report of research results regarding the moral-stage sequence, he identified principled moral reasoning among adolescent subjects. In their subsequent reanalysis of these data in conjunction with their longitudinal studies, the Kohlberg group determined that principled moral reasoning does not occur in adolescence but is a rare achievement of adult moral reasoners. The earlier Kohlberg adolescent findings were recoded as "Stage 3 (Type B, autonomous)" reasoning (Colby et al. 1983). The "Type B" assignment was a post hoc attempt to account for the fact that the adolescents provided moral justifications that focused upon universal requirements for attention to fairness and compassion, and they prioritized these concerns over issues of law or convention when such issues were raised by the interviewers. These adolescent subjects did not employ the "typical" Stage 3 references to group normative expectations. In the reanalysis of their reasoning, their judgments were assigned a Stage 3 score because the subjects did not evidence an understanding of society as a system, and thus could not provide a "prior to society" orientation requisite for a Stage 5 or 6 designation.

A domain-theory interpretation of these same results would be that the negation of convention typical of this age group would make it unlikely that their moral reasoning would make reference to social norms. Moreover, moral judgments typical of this age group (as assessed by Damon's "distributive justice" 1975, 1977, and Lapsley's 1982 "retributive justice" interviews) have many of the formal features associated with principled moral reasoning. Thus, the reasoning presented by morally sensitive adolescents might well look like principled morality. In our use of Kohlberg interviews with eighth-grade honors students, we found that we could distinguish the reasoning of these students from postconventional adults only by specifically asking questions that would demonstrate that they did not have a conception of societies as systems, and thus could not provide an articulated "prior to society" perspective (Nucci and Weber 1991).

Age 14 to 17 Years (Stage 4)

The moral reasoning associated with middle to late adolescence has not been studied from a developmental perspective outside of the Kohlberg framework. However, one can extrapolate from the existing work with younger adolescents and children that the course of moral development would be toward deepening the understandings of fairness that emerged in earlier developmental periods. A significant aspect of this deepening would stem from the person's construction of more comprehensive conceptions of society and people.

 It is in middle adolescence that children first construct an understanding of conventions as constituent elements of societies as systems (Turiel 1983). The younger adolescent's dismissal of convention as simply the dictates of authority is replaced by an understanding that conventions have meaning within a larger social framework. Thus, conventions are viewed as normative and binding within a social system of fixed roles and hierarchical organization. This hierarchy is not the concrete differentia-tion of people in power from others of lower status, as was the case in middle childhood, but rather a differentiated conceptualization of the associations among differing social roles and social positions in relation to one another within a conventional system of norms. At this point in development, violations of convention are viewed as potentially disruptive of the normative system. Thus, participants within a system are expected to abide by the norms and conventions of that system.

 The construction of the conception of societies as normative systems allows for the emergence of what Kohlberg identified as Stage 4 moral reasoning. At Stage 4, according to the Kohlberg position, morality is codified in the laws of the governing system. Adherence to the law in a moral context provides for a shared and impersonal objective basis for the right. Maintaining the social system is viewed as a way of preserving the moral order and of providing unbiased and equal protection from harm. The underlying moral conceptions of equity and equality are the same as those of Kohlberg Stage 3.

Development in Adulthood: Age 17 to 20 Years (stage 4 1/2)

During early adulthood, there is additional reflection on the relation between specific conventions and the organizational functions they serve. The arbitrariness of convention once again becomes a basis from which to negate their normative force. Specific conventions (e.g., use of titles in addressing people in authority) are not viewed as necessary to the maintenance of the social functions (e.g., conveying respect within a set of hierarchical social positions) they are presumed to serve. Whereas young adolescents negate convention as simply the dictates of people in authority, young adults negate convention as "nothing but" the expectations of society (Turiel 1983). Systems of norms are now viewed as arbitrary.

In their longitudinal studies (Colby et al. 1983), the Kohlberg group reported evidence for a transitional stage (4 1/2) between conventional (Stage 4) and postconventional (Stage 5) moral reasoning. This transition, found among some college-age individuals, is characterized by value relativism and "situational ethics." Moral positions espoused by these "sophomoric" relativists rest on the justification that morality stems from societal norms that have force only within the context of particular social systems. Systems of norms are themselves arbitrary; thus, morality is a matter of what seems right to the person in his/her situation. One can see, in this description of the moral relativism captured by the Kohlberg group, a subordination of moral justifications to the negation of convention characteristic of individuals at that same general age. This is not to say that all young adults enter a period of moral relativism, but simply to point out how a conflation of conventional concepts with morality can result in such reasoning. The fact that these young relativists hold onto a set of criteria independent of societal norms as the ultimate basis for their moral justifications points toward a latent recognition that morality stems from sources other than conventional norms.

Adulthood: Age 20 and Above (stage 5)

The recognition that conventions do not in and of themselves constitute the defining elements of social systems is maintained at the final point in the development of conceptions of social convention. However, there is an additional understanding at this level that conventions serve to coordinate the interactions of people in ongoing social systems and, thus, that conventions serve the important function of facilitating the operation of social systems. Conventions provide individual members with predictable sets of mutual behavioral expectations within a particular social frame and, thus, allow for the smooth and normalized flow of social interaction among members of a social group.

The final empirically supported stage of moral development as defined by the Kohlberg system appears only in the reasoning of a minority of adults (Colby et al. 1983; Lapsley 1996; Snarey 1985). As can be seen in Table 4.1, Stage 5 reasoning is characterized by a "prior to society" perspective in which what is moral are those values and rights that transcend particular social attachments and contracts. Such values and rights are those which any rational being would want to see reflected in the norms and mores of a moral society. From a domain theory perspective, this principled moral position is one that can be constructed once the individual has gained some "distance" from the conventional system conceptualization of adolescence. It represents a particular coordination between one's conceptions of conventional systems and morality, such that morality is structured not simply by a capacity to judge actions in terms of their application to personal interactions, absent concerns for the structure of the social system, but to provision universalizable principles for human interactions with application to a contextualized sociohistorical frame. Even though the antecedents of principled moral judgment are evident in childhood (e.g., adolescents are capable of evaluating the morality of social practices in terms of their concordance with formal moral criteria; Nucci and Weber 1991), the requirements for moral judgment, so defined, would appear to be ones that are beyond the normal life-space of most adults. The factors or conditions that would stimulate development of principled moral reasoning as defined by Kohlberg are likely to be multifaceted and to go beyond the mere interplay between conventional and moral concepts. Among the factors likely to be involved are sociohistorical context (Habermas 1991; Snarey 1985) and educational level (Lind, Hartman, and Wakenhut 1985).

On that note, I will now leave the discussion of developmental factors in cross-domain interactions to take up some of the issues regarding the impact of culture on sociomoral judgment.

CHAPTER FIVE

Morality in Context: Issues of Culture

As we saw in Chapter 4, people at any given level of development may read the moral and nonmoral components of complex social situations in different ways. One of the primary influences upon the ways in which people read social situations is the cultural frame in which they live. In their simplest form, these cultural influences result from the mere presence or absence of particular nonmoral rules or norms. For example, queuing in line to buy movie tickets can have moral implications only in a cultural setting where the convention of standing in line is in effect. Of more interest, however, is the manner in which cultures emphasize the importance of maintaining the existing social order, and the degree to which that social order emphasizes hierarchy and social stratification. Cultures, like individuals, are complex and multifaceted, and it is simplistic and even stereotypic to characterize cultures in global terms.

The discussion that follows begins with an examination of some general trends that can be observed emerging from the relative emphasis on tradition and hierarchy in cultural value systems. It moves on toward a discussion of how the heterogeneous nature of culture may lead to conflicting and even oppositional viewpoints in value orientations within a given society.

CULTURAL EMPHASIS ON TRADITION

With regard to the first point in the discussion, it is the case that all cultural groups endeavor to maintain their traditions and customs and pass them on to the next generation. Without such conservative tendencies, the very existence of culture and society would be hard to envision. Cultures differ, however, in the degree to which adherence to custom and tradition is emphasized. It is generally recognized that the so-called modern societies change their customs and conventions more readily than so-called traditional societies. One consequence of these differences is that members of traditional societies are more likely to "moralize" their conventions. For example, as was mentioned in Chapter 1, Ijo children and adolescents in Nigeria (Hollos et al. 1986), Arab children in Israel (Nisan 1987), and lower-class children in northeastern Brazil (Nucci et al. 1996) tend to affirm the importance of customs and tradition to a greater degree than do American children. Children within the more traditional cultures were less likely to view the conventional norms of their society as alterable, and more likely to generalize their conventions to other cultural settings than were American children.

One probable consequence of these differences is that individuals in more traditional cultures would be more sensitive to the salience of custom and convention in contexts where convention and morality overlap. There is some indirect evidence that this is the case. It comes from the cross-cultural work done using the Kohlberg stage sequence (Snarey 1985). One of the striking findings of this cross-cultural work is that postconventional reasoning (as defined within the Kohlberg framework) is almost absent among the adult population of traditional cultural groups. The usual explanation for these findings is that traditional cultures do not provide the kinds of disequilibrating social experiences that would move individuals to higher levels of moral reasoning. This explanation is concordant with sociohistorical analyses of the impact of modernity on moral discourse (Habermas 1996).

Without denying the role of history in shaping the context of moral discourse, we may offer an alternative explanation for the dynamics resulting in the apparent absence of postconventional reasoning among members of traditional cultures. The alternative being suggested here is that the traditional social/cultural context is one that places a very high value on societal continuity, thereby raising the salience of convention relative to moral considerations of fairness and welfare in many social situations. Thus, it is not surprising that adults from such cultures tend to bring in concerns for social organization, custom, and tradition when making moral judgments about multifaceted social situations.

It is entirely possible, however, that the moral concepts of adults in such cultural settings have been underestimated by methodologies that define moral development in terms of reasoning about mixed-domain issues (Shweder, et al. 1987; Snarey 1985). We should keep in mind that there is considerable cross-cultural evidence that children and adults across a wide range of the world's cultures conceptualize prototypical moral issues pertaining to fairness and others' welfare in ways very similar to children and adults in Western contexts, and differentiate such issues from prototypical matters of convention. By assessing moral reasoning in the context of multidomain issues, we may be looking at how members of traditional cultures coordinate morality and convention, rather than assessing their levels of moral understanding. John Snarey (1985) has made a rather compelling case for the likelihood that methodologies, such as the Kohlberg interview, developed to measure moral judgment in Western settings, may be inappropriate for analyzing the reflective "postconventional" reasoning of members of societies that emphasize attachment to the social group, and who couch their moral judgments of fairness within language that emphasizes group membership.

The power of social/cultural context as a factor in altering the mixed-domain judgments of sophisticated moral reasoners is not limited to traditional cultural settings. This was vividly demonstrated by findings from the famous Milgram (1963) study on obedience. In that study, American subjects were told that they were participating in a scientific study of the impact of punishment on learning, and were required to administer what the subjects were led to believe were increasingly painful electric shocks to learners each time the learner made an error. In point of fact, the "learners" were actors hired by the experimenters, and no electrical shocks were actually administered. The finding that is of particular interest for this discussion is that some subjects assessed as principled moral reasoners (on the basis of their responses to standardized Kohlberg dilemmas) nonetheless complied with the commands of the scientific "authority" in the "learning" situation. In fact, they continued to administer electrical shocks right up to the point where the level of shock was said to be dangerous and very painful.

The willingness of principled moral reasoners to inflict pain and to endanger another person requires some explanation. One possible explanation is that these subjects did not have the "character" to follow through with what they knew to be morally right. (We will look critically at this conception of character in Chapter 7.) A more plausible account, which is in line with reports of subjects' experiences in the study, is that the situation created genuine conflict between two competing, important sets of values: (1) to not cause harm, and (2) to contribute to scientific progress. At the time of the Milgram studies, scientific authority was held at a level of esteem few can imagine at this point in history. American cultural ideals of social progress were enmeshed with the achievements of science. Few lay people, however, had any real conception of the conventions of scientific inquiry. Thus, they were at the mercy of scientific authorities for information regarding appropriate conduct in the experimental situation. Adding to the mix was the fact that the learner/victim was located in an adjacent room away from the subject, while the scientific authority hovered close to the subject supervising his/her actions. Under these conditions, even for some of the principled reasoners (as assessed by Kohlberg stage), the salience of the social-conventional elements of this particular cultural context outweighed the moral components. As a result, in this particular cultural situation, some of the American subjects who had been assessed as principled moral reasoners responded to this mixed-domain conflict by prioritizing obedience to convention and authority over their moral concerns about harm. (For a more detailed discussion of these issues within the Milgram study, see Turiel 1983, pp. 203–10).

THE IMPACT OF HIERARCHY AND SOCIAL STRATIFICATION

As we have just seen, the degree of emphasis that cultures place on adherence to custom and convention can impact upon the tendencies of individuals to prioritize moral and nonmoral factors in multifaceted social situations. Even within the so-called modern societies, certain aspects of the social order (such as scientific authority) can take on a level of importance that rivals that of moral concern. A second cultural factor that affects how individuals construct the relation between morality and convention is the degree of social stratification within a society, as well as the individual's place within it.

The notion of social hierarchy may seem anathema to democracy and social equity and, thus, inherently at odds with morality. But some degree of social stratification and hierarchy is needed for social organizations to function. Even within the most equitable of social arrangements, some degree of stratification will arise as a function of variations in expertise and the need for at least a practical (if not optimal) level of efficiency and organization. Moreover, there are contexts in everyday life where concerns for social coordination override the unfairness that may be generated by the maintenance of hierarchy and differential authority.

For example, members of an orchestra or players on a football team render greater power and authority to the coach or conductor than to other members of the group. These inequalities are viewed as essential to the successful conduct of the group's activities. In such situations, however, in addition to shared understandings of the connections between hierarchy and group purposes, there is an element of voluntariness on the part of participants, and there is the option of exiting the situation.

This is not the case, however, with regard to the hierarchical structures of the broader societal and cultural context within which people live out the course of their daily lives. Even within an "open society," one cannot generally take oneself out of one's cultural and social context without a great deal of effort and personal cost. Thus, within the broader social context, there is an inherent tension associated with social hierarchy between the needs for social organization and efficiency, on the one hand, and fairness and equity, on the other.

Within the modern democracies, this tension between hierarchy and morality is often played out in the public arena. In the United States, for example, we are currently in the midst of a cultural struggle to establish family patterns and structures that allow for women, as well as men, to establish autonomous adult lives while contributing equitably and effectively to the necessary tasks of child rearing and household organization (Okin 1996).

Within traditional hierarchical societies, such tensions between morality and hierarchy have been less obvious to outside observers (Turiel 1996). Recent anthropological (Geertz 1984; Shweder, et al. 1987) and cultural psychology accounts (Triandis 1988) have tended to depict patterns of living and expressions of values that reflect the dominant ideologies and belief systems of cultures. The resulting portraits of culture, while rich in detail and oftentimes breathtaking in their ethnographic sensitivity (cf. Geertz 1984), do not generally capture the dissident undercurrents hidden in the beliefs of individuals, or in the surreptitious practices of subordinate groups (Abu-Lughod 1993; Spiro 1993). As a result, the picture that emerges of traditional societies is of predominantly conflict-free commitment to tradition, custom, and respect for authority. This picture has been so compelling that the anthropologist Richard Shweder (1990) has characterized such hierarchical cultures as having a second moral code of respect for authority and tradition in addition to the morality of justice and human welfare.

There is no question that traditional, hierarchical systems tend to foster adherence to convention. It is a mistake, however, to assume that compliance with convention reflects a homogeneous reading of society by its members. In fact, there are marked differences in the ways in which individuals within a culture read the morality of conventional norms that assign privilege and power to classes of people. These differences in perception are systematically related to an individual's status within the social hierarchy. This set of issues has been most carefully investigated with respect to the power and freedom men enjoy relative to women in most of the world's cultures (Abu-Lughod 1993; Okin 1996; Turiel 1998b; Wainryb and Turiel 1994).

One such series of studies (Wainryb and Turiel 1994) looked at how Arab Druze villagers thought about issues of fairness and duty with regard to gender relationships. Adolescent males and females were interviewed about decision making regarding everyday types of activities pitting husbands' or fathers' desires or wishes against those of their wives, sons, or daughters. Scenarios included such things as choices of occupational and educational activities, household tasks, and leisure activities. Conflicts were presented in such a way that half depicted situations in which the person in the culturally defined dominant position objects to the choices or activities of a person in a subordinate position (e.g., a husband objects to his wife's decision to take a job), while the other half presented the person in a culturally defined subordinate position objecting to a dominant person's choices (e.g., a wife objects to her husband's decision to change jobs).

The results of the study with regard to the responses of the males (husbands and fathers) are not surprising. In virtually all situations, including those in which the female objected to the behavior of the male, the male's decisions and choices were judged to be the position that should prevail. The adolescent and adult males in the study viewed it as not only the right of men to decide such things for themselves but also as both fair and a matter of personal rights for husbands and fathers to decide such things for their wives and daughters as well. Wives and daughters were expected to comply with the wishes of husbands and fathers as a matter of tradition and duty. Within this traditional family structure, the roles of women were defined as dependent upon the corollary and inverse roles of men acting within their responsibilities of husband and father. In other words, from the perspective of the Arab Druze males, the customs and conventions structuring the hierarchical relations between men and women conformed to a "moral order."

Interviews with Arab Druze females showed that they also saw daughters and wives as bound by culturally defined role obligations and, therefore, obliged not to act contrary to the man's wishes. Unlike the males in the study, however, the women did not simply justify their answers in terms of obligations to the existing normative order. Instead, they often referred to the need for women to comply out of *pragmatic* concerns for the possible consequences of not accepting the men's choices, including physical violence, abandonment, or divorce. Furthermore, Wainryb and Turiel (1994) reported that a large majority (78%) of the Druze females in their study thought that it was unfair for a husband or father to interfere with the choices of activities on the part of the wife or daughter depicted within the study scenarios.

The almost inverse responses of the Druze Arab men and women indicate that perceptions of the "morality" of hierarchical systems depend upon "where you sit" within the hierarchy (Turiel 2000). The compliance of the women was not the simple result of commitment to a "moral code" of respect for authority and tradition (Shweder 1990), but also included a pragmatic response to power and the attendant potential for negative consequences. The men's sense of "right" was offset by the women's sense of injustice. The picture of oppositional points of view that emerges from this study of gender relations within the Druze Arab family sits in stark contrast with the pacific depiction of traditional culture offered up by cultural anthropology (Geertz 1984; Shweder, et al. 1987). Turiel (1996) is quick to point out, however, that it would be equally simplistic to cast traditional cultures simply in terms of oppositional perspectives maintained by persons at different points within the hierarchy. Members of a culture (such as the Arab Druze men and women we have been referring to) have many commonalties and shared values. Thus, the tensions that exist within their hierarchical family system sit within a relatively stable and enduring cultural system.

Cultures, like individuals, are multifaceted and complex. For our purposes, the lesson to be gained from such cross-cultural research is that social structure may have considerable impact on the ways in which morality is experienced and thought about in everyday life. Such research should serve to shake us out of our own complacency with regard to the morality of our society's conventions, customs, and hierarchical structure. Individuals steeped in a culture are often incapable of perceiving the moral impact that their way of life has upon its members.

Like the Arab Druze men and women, we, too, are participants in a society that assigns different roles and scripts to people in different social stations.

The ways in which cultures structure the conventions and customs of society are often the accidents of history, resulting from collective efforts to structure and coordinate the social interactions of a particular group of people. But, in many cases, these norms are also informed by the factual assumptions people make about the world, and/or the presumed relations between humanity and the cosmos. For example, some of the norms people establish to structure male/female relations are based on factual assumptions made about the differing nature and capacities of members of each gender. We will close out this discussion of the ways in which our understandings of morality, convention, and personal choice may interact in contextualized social reasoning by looking at the ways in which factual assumptions may enter the picture.

Factual Assumptions and Moral Reasoning

Imagine, if you will, the following set of cultural practices. They are a set of purification rituals that would take place as the necessary precursors to another set of activities. In general, the roles played by participants are defined by gender, although this is not always the case. Typically, the central figure is an adult male. This male begins by cleansing his hands and forearms using a prescribed liquid and washing himself carefully for no less than ten minutes. He is then robed by female attendants who are careful not to allow their bodies to come into contact with and thereby contaminate either the male or the outer part of his garment. The female attendants hold his garment open so that he may slip his arms through the sleeves. The attendants then tie the garment together with strings that are themselves covered over by an extending flap of material, such that the exterior of the garment remains pure. The female attendants then provide the male with uncontaminated coverings for his head, feet, hands, and face. Only after the male has been so cleansed and covered may he then move to the next series of culturally defined activities.

Of course, what I have just described are the procedures surgeons in our society go through prior to engaging in surgery. Surgeons go through all of this in order to reduce the likelihood of the patient contracting infection caused by microorganisms, commonly known as germs. Now some of you reading this book may have actually seen germs through a microscope, but most of us have not. Certainly none of us, not even the biologists, has ever seen a living virus. Nonetheless, virtually all of us who live in modern society believe that there are such things as germs and that they may cause infection and disease. We believe there are germs because the experts in our culture whose job it is to inform us about the facts of biological phenomena have assured us that they have evidence that germs exist. Moreover, through the years of following the advice of biologists and medical experts, we have a set of shared, practical experiences that seem to conform to what their germ theory has to say about the prevention and cure of infection and disease.

Having this knowledge, we would judge as morally wrong any surgeon who conducted nonemergency abdominal surgery, such as an appendectomy, without first going through the cleansing procedures just described. However, it is interesting to note that around the turn of the twentieth century, prior to germ theory, surgeons did not follow these carefully prescribed cleansing practices. In fact, surgeons, in an attempt to deliver service as efficiently as possible, would sometimes move from completion of one surgical procedure to the start of another without changing their clothes or thoroughly cleaning up in between. This practice resulted in the surgeons themselves being the source of sometimes fatal infections.

When I raise this example in my education classes, I never encounter a student who believes that the doctors who acted prior to knowledge of germ theory were engaging in conduct that was immoral. Nor have I had a student take the position that today's surgeons, by following cleansing procedures, are morally superior to the surgeons of the nineteenth century. From my students' point of view, the morality of doctors hasn't changed but, rather, their knowledge of what actions can cause or prevent harm.

The issues raised in this illustration may help us to account for some of the findings of apparent cultural variability in morality reported by anthropologists. As an example, let's consider the rather shocking findings reported in an anthropological study of the moral values of devout Hindus living in the temple community of Bhubaneswar, Orisa, India (Shweder et al. 1987). In one part of this study, Shweder and his colleagues presented their subjects with descriptions of thirty-nine different behaviors that entailed breaches of their community norms and asked them to judge each in terms of its "seriousness." The act rated as the most serious breach was the eldest son in a family getting a haircut and eating chicken the day after his father died. Rated thirty-fifth in seriousness among the thirty-nine behaviors was a man beating his disobedient wife black and blue!

Certainly, on the face of it, these data would appear to be evidence that this community of Hindus has a very different way of conceptualizing morality from what is generally considered moral in the West. Shweder and his colleagues (1987), however, provide additional information in their report that helps to account for the ways in which the subjects in their study reasoned about these issues. As it turns out, the Hindu judgments of the actions of the eldest son getting a haircut and eating chicken the day after his father's death, while morally neutral from a Western point of view, take on a different meaning within the context of the Hindu sub-jects' beliefs about the impact of these actions upon the father. In particu-lar, the judgments of these subjects must be seen from within the context of their beliefs about the ways in which events in the natural world oper-ate in relation to *unobserved entities*, such as souls and spirits of deceased ancestors. In this case, the father's soul would not receive salvation if the norm prohibiting the eating of chicken is not observed.

If we allow ourselves to role-take for a moment, and imagine that we are in the son's position, we can see how the act of eating chicken becomes a serious matter of causing grave harm to another being. We don't need to assume a new set of *moral* understandings but, rather, to apply our moral conceptions of harm and fairness to this situation once the *facts* of the matter are understood. Our relation to Shweder's Hindu subjects is quite analogous to that of the twentieth-century surgeon to his nine-teenth-century counterpart with respect to germ theory and the morality of maintaining a sterile environment for surgical procedures. Now, it might be argued that knowledge derived from science has a different epis-temic claim to validity than knowledge provided by religious belief. What cannot be argued, however, is that the assumptions one has about the nat-ural world, however arrived at, have an impact on our moral evaluations of actions.

Within our own culture, for example, people hold different views about whether it is morally wrong or all right to engage in the physical punishment of children. In her research on this issue, Wainryb (1991) found that pro–corporal punishment parents held the view that this be-havior was all right because it was a highly effective, educative act, rather than one of unprovoked harm or abuse of the child. When such parents were presented with information that spanking is no more effective than other methods of disciplining children, significant numbers of parents shifted in their view of corporal punishment and maintained that it was not all right for parents to engage in the behavior. Conversely, when par-ents who maintained that it was wrong to engage in corporal punishment were presented with information that experts had found spanking to be the most efficient method of teaching young children, there was a ten-dency for such parents to shift toward a view that corporal punishment would be all right.

In this example, the morality of an action shifted as a function of the informational assumptions people had regarding the effect of the act. In other cases, informational assumptions can alter people's views of the moral culpability of the actor. Many people in our culture, for example, have been found to hold the view that homosexuality is an immoral lifestyle choice (Turiel, Hildebrandt, and Wainryb 1991). From that perspective, being a homosexual entails a conscious decision to engage in behavior that they consider to be offensive and indecent. Leaving aside such questions as to whether homosexuality should be viewed in such normative terms or as a matter of private, personal conduct, the issue of choice is central to whether the individual may be held accountable for his or her sexual orientation. Information that would bear on that issue (e.g., findings of a substantial genetic component in determining sexual orientation) would undoubtedly impact the moral evaluation many people would make of homosexuals, even if it had no impact on their view of homosexual acts.

EDUCATION, CONTEXT, AND CONTROVERSY

The analysis of moral and social reasoning afforded by domain theory has allowed us to identify the nature and sources of moral understandings and to differentiate morality from other basic normative frameworks. That differentiation provides an invaluable tool for educators by centering the core focus of moral education around the development of students' conceptions of fairness and concern for the welfare of others.

In this chapter, we have explored some of the sources of variation that enter into the application of our moral understandings in our daily lives. A part of that variation arises from the inevitable overlap that exists between morality and the cultural framework in which we operate. Even though conventions are not in themselves moral norms, the frames established by the conventions of our culture often influence the ways in which we interact with others, along with our ability to see the moral impact of those interactions. As we become socialized within a cultural framework, we adopt the conventions of our social class, gender, and ethnic group. For those members of a culture for whom the conventional system ascribes status and privilege (e.g., males in most cultures), the immoral features of those aspects of the conventional system (e.g., relative subjugation of women) are generally unrecognized. On the other hand, members of a culture for whom the conventional system ascribes subordinate roles (e.g., women) are generally more aware of and sensitive to the immoral features of their society's norms as they impact them personally, but are also cognizant of the risks inherent in challenging the status quo. As we have also seen, the emphasis that a culture places on the maintenance of tradition and social hierarchy influences whether its members, whatever their social position, will even be open to reflection upon the potentially immoral features of the social system.

Added to the variations in moral meaning of acts that result from overlaps with the conventional system are the variations that emerge from differences in the informational assumptions people hold about the natural world. Informational assumptions are at the heart of the child's construction of basic moral understandings. The child's early moral intuitions emerge out of attempts to assign meaning to the consequences of directly accessible acts. For example, the child's earliest concepts of harm emerge from their direct experiences with the impact of hitting another person. As children are socialized, however, they are exposed to sources of information for which they have no personal means of independent verification. If the information provided by the culture indicates that a given action will result in harm or unfairness to others, the child will extend their moral understandings to include the particular action as an issue of moral concern. Thus, while the morality of children appears very similar across cultures, the morality of adult members of a culture may appear to be quite divergent in content from that of adult members of a different culture or historical period (Shweder et al. 1987).

From an educational perspective, these interactions among cultural normative systems, informational assumptions, and morality make the task of engaging in moral and character education a considerable challenge. Educating a "good" person entails the teaching of someone within a particular cultural context. As we have just seen, those cultural factors may or may not be concordant with what is morally right. The conventions that structure the social order may establish systematic biases favoring the rights of one group of persons over another. The factual assumptions maintained by a culture's basic belief systems may lead to mischaracterizations of actions and of classes of people and, in turn, be the sources of harm and injustice. Finally, the interpretation of the moral impact of these nonmoral cultural factors may vary as a function of the social position and ideological perspective of the person reading the situation. One cannot, therefore, simply inculcate children in the norms of a culture without thereby recapitulating the immoral features of the existing social system. On the other hand, it is a great deal to ask of individual educators to set themselves up as the arbiters of cultural moral discord.

The educator's task requires a degree of detachment and neutrality that sets this profession apart from others, as well as from other facets of the educator's own lived experience. For the educator needs to recognize and respect the diversity that exists within moral orientations without succumbing to the nihilistic relativism inherent in the postmodern retreat from the core insights of Enlightenment philosophy, and to the doctrinaire chauvinism that reduces moral differences to a falling away from or decay of traditional Western values. The position of neutrality being suggested here is not value free but, rather, centered around the identification of a universal domain of moral cognition around which the educator may construct a meaningful educative process that enables students to engage as moral beings in a world filled with contradiction and controversy.

In the second part of this book I will take up specific suggestions for educational practice that will flesh out the approach being suggested here. But, before doing so, we need to examine two more pieces of the puzzle that will help us understand the factors that enter into the formation of individual morality and character. The first of these is the role of affect and emotion in moral decision making and action. The second is the emergence of personal characteristics, in addition to moral development, that form an individual's character.

CHAPTER SIX

Morality and Emotion

If we were to ask the protagonist in the train platform scenario from Chapter 2 to explain what he was thinking about when he stepped in front of the gunman, it is unlikely that he would have provided an articulated, thorough-going analysis of the practical and moral aspects of the situation. He would probably have said something along the lines of: "I didn't really have time to think about it. I simply reacted. It felt right. I think anybody else would have done the same thing." While the drama and seriousness of that particular scenario is not an everyday occurrence, the act of unreflectively doing something because it "feels right" is fairly commonplace. Such simple acts of kindness as giving a homeless person some spare change, giving a stranger directions, or helping someone up who has fallen on an icy pavement don't generally involve careful reflection and analysis. Instead, they seem to involve a feeling, perhaps of sympathy, empathy, care, or an unidentifiable sense of the "right thing to do," and a corresponding action that seems to flow automatically.

The commonality of these latter experiences in the everyday lives of people raises some interesting questions about the role of cognition and rationality in everyday morality, and the role of habit and moral feelings. To understand these relationships in the moral domain, we need to begin with a more general examination of the role of affect and emotion in relation to cognition.

THE RELATION BETWEEN THOUGHT AND EMOTION

Only intelligent living systems have feelings. Artificial systems of intelligence, such as computers, do not. This is not simply an aesthetic or metaphysical distinction, but one that gets at the heart (if you will) of what makes living systems more intelligent than their artificial analogs. Within intelligent living systems there is no cognition without affect. Jean Piaget (1981), the Swiss developmentalist most generally known for his work on cognition, rejected the dualism that is usually maintained between intelligence and affectivity. As Bearison and Zimiles (1986) summarize, "for Piaget, the dichotomy between intelligence and affectivity has been artificially created by analytic abstractions to serve as an axiomatic device for the convenience of exposition, whereas in reality, neither can function without the other" (p. 4). The construction of any cognitive scheme, such as the simple means–end relationships involved in reaching and grasping a ball, doesn't only involve the generation of computational subroutines (as would be employed by a computer) but also incorporate the associated affect (e.g., desire for the ball, joy at grasping it).

These coextant feelings serve two functions for living systems of intelligence. In Piaget's analysis (1981), affect provides the energetics of behavior, while cognitive structure provides the directive framework. The desire and joy are what move the child to grasp the ball. The cognitive structure directs the movements of the arm, fingers, head and eyes to accomplish the task. This energetic aspect of affect carries along with it a second and perhaps even more critical function. Terrance Brown (1996), building from Piaget and the work of the cognitive scientist George Pugh (1977), has argued that the affects incorporated within cognitive schemes and schematic structures comprise a system of valences or "values" that weight them relative to one another. The significance of these "values" is that they prime given schemes or schematic sequences (procedures) for selection by the overall cognitive system within a particular problem space. One need not experience these remembered affects as conscious feelings in order for them to operate. But it is their integral presence that gives even the "coolest" human cognitive activity, such as performing a logical proof, its flesh-and-blood nature.

The importance of affective tags for the cognitive system is that without some such value heuristic, there wouldn't be enough cognitive capacity or time for the most capable person to examine exhaustively all possibilities and arrive at optimal solutions that arise in common situations. Writing in 1987, Brown (Brown and Weiss 1987) illustrated this point by noting that it would take a computer a thousand years to calculate all of the moves and outcomes that would result from six turns within a chess game. Any living cognitive system would certainly be maladaptive if it attempted to operate in such a hyperrational manner. Instead, living systems have evolved to generate "good enough" rather than optimal solutions to life's problems. Selecting the "good enough" option is accomplished by living systems, according to the Brown–Pugh hypothesis, through the heuristic of the affective "values" or weights integrated within the construction of cognitive schemes and procedures. Our feelings, then, not only accompany our thoughts but also have a role in directing our decisions. With the evolution of the frontal cortex, the human capacity for reflection afforded our species the capacity to generate structures of logic that constitute a second, more exact way of knowing than can be achieved through the "good enough" heuristics guided by affect.

With respect to morality, we see an analog to logical analysis in our deliberations over what constitutes a necessarily right thing to do. For example, a child's statement that the act of unprovoked harm is wrong, even if there is no social or religious rule about the action, stems from the child's rational conclusion that the act of hitting requires a particular nonarbitrary moral evaluation. The child judges the moral right or wrong of the action not simply on the basis of what "feels" right but on the basis of what the child rationally concludes *must* be the moral evaluation of the act. However, even logic is accompanied by feelings (e.g., certainty, necessity), and the procedures that are generated in the service of logic operate through the cognitive-affective heuristic apparatus.

The efficiency gained for living intelligent systems by integrating affective "value" within cognitive processes and structure should not be misunderstood as giving primacy to affect in psychological functioning. Affect does not substitute for cognitive structure (feelings are not knowledge); rather, affect is part and parcel of adaptive intelligence. The observation that we approach problems with interest or disinterest and appear to generate solutions to problems on the basis of hunches, intuitions, and feelings of certainty or uncertainty comports with views, such as those offered by Pugh (1977) and Brown (1996), that affect is involved in the selection of procedures employed in solving problems or directing our behavior. But the structures of those procedures, as well as superordinate structures of logic or domain-specific knowledge, are not contained within, nor reducible to, their attendant feeling states. As Piaget (1981) put it with respect to math, irrespective of a child's feelings about the subject, "the structure of mathematical operations will not be changed" (p. 6).

While this functional differentiation may seem fairly uncontroversial with respect to logical-mathematical knowledge, it is not as obvious with respect to issues of morality. Questions of morality are fundamentally about human relations and the coordination of human desires, wants, and needs. Emotions and feelings are not simply implicated in the decision-making process; they are part and parcel of the very content of the domain. Thus, to understand the role of emotion and affect in morality, we need to move beyond the general discussion of affect and cognition to explore the particular relations between affect and knowledge in the moral domain.

EVOLUTION AND MORAL EMOTION

Beginning with Charles Darwin (1872/1965), scientists have speculated that the precursors of human morality emerged within social animals as a means of regulating intraspecies aggressive conduct and fostering within species nurturance. These behaviors are thought to be regulated by a system of inborn emotions and associated physical displays, such as facial expressions, body posture, and vocalizations. As an illustrative example, anyone who has a dog is familiar with its capacity to present what a human would interpret as a "guilty" look when it has misbehaved. Ethologists, such as Lorenz (1960) and Lopez (1978), have provided accounts of how such displays serve to sustain the social fabric of canine social groups.

Frans de Waal (1996) has provided compelling evidence that primates have, to varying degrees, evolved behaviors that closely approximate human morality. Among the behaviors he and others have observed within chimpanzees and/or bonobos are sharing, reciprocity, revenge, reconciliation, and prosocial conduct. Evidence of this sort, along with accounts of primate aggression and sexual behavior, has generated a cottage industry of speculative accounts in which human conduct, from war (Morris 1969, 1994) to marital indiscretions (Buss 1994) to morality (Wright 1984), is reduced to our presumed membership within the primate order. Primatologists, however, are generally far less prone to engage in such romanticism. De Waal (1996), for example, reminds us that no serious primatologist has made the claim that great apes engage in moral philosophy. Nevertheless, there is more than a century of careful observational and experimental work that points to continuities in the evolution of mammalian social behavior that are consistent with the assumption that part of the substrate of human emotion and related social behavior has its roots in our evolutionary history.

There is some evidence that humans are born with both productive and receptive behaviors that would prime them for life as social animals. Research has demonstrated that human infants respond to emotions shown by other people. Infants as young as one day old have been reported to cry intensely and spontaneously in response to the distress cry of another infant, but not to a tape recording of themselves crying (Martin and Clark 1982). This rather remarkable finding (replicated in several studies) has been interpreted as evidence that feelings of distress at another's pain may be an evolutionarily selected component of human nature (Plutchik 1987). By around six months of age, infants become capable of differentially responding to diverse facial expressions associated with particular emotions (Ludemann 1991; Nelson 1987). By the end of the first year of life, infants employ the emotional expressions of mothers as indicative of a situation's being one of safety and comfort or one of danger (Campos and Barrett 1983).

While there is considerable evidence of cultural influences in the ways in which we learn to interpret or respond to our feelings, there is also evidence of a remarkable degree of cross-cultural similarity in the facial expressions used to convey basic emotions (Ekman 1993). These emotional displays appear very early. For example, researchers report being able objectively to code anger expressions in four-month-old infants (Sternberg, Campos, and Emde 1983) accompanied by behaviors consistent with anger feeling. Children born deaf and blind have been found to provide the same basic emotional displays of laughter, crying, and anger as children with intact sensory systems (Eibel-Eibesfeldt 1970). Thus, it would appear that the human infant is primed with affective schemata that afford access to the feelings of others, and that allow the infant to convey basic feeling states.

Evidence of this sort has been taken by researchers, working within what is called differential emotions theory, as evidence that there are biological determinants of emotion states (Izard 1983, 1986). These researchers (Izard 1983, 1986; Zajonc 1984) maintain that emotions may occur as a function of untransformed sensory input. Their position is that one can feel emotion prior to cognitive evaluation of the experience. One can sense anger, for example, before one has had time to reflect upon and interpret the feeling as anger. If one takes an evolutionary/adaptive view of intelligence, one can attribute to these basic emotional schemata the sort of "quick and dirty" response to social problems that might be a part of our evolutionary heritage. Unmediated "raw" emotion, however, is hardly adaptive in the social world. What we generally refer to as emotional development is largely about the integration of affect into cognitive systems that are more adaptive for life within a sociocultural frame than the outbursts available to us as infants.

As we consider this with respect to the moral domain, we are interested in how the affective schemata available during infancy and early childhood are incorporated into the construction of our moral understandings, and how the energetics of affect contribute to the selection and enactment of moral behaviors in context. From an educational point of view, we want to come to an understanding of how the emotional or affective climate of a child's social world enters into his or her moral constructions.

EMOTION AND THE CONSTRUCTION
OF MORAL UNDERSTANDINGS

A question we might ask regarding the relations between emotion and the child's construction of moral understandings is whether morality is associated with particular emotions. There are at least two ways to understand this question. The first is whether there are particular kinds of emotional experience that lead to moral constructions, rather than to the development of knowledge about other social-cultural rules, such as conventions. The second, related question is whether certain kinds of feelings help to motivate and direct moral behavior.

A good place to begin consideration of the issues raised in these questions is the work of William Arsenio (Arsenio 1988; Arsenio and Lover 1995). Arsenio set out to discover whether social events that involve moral forms of "right and wrong" elicit different emotions than do events that have to do with conventional or personal matters. In his initial studies, Arsenio (1988) presented kindergarten, third-, and fifth-grade children with drawings depicting children engaged in actions that fit within six social or moral rule systems. Four of these rule types were within the moral domain. These were

- active morality (interventions on behalf of victimized others, such as stopping a child from hitting another child);
- distributive justice (distributing group-earned resources, such as dividing up the money earned by a group of children working together to clean someone's yard);
- prosocial morality (engaging in helpful behavior toward another, such as carrying the groceries for an aged person); and
- inhibitive morality (actions in which one should refrain from engaging; acts which cause harm or unfairness to others, such as stealing another child's toy).

The remaining two rule types were violations of conventions, such as wearing inappropriate attire to school and engaging in behavior that the

child might consider personal, but which an adult authority wishes to regulate (e.g., a child writes something in a notebook at recess and the teacher
requires the child to reveal what was written).

Children were asked to indicate how three actors in each of the scenarios would feel. These three were the child engaged in the action, the
person who was the recipient of the action, and a third child, an observer.
The drawings depicting each of the scenarios presented the characters
with neutral facial expressions so that the children would have to infer
what the characters felt from their own personal experiences and understandings of these situations, rather than by reading the facial expressions
of characters shown in the drawings.

Findings were that with respect to violations of convention, children
judged that the child violating a convention would be neither happy nor
sad about it and would experience essentially neutral affect. They also expected neutral affect from a child third-person observer, and thought they
(the child subjects) would themselves have neutral affect if they were to
observe the situation. On the other hand, they expected an adult governing the convention (teacher) to be upset about the violation and to experience some degree of negative affect. In terms of personal issues, the children expected the governing adult and the third-person observers to have
relatively neutral affect, but expected the main actor in the personal scenarios to experience negative affect, such as anger or sadness at having
his/her personal forms of conduct controlled by an adult authority. This
latter reaction is consistent with children's and adolescents' views that the
personal domain constitutes a zone in which it is illegitimate for adults to
intercede or regulate.

With respect to the four moral scenarios, the results were as follows. In
the case of inhibitive morality, children judged all parties, including themselves, to experience considerable negative affect (sadness, anger, fear) in
the face of such events, with the exception of the perpetrator of the act,
who was judged to experience positive affect (happiness) with his/her behavior. (This "happy victimizer" effect is something that will be discussed
in greater detail in the section on the directive function of affect.) In contrast with the findings regarding inhibitive morality, they expected all
parties involved to experience positive affect (happiness) in response to
acts that entailed distributive justice or prosocial conduct. Not only were
the recipients of such actions thought to be happy, but so were the actors
themselves.

In the second part of the study, Arsenio (1988) investigated whether
children would use emotional information conveyed by drawings of peo-

ple's emotional expressions to make inferences about what sort of interaction produced the depicted emotions. Specifically, children were presented with drawings of individual characters displaying various emotional expressions. These were based on emotions that the children had
attributed to the actors in various situations depicted in the first part of
the study. They were then presented with two story boards in which the
actors had neutral expressions. One story board depicted a scenario consistent with the emotions shown in the individual character drawings; the
other did not. Children were shown the two story boards and asked which
depicted the scenario most likely to have produced the emotions displayed by the characters shown in the individual drawings. Findings
were that children, including preschoolers, accurately matched the emotional displays of the actors with the scenario most likely to have produced the depicted emotions.

As Arsenio's work demonstrates, children associate different feelings
with different domains of social events. Issues of social convention generally elicit "cool" affect on the part of children, who expect both compliance and violations of conventional norms to elicit neutral affect from children. To the extent that emotion is generated by convention, children see
it as emerging on the part of adults, who might become upset at the violation of such norms. Thus, it would appear that children do not experience the conventions of society as containing much in the way of intrinsic emotional content. However, as Shweder's work in India (Shweder et
al. 1987) and our work in Brazil (Nucci et al. 1996) has shown, children
may well experience "hot" emotion, such as anger, in the context of violations of conventions emanating from adults responding to transgressions of importantly held cultural norms.

Issues of morality, however, are viewed by children as rife with emotional content. All parties to moral interactions, not just the guardians of
the social order, as with convention, are thought by children to experience
identifiable emotional responses to moral events. This is the case whether
the moral behavior is positive or negative in impact. In Arsenio's (1988)
study, children described the participants in distributive justice situations
as experiencing happiness – or a sense of satisfaction – that things turned
out fairly. They likewise attributed positive emotions to all participants in
prosocial moral situations. In contrast, moral transgressions entailing violations of inhibitive morality were seen by children as arousing feelings
of anger, sadness, and fear in victims and bystanders alike. Only the perpetrators were viewed by young children as having positive feelings in
the context of moral transgressions.

Morality, then, is an area of human conduct associated with "hot" affect. In addition to the emotions identified in Arsenio's (Arsenio and Lover 1995) work, prosocial morality has been associated with feelings of care (Gilligan 1982) and empathy (Eisenberg 1986; Hoffman 1981). Inhibitive morality has been associated with shame and guilt (Ferguson, Stegge, and Damhuis 1991) and with disgust (Haidt et al. 1994). And the victims of moral transgression are said to respond not simply with anger but with outrage, an emotion which the German philosopher Ernst Tugendhat (1993) interprets as indicative that the victim holds the perpetrator personally responsible for his actions.

It is not my purpose here to offer a list of moral emotions but to call on both the formal research literature, as well as the reader's own experience, to see that part of what goes into the recognition of moral events are the evoked emotional reactions. As Arsenio explains, "emotions appear to be routinely stored as a part of our basic cognitive and social-cognitive representations" (Arsenio and Lover 1995, p. 90). Not all social events elicit similar emotions. Children extract different affect-event links, depending on the particular nature of the acts. Repeated experience with events with similar emotional outcomes allow children to form generalized scripts. The automatic reactions to familiar events, or to events of similar type, result from the affective triggering of these scripts or habits. Thus, we begin to see how the basic connections between affect and cognition play out in the domain of morality.

Arsenio (Arsenio and Lover 1995) adds an additional step to the processes of moral knowledge formation. He states: "Children coordinate their knowledge of sociomoral affect to form more general sociomoral principles. For example, commonalties in the expected emotional outcomes of being a target of theft, a target of undeserved aggression, and a target of verbal abuse might all be combined to form a concept of unfair victimization" (Arsenio and Lover 1995, p. 91). As we saw in Chapter 1 of this book, there is considerable evidence that children experience qualitatively different forms of interaction in the context of moral and nonmoral social events. For Arsenio, the most important feature of moral interactions is their affective content. In Arsenio's view, sociomoral affect provides the raw data from which more general abstract principles are formed by using a variety of cognitive abilities. The cross-cultural consensus that we observe in the meaning of moral acts may be accounted for, according to Arsenio, because of the basic similarities in meanings that people attribute to the emotions that accompany moral events.

My own reading of the research evidence as discussed in Chapter 1 of this book is that there are more inherent commonalities to moral events than simply the emotions that accompany them. The harm caused by moral transgressions, for example, has objective consequences beyond the emotions that are generated. Thus, it would be an overinterpretation to identify emotional experience as the sole form of "raw" data that results in the cross-cultural similarities we observe in moral concepts. Nonetheless, the work of Arsenio and others makes it abundantly clear that emotions and feelings are an integral part of the construction of our social and moral cognition.

DEVELOPMENT AND THE DIRECTIVE FUNCTION OF AFFECT

To recapitulate, beginning in infancy we initiate the process of constructing the schemata that form our social and moral values. Incorporated within those schemata are the emotions associated with particular event types, including the affect associated with adult reactions to children's compliance with or violation of social norms (Hoffman 1983; Kochanska 1993; Zahn-Waxler, Radke-Yarrow, and King 1979). The development of these early social and moral schemata form the substrate of our moral habits and, in the view of some researchers, the beginnings of our moral character (Kochanska 1993). Variations in the nature of these interactions, stemming from such things as differences in children's temperament (Kochanska 1993), the degree of anger displayed by adults in reaction to children's transgressions or of warmth in reaction to children's prosocial conduct (Emde et al. 1991), and the overall affective climate of the household (Katz and Gottman 1991; Zahn-Waxler and Kochanska 1990) appear to impact the ways in which young children construct the basic underpinnings of their concepts of how to react within interpersonal situations.

The basic social-action schemata developed in infancy are incorporated within the construction of the overall conceptions of moral and social norms that we observe in preschool children. Thus, the affective content associated with the construction of particular moral-action schemes (e.g., hitting hurts and makes one sad or angry) becomes integrated within the overall conceptual framework guiding the child's morality. As the child develops, the meaning and relations among those affective components is altered as the child attempts to coordinate or bring into balance the competing needs, desires, and deserts of individuals and groups impacted by the child's moral judgments and actions. This is an interactive process wherein the child's moral understandings alter the meaning or salience attributed to affectively laden events, and the child's emotional experiences impact the child's constructions of moral positions. Perhaps Martha Nussbaum (2000) best captures the latter form of this interactive process in her description of emotion as "collisions of thought." Educators will recognize this role of emotion in their efforts to generate feelings among students as a way of moving them to reconsider their positions on things.

This developmental process can be seen in the results of recent research on what has been referred to as the "happy victimizer" phenomenon (Barden et al. 1980; Nunner-Winkler and Sodian 1988). This is also one of the more interesting contexts within which to observe both common threads and disruptions in the relations between children's emotional development and their morality. The happy victimizer phenomenon refers to the tendency of preschool-age children to attribute positive emotions to the perpetrator of moral transgressions.

In the Nunner-Winkler and Sodian (1988) study, children between 4 and 8 years of age were presented drawings depicting a scenario in which a child is shown deliberating over whether or not to steal candy from another child's coat, which is hanging unattended in the cloakroom. In one version of the scenario, the child resists the temptation and does not steal. In the other version, the child steals some candy. Subjects in the study were asked to indicate how the protagonist in each situation would feel, and why. There were no effects of the sex of the subjects in terms of children's answers. All of the children included in the research indicated that they thought it was not right to steal the candy. Nonetheless, 74% of the 4-year-olds and 40% of the 6-year-olds expected the protagonist in the story to feel "good" or "happy" about having stolen the candy. In contrast, 90% of the 8-year-olds expected the (thief) protagonist to feel "sad," "bad," "not good," or "not happy" having committed the theft. With regard to the scenario depicting the child who resisted temptation to steal the candy, the majority (67%) of the younger children thought that the protagonist would experience negative emotions, while a minority (41%) of the 8-year-olds thought that the child resisting the temptation to steal would have negative feelings about having done so. Few children at these ages in either situation reported that the protagonist would have mixed feelings.

The younger children explained their reasoning by focusing on the outcome. The child in the story would be "happy that he got the candy," or "sorry because he didn't take the candy, and now he doesn't have any." The 8-year-olds, on the other hand, tended to focus more on the moral consequences of the act. The child "would be sad because he had stolen his friend's candy; she was nasty to do that; because he is a thief and he shouldn't do that," or "He would be happy with himself for not taking the candy, and being good"; "She would be sad at having thought about taking her friend's candy." These age-related patterns of emotion attributions and justifications held up for situations depicting the victimizer engaged in actions that had no direct benefit to the protagonist (i.e., teasing another child), and in actions in which the victimizer physically harmed another child. In all cases, the majority of 4-year-olds expected the victimizer to be pleased with the outcome of his or her hurtful behavior, while the majority of 8-year-olds expected the victimizer to experience remorse, sadness, or other negative feelings in response to transgressions.

Finally, Nunner-Winkler and Sodian (1988) reported on children's judgments of who they thought was worse: a child who appeared happy or one who appeared sad with what s/he had done. Findings were that 90% of the 8-year-olds thought that the child who appeared happy with the acts of victimization was worse than the child who appeared sorry for the action. A majority of 4-year-olds, on the other hand, judged both children to be about equally bad.

These findings are interesting in light of consistent reports that young children judge actions of moral harm to be wrong. The complexity of the findings with young children is inconsistent with simple accounts of morality as emerging from an inherited moral sense of right and wrong. Subsequent work in this area has indicated that there is a developmental progression in children's abilities to coordinate the mixed feelings that acts of victimization generate, and to bring these mixed feelings together with their moral understandings of the actions. The well-reported finding that children, some even as old as age 11, expect the victimizer to feel happy has to be placed alongside the fact that children as young as age 4 know and express that the victims of such actions suffer and experience negative emotions. Moreover, a study by Arsenio and Kramer (1992) reported that children do not view victimizers as atypical children or bullies; rather, they expect that positive emotions are experienced through obtaining one's desired goals through immoral acts.

As children get older, they understand that one can maintain more than one emotion in response to a given event. The work of Harter and Buddin (1987) has demonstrated that children do not understand mixed emotions (that one can maintain opposite feelings) until about age 11. Arsenio and Kramer (1992) found that this developmental pattern matched children's tendency to attribute mixed emotions to the victimizer in moral situations. According to Arsenio (Arsenio and Lover 1995), what seems to occur is a gradual coordination of the knowledge that children have of the victim's suffering with their assumptions of positive emotion that would come from the victimizer's goal attainment. A part of that development is the modulation of positive feelings children might have as they contemplate engaging in immoral actions. As children progress through the normal course of development, they begin to weigh the positive feelings that come from maintaining positive peer relations against the gains that they might achieve through victimization. Their developing sense of justice integrates this balancing of emotional gains and losses to form a moral position rejecting victimization as a positive course. Thus, the interplay between changes in how children think of persons and their feelings, and developing understandings of reciprocity, equity, and human welfare leads to shifts in the ways in which affect guides moral behavior.

The juxtaposition between the suffering caused by one's victimization and the positive feelings that result in gains to oneself provides opposing motivations for one's actions. Piaget (1962) was aware of these affective conflicts, which he referred to as the "problem of will." Pitting one's duties and obligations against one's desires is an old notion often captured in religious symbolism, which poses the devil within against the "better angels of our nature" (A. Lincoln 1861). Coordinating these affective opposites was viewed by Piaget as analogous to intellectual decentration. For Piaget (1962), an act of will requires the subordination of desire to what is necessary as determined by coordinated reversible values. While Piaget never directly addressed the issue, his notion of will may be seen as placing what is rationally understood to be morally necessary as superordinate to one's personal desires in a given context. To be moral, then, is to do what is right, even when it is counter to one's immediate desire. We are obligated to act morally even toward those for whom we don't have an affective connection.

For the child growing up in an affectively supportive environment, the construction of moral reversibilty (fairness) is supported by the experience of "goodwill" that comes from acts of fair reciprocity. Moreover, this goodwill complements the positive feelings and happiness that children experience when engaged in acts of prosocial conduct (Eisenberg 1986). In contrast with this positive picture, Arsenio (Arsenio and Lover 1995) uses evidence from studies of aggressive children to suggest that some children's early experiences are ones that establish a pattern of "ill will," in which long-term patterns of victimization and peer rejection distort the construction of moral reciprocity, such that the child feels "entitled" to act aggressively toward others. Aggressive children are found to be outliers in most of the studies of children's concepts of victimization, in that aggressive children are more likely to attribute positive emotions to the victimizer and to do so at later ages than nonaggressive children.

Along these same lines, Nancy Guerra and I found in a recent study that although children seen by their peers as engaging in high rates of aggressive behavior were just as likely as their peers to rate harmful acts as wrong, the aggressive children were the only ones who also stated that it was their right to hit someone else if they wanted to. We interpreted this to mean that aggressive children do not view the moral component of harm as the necessarily salient feature of such behavior but, rather, viewed their own commission of acts of victimization as matters of personal choice.

The deviations that we see in aggressive children's moral judgments and actions point to the importance of gaining greater understanding of the role of affect in children's moral development. At a more general level, the developmental work on children's affective development has demonstrated the process by which normal affective experiences are integrated into the child's moral constructions. Morality is not simply guided by "feelings" as the emotivist philosophers (Moore 1903) would have it. Nor is it cold-blooded rationality as depicted in some misreadings of cognitive accounts of morality (e.g., MacIntyre 1984). Our feelings are an integral part of the very schemes that constitute the whole of our so-called moral habits. Our moral reasoning and processes of reflection are in reciprocal relation with the schemes that generate our moral behaviors.

CULTURAL INFLUENCES ON MORAL EMOTION

While there are broad cross-cultural commonalities in human emotion, there are significant cultural variations in the salience afforded to particular feelings, the contexts which give rise to particular emotions, and the manner in which emotions are expressed. Although nature has afforded us stereotypic physical displays (e.g., crying, laughter, rage) of basic emotional events, our feelings take place within our bodies beyond even our own direct observation. Our shared emotional experiences are, thus, largely a function of our shared language for describing those feelings (Nussbaum, 2000). Because the language of emotion is about our interior states, it is rich with metaphor about bodily events (Sarbin 1995). We say that we had a "gut-wrenching experience," our "heart aches" or is "broken," our "blood boils," we get "butterflies in our stomach," we are "moved to tears," and we "leap with joy." Placing language and metaphor around our feelings allows for considerable slippage and for variation in what we attend to and how we couch things. Most importantly, our emotions are not interpreted out of context, but within the frame of surrounding events. Thus, for example, the feeling of jealousy does not occur outside of the context of a series of events that would be interpreted as ones that should evoke jealous feeling. As a result, our tendency to feel certain things is not simply a function of what Martha Nussbaum calls our "common animality" but also a result of the cultural narratives and language that frame and interpret our feelings (Mancuso and Sarbin 1998).

Not surprisingly, then, anthropologists have uncovered cultural variations in human emotional experience. Anthropologists employ common emotional displays as a way of studying cultural variations in the emotions that are emphasized and how they are incorporated into social life. For example, observations of emotional displays of crying are used as a way of studying variations in cultural views of how one should grieve (Levy 1984). Tahitians, for example, view it as unhealthy to grieve for too long and reinterpret prolonged sadness as the state of "fatigue." The interior feeling is acknowledged, but it is not interpreted as an emotion (Levy 1984). Utka Eskimos and certain Tahitian groups find the overt expression of anger so dangerous that it is an emotion rarely expressed overtly (Solomon 1984). The Utka do not even have a word for anger as such, but label angry behavior as "childish" (Solomon 1984).

These cultural variations apply not only to differences across cultural groups but also to subgroups within cultures. Perhaps the most important of these for our purposes are variations associated with gender. Robin Fivush (1993), for example, discovered gender differences in the emotional content of parent–child conversations. In her study, parents and children were asked to talk about significant events in their lives. Fivush observed that when mothers spoke with their daughters, the mothers focused on elaborating narratives dealing with sadness, showing concern about resolving the sadness episodes through adult comfort and reassurance. With daughters as compared with sons, mothers less frequently framed events in terms of anger, tending to focus on restoring relationships damaged through anger episodes. Finally, when mothers discussed fear, they did so more with respect to fear in their sons than in their daughters.

These and other findings showing gender differences in the emotional socialization of boys and girls has led Nussbaum (2000) to wonder whether, in fact, the two genders even share the same emotional lives. Over the past two decades there has been heated debate over whether gender differences in emotional sensitivity and expression spill over into

morality (Gilligan 1982). The most interesting discussion over gender differences has focused on whether males and females differ in their tendency to frame morality around issues of care, rather than justice (Gilligan 1982). While the simple dichotomy distinguishing two purportedly
different gender-based moralities has been dismissed (Gilligan and Wiggins 1987), there is considerable evidence that gender is associated with
differences in the relative tendencies of males and females to read moral
situations as evoking feelings of care or justice (Turiel, 1998a). That is to
say, some situations tend to evoke a greater proportion of care responses
from males and justice responses from females, and vice versa (Nunner-
Winkler 1984).

We can attribute these cultural and gender differences in emotional responses to moral situations as resulting from the cultural narratives that
help to frame the construction of our moral schemes. The incorporation
of affect into our moral concepts is in part guided by the cultural narratives that help us to interpret those feelings in the context of culturally defined social events. For example, feelings of anger and aggressive behavior in the form of revenge is often a culturally prescribed remedy for
culturally defined affronts toward one's masculinity (Sarbin 1995). Recent
work with Latino and African American urban gang members indicates
that their willingness to engage in aggressive acts is a function of their
reading of aggression and anger as appropriate responses to perceived
threats to their "manhood" (Astor 1994). In a similar vein, tendencies to
respond to one's own moral transgression with feelings of guilt or shame
are influenced by cultural views of one's conduct as reflecting upon others (e.g., family) or solely upon oneself. In the former case, one feels
shame, and in the latter, guilt.

CONCLUSIONS

The emphasis placed in this book on moral reasoning and educational approaches to developing children's moral cognition stems from recognition
that the central feature of human morality is our capacity for choice and
judgment. That emphasis, however, should not be taken as an exclusive
view of morality or of moral education. As we have seen in this chapter,
moral reasoning and judgment occur in conjunction with feelings and
emotions. To educators, the interplay between emotion and moral development implies, among other things, that our efforts to contribute to children's growth must include attention to the affective climate and content
of our classrooms. The culture of our schools and classrooms helps to con-

textualize and to direct children's constructions of the meaning and import of the feelings they experience in conjunction with social events. These experiences can both build from and offset the social-affective constructions children forge at home and in their communities. Well-run schools can do these things by providing emotionally safe and fair contexts within which to explore ways of interacting with others.

Attention to the affective side of morality and moral education goes beyond the obvious connections to direct moral experience associated with the moral atmosphere of the school and classroom. It includes the emotions generated through exposure to curricular assignments in such areas as literature or history, which engage the reader in the moral conflicts and events that broaden one's moral world. While we are accustomed to bracketing such curricular activities under the rubric of "cognitive" teaching goals, there is no question that their effectiveness rests in our ability as educators to engage students in Nussbaum's characterization of emotion as "collisions of thought."

We will deal with these educational issues at length in the second part of this book. At this point we have one set of issues remaining in our account of moral and social development. Those are the issues having to do with moral character. It is those issues which are addressed in Chapter 7.

CHAPTER SEVEN

Reconceptualizing Moral Character

The preceding chapters have dealt with issues of social cognition and moral reasoning. Morality, however, is more than a matter of understanding what is right. It requires that one act in ways that are consistent with one's moral judgment. This, in turn, requires that one's moral understandings be translated into a sense of personal responsibility.

One of the open questions in contemporary moral psychology is how to account for the linkage between objective judgments of moral obligation and personal responsibility. In philosophy, a distinction is made between deontic judgments of what is morally obligatory and aretaic judgments of the moral worthiness of individuals and their actions. Since the question of moral action turns on the notion of personal responsibility, accounts of moral action often evolve into aretaic evaluations of what it means to be a good *person*. In everyday language, the term "character" is used to convey such aretaic judgments. A person of good character is someone who attends to the moral implications of actions and acts in accordance with what is moral in most circumstances. This everyday usage of the term character captures an important feature of what is ordinarily meant by a good person. It is also at the core of the current interest in character education.

While some notion of moral agency is necessary for a complete moral psychology, it has been clear to most psychologists for decades that the traditional character construct has fundamental flaws and cannot serve as the basis for an account of moral action. Unfortunately, much of the current rhetoric about character education has little to do with what people are really like, and more to do with a political agenda (Kohn 1997). It is important before moving on to more contemporary thinking about these issues to recount why character education fell out of favor in the first place.

LIMITATIONS OF TRADITIONAL VIEWS
OF MORAL CHARACTER

Traditional character education, which had its heyday in the early part of the twentieth century, had as its central aim the fostering of the formation of elements of the individual's personality and value structure that would constitute socially desirable qualities or virtues. This is a venerable tradition, drawing on commonsense perspectives and buttressed by a particular, narrow reading of Aristotelian philosophy (Ryan and Lickona 1992; Wynne 1986).

In the late 1920s, a major research effort was undertaken by Hugh Hartshorne and Mark May (1928, 1929, 1930) to identify the factors that contribute to the formation of character. Their research was based on the reasonable premise that the first step should be to identify those individuals who possessed moral virtues. What they had expected to find was that the population of 8,000 students they studied would divide up into those who displayed virtuous conduct nearly all of the time and those who would not. To their surprise and disappointment, the researchers discovered that few students were virtuous and that most children cheated, behaved selfishly, and lacked "self-control" some of the time. Virtue, according to their data, seemed to be context dependent, as students cheated or lied in some situations and not in others. As Clark Power (Power, Higgins and Kohlberg 1989b, p. 127) noted, Hartshorne and May concluded that there were no character traits *per se* but "specific habits learned in relationship to specific situations which have made one or another response successful."

In hindsight we can see two major flaws in the view of character that guided the educational programs of that era, as well as the research program of Hartshorne and May. The first is a mistaken view of personality as defined by global dispositional tendencies or traits. This venerable trait conception of personality comports with commonsense attributions that we make toward others as we attempt to assign categories or labels to persons that allow for some predictability in interpersonal interactions.

It is not difficult to get individuals to generate lists of characteristics that are thought to capture certain types of people. For example, in a recent study (Walker 1998), a sample of 120 undergraduates were asked to freely list their perceptions of traits or attributes they thought would be characteristic of persons who were defined as moral exemplars. Analyses of these trait lists turned up *agreeableness* and *conscientiousness* as dominant factors, followed by *openness to experience* as the main attributes of persons considered to be morally exemplary. There were also variations in the salience of these general traits accorded to moral "types" as a function of their presentation as secular moral, religious, or spiritual exemplars. For example, agreeableness was attributed less to religious exemplars than to the secular moral or spiritual types. This study demonstrates that commonsense psychology contains the assumption that people have reasonably consistent ways of acting, and that persons of moral character can be expected to exhibit some shared general dispositions. Such attributions, however, are neither a demonstration that any actual person fits the general profile attributed to moral exemplars (for example, it is not hard to imagine a "disagreeable" secular social activist), nor a demonstration that morally exemplary people are as consistent in their personal tendencies across contexts as would be expected from a trait theory of personality.

Beginning in the 1950s, personality and social psychologists conducted several decades of careful research into whether there is behavioral consistency within individuals with presumed personality traits. This work turned up the same sorts of contextual variations in the behavior of individuals as was reported in the character studies of Hartshorne and May (Mischel 1973; Ross and Nisbett 1991; Sarbin and Allen 1968). These researchers concluded that people cannot be accurately described in terms of stable and general personality traits, since people tend to exhibit different and seemingly contradictory aspects of themselves in different contexts. People don't possess personality traits or moral virtues in the same way that they have eye color or stature. We can't speak of someone as an "honest person" in the same way that we can speak of someone as being a blonde or as having brown hair.

Instead of articulating trait theories, contemporary personality psychologists tend to view personality as something one *does* in particular settings, rather than as something one *has* independent of context (Mischel 1990; Ross and Nisbett 1991). As Lapsley (1996) summarizes in his review of this literature, people have scripts, knowledge systems, and reasoning capabilities that allow them to pick out what are to them the salient features of immediate situations and to act accordingly. Thus, one should view dispositional tendencies as a set of "if-then" propositions, rather than traits. From the domain-theory perspective of this book, one can understand these "if-then" sequences as emerging from the domain-salient features of social events, the domain-specific knowledge that a person has, and the affective weights that are incorporated within the person's social-moral schemata.

As was discussed in Chapter 6, these affective weights comprise a significant factor in how situations are perceived and responded to, and contribute to observed individual differences in responses to social situations. What one does in a moral sense is, thus, more fluid than would be expected from a simple trait account of virtue. It is also more fluid than would be expected from an account of moral action as stemming from inculcated social values and deeply ingrained habits of conduct. Yet, it is these companion notions of inculcation and habit formation that form an integral part of the traditional account of the emergence of virtue. Not surprisingly, then, the emphasis on habit and inculcation as sources of virtue comprise the second major limitation of traditional accounts of character formation and education.

Since Aristotle, the development of virtue has been thought to emerge out of the progressive building up of habits. Contemporary character educators (Benninga 1991; Wynne 1989; Wynne and Ryan 1993) likewise rely heavily on psychological theories that emphasize punishment and reward systems to reinforce desired behavior, and systems of inculcation that are presumed to instill values and virtues in the young (Kohn 1997). It is worth remembering that in response to their findings, Hartshorne and May (1930) concluded that such traditional approaches to character education through the use of didactic teaching, exhortation, and example probably do more harm than good since such practices do not take into account the practical demands of social contexts. In other words, such rigid instruction runs counter to the evaluative and contextualized nature of moral life. By focusing heavily on efforts to instill proper values and habits, such approaches fail to develop students' capacities to make the social and moral judgments that contextualized actions require.

Ironically, Aristotle was not as limited in his approach to virtue and moral habit as some of his twentieth-century interpreters. For Aristotle (1985), mature morality was identified by the subordination of particular habits and virtues to the master virtue of justice. A just person was not an automaton, ruled either by passion or thoughtless conformity to social norms, but a person of reason and judgment.

The limitations of a reliance on modes of inculcation and habit formation have not been lost on all character educators. There is an emerging trend among those Clark Power (Power and Khmelkov 1998) refers to as "generalists" (e.g., Battistich et al. 1991; Lickona 1991) toward an integration of practices of reflection, borrowed from developmentalist moral educators, such as Kohlberg, into programs of character education. This eclectic integration has not occurred, however, with a corresponding reconceptualization of the character construct. Thus, we are entering an interesting period in the field where the term "character education" is serving as the generic, publicly accepted label for a range of approaches to moral education, without any clear conceptual framework for what the term "character" even refers to.

There would seem to be two options open to resolving this situation. One would be to take a narrow reading of character education and reserve the term for the traditional approaches, plagued with the limitations I have just outlined. That is the approach recently taken by Kevin Ryan (1996) in an article attempting to distance traditional character educators from what he refers to as the "character education bandwagon" (p. 77). The second would be to reconceptualize what is meant by moral character in a way that does not rest on assumptions about personal virtues or traits, while capturing the essential notion that morality cannot be divorced from the person as a moral being.

THE MORAL SELF

Over the past decade, there has been a gradual convergence among some moral educational researchers (Blasi 1983, 1984, 1993; Blasi and Glodis 1995; Colby and Damon 1992; Lapsley 1996; Noam 1993; Power and Khmelkov 1998) toward the idea that a more fruitful way to begin understanding how a person's moral concepts relate to the person as a moral agent is to look at the ways, and the extent to which, individuals integrate their morality into their subjective sense of personal identity. The most influential source for this shift has been the work of Augusto Blasi (1993). For Blasi, moral responsibility is the result of the integration of morality in one's identity or sense of self. From moral identity derives a psychological need to make one's actions consistent with one's ideals. Thus, in Blasi's (1993) words, "self-consistency is the motivational spring of moral action" (p. 99).

In a similar vein, Clark Power (Power and Khmelkov 1998) redefines character as the specifically moral dimensions of self. Like Blasi, Power states that the motive for moral action is not simply the direct result of knowing "the good" but derives from the desire to act in ways that are consistent with one's own sense of self as a moral being. As Power puts it: "Individuals may undertake a particular course of action, even at some cost, because they want to become or remain a certain kind of person" (Power and Khmelkov 1998). In contrast with the traditional character construct, the approach taken by Blasi and Power, "does not attempt to replace moral ideas with a set of noncognitive personality characteristics: it sees personal identity as operating jointly with reason and truth in providing motives for action" (Blasi 1993, p. 99). Thus, one's moral character is not something divorced from moral cognition and the complexity that it entails.

General Issues in the Construction of Self

The construction of personal identity is itself multifaceted, incorporating values and social roles from a number of contexts. There is both a personal, idiosyncratic element to who we are and what we care about, as was discussed in Chapter 3, as well as an integration of shared normative concerns and objective factors inherent in social life. Our personal tastes, talents, opportunities, and experiences enter into the construction of "self" in ways that capture both the particular sociohistorical context of the individual's life space, and the particulars of the person's own reading of what matters in his or her own life. Self, in this view, is not so much an entity as it is a story or a narrative we tell ourselves in which we are the featured character (Sarbin 1986). Who we are emerges as we engage the social world and attempt to provide ourselves an account of how we initiate actions (a sense of agency), who that agent is (a sense of identity), and who we wish that agent to be (a combination of agency and identity).

Research on the development of children's conceptions of self (Damon and Hart 1988; Harter 1983) provides evidence that with age, children construct increasingly differentiated notions of themselves as actors within different contexts or domains. These differentiated constructs emerge as a result of children's efforts to interpret their differential competence and involvement in various areas of activity (academic, making friends), as well as a corresponding tendency with age to assign meaning to those levels of competence and commitment. Harter (1983) has suggested that development of self-concepts may very well entail a reiterative process whereby a child's initial attempts to construct an integrated notion of self (e.g., in terms of characteristic behaviors) is followed by a period of differentiation (e.g., good at some things, bad at others). These differentiated general descriptions are then incorporated within a higher level of integration (e.g., general traits), which are then subsequently differentiated. This process eventuates at the most advanced levels of development in a conceptualization of self in multidimensional and contextual terms (Broughton 1978; Damon and Hart 1988).

The inherent complexity of self-definition has its counterpart in children's efforts at self-evaluation. As a way of beginning to think about how this might apply to the area of morality, let's look for a moment, by way of analogy, at the highly researched area of how children apply their sense of self to academic performance. Educators have long been concerned with the relation between self-esteem and school variables, such as academic achievement. At issue is whether children have a global sense of self-worth, or whether self-esteem varies by domain of activity. There have been proponents of the view that self-esteem is a global construct (Coopersmith 1967), as well as views that self-esteem exists as a differentiated aggregate of evaluations (Mullener and Laird 1971). Current evidence, however, supports the proposition that children construct both a general sense of self-worth and domain-specific evaluations of their own competence (Byrne 1984; Harter 1985, 1986; Rosenberg 1965).

In line with those findings, there is little evidence to suggest that students' view of themselves in terms of academic capabilities (academic self-esteem) is necessarily tied to students' general sense of self-worth (Harter 1983; Marsh, Smith, and Barnes 1985). Correlations between general self-esteem measures and academic self-concept tend to correlate between 0.30 and the low 0.40s (Nucci 1989). What is more, there is evidence that children's academic self-concept may be differentiated according to area of activity, for example, math versus reading (Harter 1983).

In one such study, Marsh and colleagues (1985) found that math and reading achievement scores and teacher ratings of fifth-grade boys and girls were positively correlated with each other and with academic self-concepts in the matching area. Children's academic achievement was uncorrelated, however, with nonacademic self-concept, and the two academic self-concepts (math and reading) were nearly uncorrelated. It also appears that the areas of activity important to children's self-image may be a function of gender or ethnic/cultural background (e.g., first-grade girls may not consider their ability in math to be relevant to their academic image) (Entwisle et al. 1987). The importance of distinguishing between academic self-concept and general self-image is underscored by findings that there is no causal relationship between academic self-performance and general self-image, as measured by such global instruments as the Coopersmith (Harter 1983). The loose relationship between academic self-concept and general self-worth means that attempts to improve children's academic performance and academic self-image are unlikely to result from attempts to raise children's general self-esteem. These findings also illustrate that our overall sense of self may or may not be importantly related to any particular area of our social or practical activity.

Morality and the Self

If we move from the area of academics back to the issue of the moral self, one can see both parallels and differences. One significant difference is that people aren't as free to discount their moral selves as they are to discount other aspects of their personal endeavors, such as their performance in mathematics or on the dance floor (Power and Khmelkov 1998). This is because morality is inherent in human interaction and engages us in binding "objective" ways. As we have seen, very young children construct intuitions that harming someone is wrong. The objective or binding nature of morality should not, however, be overstated as a basis for its centrality in the construction of personal identity. Whether one attends to the moral implications of events may be more compelling than whether one develops skill as a dancer, but it may not attain the same degree of salience or centrality for everyone. There is no reason to assume that the basic process of constructing the moral aspect of self is fundamentally different from the construction of other aspects of personal identity. Thus we should expect interpersonal variations in the connection between self and morality.

This assumption of interpersonal variation in moral identity has not been extensively researched. However, recent work by Augusto Blasi (1993) and his colleagues has provided evidence that some individuals let moral notions penetrate to the essence and core of what and who they are, while others construct their central defining features of self in other ways. This is not to say that morality is somehow absent from many people but, rather, that the moral aspects of self may be subjectively experienced in different ways. Blasi (1993, p. 103) puts it this way:

> [S]everal individuals may see morality as essential to their sense of self, of who they are. For some of them, however, moral ideals and demands happen to be there, a given nature over which they feel little control. In this case moral ideals exist next to other characteristics, all equally important because they are there. Others instead relate to their moral ideals as being personally chosen over other ideals or demands, sense their fragility, and feel responsible to protect them and thus to protect their sense of self.

To explore the relationship between moral identity and motivation for moral action, Blasi and Glodis (1995) examined whether people who define morality as a central part of their personal identity experience a sense of "personal betrayal" when they act in opposition to those moral values. They hypothesized that such a sense of personal betrayal would be more

evident in persons whose sense of identity stemmed from their own active efforts at becoming the person they were, than among persons whose
identity emerged from a relatively passive, unreflective acceptance of
themselves. In their study, they asked 30 women to indicate an ideal that
they considered to be very important to their sense of self, one that they
cared deeply about and to which they were deeply committed. Among the
ideals listed were friendship, caring for others, morality and justice, self-
reliance, and improving one's mind and knowledge. Six to ten weeks later,
each of the women was presented with a story in which a fictional character chooses a course of action advantageous financially and careerwise,
but which compromised her ideals. The compromised ideal in each case
was the one listed by the subject as a central value in her earlier interview.

What Blasi and Glodis (1995) found was that some of their subjects
tended not to see the situation as relevant to their ideals. Instead, they focused on the pragmatic consequences of the decision presented in the
scenario and expressed feelings of satisfaction with the protagonist's
pragmatic choice. However, others saw the situation as entailing a serious
contradiction of their ideals, and they expressed such feelings as shame,
guilt, and depression over the protagonist's choice to violate those ideals.
The feelings expressed by subjects in the study were a function of their
own sense of identity as being one for which they were actively involved.
Subjects whose ideals were not experienced as passively received from
outside influences, but rather as central concerns to be pursued, were
those who reported the most distress in response to the scenario's entailing a contradiction or betrayal of those ideals.

In discussing their findings, Blasi and Glodis avoid claiming that it is
essential for a person to have constructed a moral identity of this sort in
order for someone to act in morally consonant ways. They recognize that
morality may be viewed as important for other reasons, such as social approval, or simply out of concern for the objective consequences of actions.
They also suggest that such intense personal involvement may not be implicated in many day-to-day moral interactions that don't entail dilemmas pitting one's pragmatic self-interest against the needs of someone
else. One's personal identity may only be at stake in cases requiring substantial subordination of other motives. Of course, whether one views
such situations as placing the self at risk is a function of the degree to
which morality exists as an ideal central to one's self-definition. Blasi
(1993) asserts that moral and other ideals are chosen as core values because they are understood to be important. Thus, "to some extent per-

sonality is shaped by what one knows to be worthy of education and commitment" (Blasi 1993, p. 119).

Blasi's work is provocative in that it links Aristotelian notions of eudaimonia (self-flourishing) to the work that has been done on moral cognition. It also implies that constructivist assumptions of how one generates moral knowledge are also important to the active construction of the moral self and the consequent moral responsibility and character. A major (self-acknowledged) limitation of his work is that it is centered around a sophisticated form of personal identity that does not typically emerge before adolescence or adulthood. Thus, Blasi's work does not provide us with an account of the developmental antecedents of moral identity, nor does he provide an account of moral motivation for children prior to this adolescent period of identity formation.

Childhood Antecedents of the Moral Self

Other research on children's construction of self has indicated that children use moral language in their self-definitions from at least 6 years of age (Power and Khmelkov 1998). At these young ages, however, the terms used are very global, evaluative labels, such as "good," "bad," and "nice," which appear to have little to do with the children's own efforts at self-reflection. Young children do not differentiate between descriptions of themselves as they are and descriptions of themselves as they would like to be, and they rarely offer moral self-criticism, even when probed to do so (Power and Khmelkov 1998). Instead, when describing the moral aspects of themselves, they tend to use positive terms such as "good," and "nice." The absence of self-criticism means that self cannot serve as a source of moral motivation for young children. That is, while children may view hurting as wrong, and refrain from engaging in the action because of their perceptions of the objective harm that would be caused by the act, engaging in wrong actions does not seem to be tied to conceptions of the self as "bad."

This lack of self-reflection is consistent with Freudian assumptions that the morality of young children is tied to remorse for consequences after the fact, rather than to an internally directed anticipatory experience of guilt. Roughly between 8 and 10 years of age, children begin to apply moral language to describe not only their typical dispositions for action, such as kindness or helpfulness, but also their behavioral goals for themselves to become free of any bad habits or dispositions that they might possess. These goals are in relation to their recognition of aspects of their own current behavioral tendencies that constitute "bad habits" or dispositions. Thus, it is in middle childhood that children begin to evidence early signs of moral self-evaluation (Power and Khmelkov 1998). The moral goals of middle childhood, however, are framed in terms of the behavioral language of self-understandings of this developmental period and, therefore, center around overt behaviors, such as responding to the needs of others, rather than affecting interior psychological characteristics, such as becoming a more caring or sensitive person.

These more complex "psychological" aims emerge in early adolescence as self-understanding becomes based around a conception of self and personal identity as comprised of a unique personal configuration of interior thoughts, feelings, beliefs and values (Damon and Hart 1988; Nucci and Lee 1993). The moral content of one's self is now as seen as a component of this psychological self-definition, and moral terms are now spontaneously applied to describe the self (Power and Khmelkov 1998). Finally, in late adolescence and adulthood, the self is seen as an integrated system, and personal identity is viewed as integrated with one's moral character (Power and Khmelkov 1998).

Power and Khmelkov's (1998) work on moral self-concept has led them to conclude that whatever precursors may exist for moral character, they do not reveal themselves in the form of conscious self-reflection in young children. Middle childhood and early adolescence, however, appear to be crucial in the integration of morality into the self-system (Damon 1984; Power and Khmelkov 1998). It is at these ages that children begin to link their conceptions of what sort of person they would like to become (*Ideal Self*) and what sort of person they hope never to become (*Dreaded Self*) to evaluations of the person that they are (*Real Self*) (Power and Khmelkov 1998). This integration allows the child to become capable of being self-critical and provides the capacity for motivating the child to begin to be concerned about living up to his or her own expectations.

There is some empirical evidence that the integration of moral concerns into personal identity has an impact on the positive social behavior of adolescents. Hart and Fegley (1995) studied the moral identities of a group of inner-city adolescents who exhibited a high degree of community-service voluntarism and care for others. These adolescents were identified by community leaders, teachers, and churches as youth who had done such things as organize youth groups and work in homeless shelters. They and a comparison group of adolescents from the same community were asked to generate a list of all of the important characteristics they could think of that described themselves as they are in the present, the person they were in the past, the person they dreaded becoming, and they kind of person they would ideally like to become. What Hart and Fegley (1995) assumed was that persons whose actual selves incorporate a subset of their ideal selves will be more driven to realize the goals of the ideal self than persons whose ideal self and actual self are unrelated. What they discovered in their study was in line with that hypothesis. Two-thirds of the adolescents high on voluntarism and care and less than a third of the comparison adolescents exhibited overlap between the characteristics of their actual and ideal selves.

The comparisons adolescents draw among their potential selves, however, do not always lead to good outcomes. Power and Khmelkov (1998) note that early adolescence provides a period of risk for children who perceive themselves not only falling short of an ideal but "becoming what they fear" (Power and Khmelkov 1998, p. 16). Such children appear to engage in a form of debilitating self-criticism that undermines their sense of agency. In some cases, this debilitating view of self becomes a self-fulfilling prophesy in which the child's sense of becoming what he or she most dreads ends up defining the self that emerges. In other cases, the effort to save face (as in the case of violent antisocial youth) leads to a set of self-serving cognitive distortions to justify or excuse their actions. An educational implication Power and Khmelkov (1998) draw from their research findings is that character education needs not only to engage children in constructing moral understandings, but also to provide a context within which to construct a positive sense of self and personal agency, a view echoed in our work on the relationship between morality and the personal domain (Nucci 1996).

The consistent picture that emerges from diverse studies of the development of self-understandings is that morality and the self-system develop independently until middle childhood. Prior to this integration, however, children begin to construct modes of responding to moral situations that reflect, at least in part, their sense of how such actions relate back to their own goals, aims and their sense of what is right in relation to themselves. Gil Noam (1993) has captured much of the results of this research, as it relates to the eventual construction of the moral self, in his conclusion that early, secure emotional attachments, predictable contexts, and a zone of trust and reciprocity are conducive to formation of the moral self.

Noam's position is consonant with an overwhelming body of evidence on the social and emotional development of young children. It is also consonant with the work on emotional development and morality reviewed in Chapter 6. As we saw there in the discussion of the "happy victimizer" phenomenon, the gradual coordination of early-childhood conceptions of moral transgressions as wrong with the sense that knowledge of the pain caused to the victim should outweigh possible gains to the perpetrator is fostered by affectively supportive environments in which fairness and moral reciprocity are supported by the experience of "goodwill" that comes from such interactions. As Arsenio and Lover (1995) discuss, some children's early experiences lead to the construction of a pattern of "ill will" in which long term patterns of victimization and peer rejection distort the construction of moral reciprocity such that the child feels "entitled" to act in aggressive or exploitive ways toward others.

The importance of early emotional experience in the construction of one's moral orientation has long been the subject of psychological accounts of moral development and character formation (Hoffman 1983; Kochanska 1993; Wilson 1993). Clearly, early-childhood patterns that emerge from such things as experiences of goodwill and ill will, if unchecked, become integrated into the construction of moral self in middle childhood and form the base for constructions of personal biases in the reading of social-moral situations later in life. The tendency to read situations as having moral, rather than primarily pragmatic or conventional, features and to link moral situations to oneself will be affected by the ways in which lifelong patterns of responding to social situations predispose one to reason and act. Because of the sheer logic of the temporal primacy of early-childhood events, there is a tendency to overestimate the influence of such early experiences on later social and moral functioning. In addition, because these events take place during a period of relative unsophistication, there is also a tendency to view such early-childhood experiences as forming a nonrational base for morality and character (Wilson 1993). These two notions come together in a view of early childhood as a critical period for moral character formation (Wilson 1993).

Psychotherapist and clinical researcher Gil Noam (1993) takes issue with the idea that formation of a moral self is an all-or-none phenomenon. The formation of the moral self is not the outcome of the socialization of a nonrational childhood "sense" (Wilson 1993) but, rather, "a lifelong experience of intersubjectivity, of selves merging and differentiating" (Noam 1993, p. 233). Noam reminds us that the early pioneers of object relations and attachment theory, such as Anne Bowlby, have pointed to the healing power of new relationships that can be formed throughout one's life. For Noam, having missed out at first on the types of emotional experiences conducive to constructing a positive moral self "makes it harder later," but new opportunities may arise from which a person may create a new "vitality" (Noam 1993, p. 233). It is interesting to note that Noam views moral reflection and engagement in moral action as an avenue not just for development of the moral aspect of self, but as a way in which to heal the self more generally (Noam 1993, p. 35–6).

Developmental Summary

The developmental picture that emerges of the construction of the moral self may be summarized as follows. Early-childhood constructions of morality incorporate the affective experiences associated with moral events, resulting in schemas that establish tendencies toward moral action. A part of the affective information that goes into the generation of early moral schemata is the overall climate of social events, which children may interpret as constituting a context of "goodwill" or "ill will." This early-childhood interpretation of the social world as benign and supportive or as malevolent may contribute to the likelihood that emerging capacities to understand morality in terms of just reciprocity will result in the view that the affective consequences of harm or perpetrating injustice toward another should outweigh the possible benefits that would accrue from engaging in moral transgression. This act of "will," as Piaget (1962) defined it, constitutes an early instance of character, in that it entails the subordination of personal gain to what is morally right. This construction of will forms the entry point in the child's incorporation of moral ideals of conduct into his or her construction of self.

The continuing construction of self that takes place during adolescence and adulthood involves a series of differentiations and integrations, of which morality is but one component. Because of the objective nature of morality and its presence in all human interaction, it is more difficult to discount the moral aspect of self than other aspects of one's self-system. Nonetheless, individuals vary in the degree to which morality becomes integrated into the core of one's personal identity. Moral responsibility is at stake in those situations which the individual reads as moral, and for whom morality is an integral part of personal identity.

Character, then, is not a constellation of personality traits or virtues but, rather, the operation of the moral aspects of the self in relation to the self as a whole. As such, the expression of character is subject to contextual variation, even if the structures of moral reasoning themselves are contextually invariant. Finally, character, defined in terms of the moral self, is not static but may evolve over time, both in terms of its own structure and in relation to the totality of the self as a system.

EDUCATION AND THE MORAL SELF

There are several educational implications in reconceptualizing character in terms of the moral aspects of self. Perhaps the most important is the recognition that what is being developed in terms of moral character is not a set of traits but, rather, an integration of moral and social understandings, affects, and skills with the way in which one defines oneself in moral terms and in relation to the given social context. This is an undoubtedly less straightforward and more complex way of looking at things than being able to size people up in terms of such virtues as honesty, diligence, and the like. It also makes it much more difficult for us as educators to clearly identify students as either having good character or not. For if we recognize that being able to identify a good person is often a matter of being able to see the world from the vantage point of the actor, the enterprise of aretaic evaluations becomes, as Socrates acknowledged in The Meno, a very difficult task, beyond even his wisdom.

Yet, to ignore the agentic aspect of moral development is to abdicate a fundamental role of any educator. It matters a great deal whether or not students grow up to be people for whom morality is a central element of their identity, and whether their moral understandings inform them in ways that direct them to attend to the embedded, as well as highly salient, moral features of the social world. Thus, we needn't throw up our hands in dismay at the prospect that we cannot create people of virtue. What we can do instead is contribute to the ways in which children construct their moral understandings, their interpretations of the moral and social world, and the linkages between those understandings and how they self-define. This integrative view of moral education addresses the agentic side of morality without reducing moral education to a series of futile efforts at indoctrination. Viewed in this way, the process of moral education becomes consistent with the more general constructivist approach to teaching that is emerging as the general paradigm for contemporary education. It is also consistent with what we understand to be the psychology of children's moral and social development.

With this chapter, we have reached the end of the overview of research on children's moral and social development. Let us then turn to a more detailed discussion of the implications of this psychological research and theory for educational practice.

PART TWO

Classroom Applications

CHAPTER EIGHT

Creating a Moral Atmosphere

Caitlin and Lauren are girls who live in the same neighborhood but attend different schools. At Caitlin's school, children all wear uniforms. In the morning they all line up with their classmates and are led into the school by their teacher. There is no talking allowed as they walk into school in single file and take their assigned seats. During class, students must raise their hand to speak or to get permission from the teacher to sharpen a pencil or go to the bathroom. No one is permitted to chew gum or eat in class. There are clear rules against using swear words or fighting on the playground.

Lauren, on the other hand, can wear jeans or shorts to school, but she can't wear extrashort skirts. When the bell rings, she and her classmates enter the school together, laughing and talking to one another. Once they get to the classroom they take whichever seat they wish. If they have something interesting to say during a lesson, they can speak up without raising their hands so long as they don't interrupt another speaker. If they need to sharpen a pencil, they can do so whenever they wish so long as they don't interfere with other students. Bathrooms are built into each classroom, and students may use them freely whenever they need to. As in Caitlin's school, students are not allowed to eat or chew gum in class. Also as in Caitlin's school, there are clear rules against fighting, and kids aren't supposed to swear, though that rule isn't strictly enforced.

Lauren and Caitlin attend schools with different social norms, which reflect divergent educational philosophies and ideologies. Readers familiar with variations in school structure can envision even more divergent forms than the examples illustrated by Lauren and Caitlin's elementary schools. Schools constitute minisocieties within the larger culture. They are structured by norms and conventions that frame the affective, personal, and moral elements of the school experience. As a consequence, the sociomoral curriculum of school, unlike its academic curriculum, is not confined to periods of instruction and study but includes the social interactions established by school and classroom rules, rituals, and practices (Jackson, Boostrom, and Hansen 1993), and by the less regimented peer interactions that take place on the playgrounds, in cafeterias, and in hallways.

The standard approach to this "hidden curriculum" has been to treat the entire complex of school rules and conventions as rife with moral meaning (Durkheim 1925/1961; Hansen 1996), and to treat adherence to rules as a cornerstone in the formation of moral character (Wynne 1986, 1989). Whereas it is the case that some school rules deal with matters of morality, and also true that the manner in which even trivial rules are enforced can have moral consequences, it is a mistake to equate school norms with moral standards. It is equally mistaken to view student compliance with or resistance to school rules per se as indicating much about a student's moral character. This is because the same differentiations that exist within the larger social system among convention, morality, and personal discretion also hold within the microsociety of the school. As teachers and administrators wrestle with how best to establish and maintain educationally constructive school rules and discipline, they are constantly confronted with the qualitatively different characteristics and functions of the moral, conventional and pragmatic/procedural norms of their institutions and classrooms, and with the qualitatively different ways in which students at different ages react toward those norms. For the most part, teachers and administrators are unaware of the systematic way in which these classes of norms vary. Nor are they generally cognizant of the tacit ways in which their own classroom interactions are often guided by these qualitative differences.

In the remainder of this chapter, we will take up the issues surrounding the domain-related features of school rules and norms and the ways in which students and teachers at different grade levels deal with matters of social regulation. In doing so, opportunities will be created for educators to reflect upon how best to incorporate this information within their own school setting in ways that constitute *domain appropriate practice* (Nucci 1982). While some approaches to classroom management and school structure will be presented as examples of effective practice, they are offered as a way to look at general principles, and not as the sole or necessarily best ways in which to achieve a positive sociomoral school climate within a particular school setting.

DOMAIN APPROPRIATE PRACTICE: GENERAL ISSUES REGARDING SCHOOL AND CLASSROOM NORMS

Teacher Authority and Children's Conceptions of School Rules

As one might expect, children's differential understandings of the nature of morality and convention have implications for the ways in which children evaluate school rules and teachers' authority. One might argue that how children view such issues doesn't matter very much since teachers exert considerable power over their student charges. However, as Metz (1978) indicated more than twenty years ago, the authority–child relationship is not a one-way street. Just as teachers and schools establish rules and policies for behavior, so too do students evaluate those rules. Barnard (1963), writing in the 1930s, pointed out that authority is successful only when its commands further the moral or social order as the subordinate understands it. Research on children's moral and social concepts has begun to provide a consistent set of findings that children's interpretations of acts as matters of morality or convention affect their evaluation of the legitimacy of social rules and authority.

With regard to the moral domain, children expect schools to have rules governing such actions as hitting and hurting or stealing personal property. They state that it is wrong for schools or teachers to permit such behaviors because they result in harm to persons (Laupa and Turiel 1986; Weston and Turiel 1980). In addition, Laupa and Turiel (1993) reported that children generalize their reading of actions to their evaluation of the legitimacy of adult authority. In their study, Laupa and Turiel (1993) found that elementary school children accepted as legitimate those instructions from teachers that would prevent harm to another child, but they rejected the instructions of teachers that, if followed, would result in harm to another child. The Laupa and Turiel (1993) study dealt with hypothetical scenarios so that children could provide responses without fear of coercion from an actual teacher. It is possible, and perhaps even likely, that a child would follow a teacher's command to hurt another out of fear of the teacher's power. Nonetheless, the study suggests that children might not view such a teacher as a legitimate authority. Finally, teacher fairness and impartiality constitute important criteria for students' judgments of teacher adequacy (Arsenio 1984; Lee, Statuto, and Vedar-Voivodas 1983; Veldman and Peck 1963). This latter finding is consonant with a central theme addressed by Philip Jackson and his colleagues (Jackson et al. 1993) in their depiction of the pervasive nature of moral issues in every-day classroom interactions. Thus, it would appear that, with respect to morality, it is less the case that teacher authority and rules establish what is right or wrong as it is that teacher authority stems from the extent to which the rules they establish, and the actions they engage in, are conso-nant with the child's conceptions of justice and harm.

The one caveat that must be added to this conclusion, however, is that teachers, because of their presumed access to accurate information, have great potential to alter the ways in which children read the meanings of people's intentions and actions. As was covered in Chapter 5, recent work has shown that the informational assumptions people bring to social sit-uations can radically alter their reading of events (Turiel et al. 1991; Wain-ryb 1991). Teachers who provide children with highly biased and preju-dicial accounts of historical events, and of the intentions and capacities of groups along racial, ethnic, and gender lines, have the capacity to alter the ways in which children view the actions of others. The impact of such teacher bias, particularly when enacted within the context of a shared community-wide viewpoint, has not been well studied in relation to chil-dren's moral understandings, and further research in this area is needed. One needn't wait for definitive research, however, to be aware of the po-tential for harm that might stem from a teacher's prejudicial framing of events for children. A moral responsibility of teachers and administrators is to mitigate such tendencies within themselves. This will be dealt with again when we look in Chapter 9 at the role of factual assumptions when generating moral lessons from the academic curriculum.

If we move from the moral domain to consideration of classroom con-vention, we see a very different pattern regarding children's acceptance of teacher authority. With respect to conventions, students acknowledge that school authorities may legitimately establish, alter, or eliminate school-based norms of propriety (e.g., dress codes, forms of address) and the rules and procedures for academic activity (Blumenfeld, Pintrich, and Hamilton 1987; Dodsworth-Rugani 1982; Nicholls and Thorkildsen 1987; Weston and Turiel 1980). As we saw in the examples presented at the be-ginning of this chapter, schools may vary widely in terms of these con-ventional and procedural norms, while sharing a common set of core moral rules.

The scope of the school's legitimate authority in establishing conven-tional norms is limited from the child's point of view by whether they en-croach on areas of activity perceived by children as within the personal domain. This was illustrated in a study of children's positive and negative feelings about classroom rules (Arsenio 1984). Arsenio reported that nearly 62% of all negative rule evaluations provided by fifth-grade boys involved undue teacher control of such nonacademic activities as bathroom and drinking-fountain procedures and restrictions on free-time activities. As was noted in Chapter 3, the definition of what counts as personal is not, however, solely a matter of individual decision making. The precise content of what is personal will vary as a function of the general system within which the child operates and the degree to which the child has successfully established an area of personal authority.

Schools are social institutions that place different sets of constraints on personal behavior than might exist in other social settings, such as the family and the general outside environment. Thus, schools represent a rather unique context within which children must learn to negotiate and accommodate their own personal freedoms in relation to the organizational conventions imposed by the varying institutions of general society. As we will discuss more thoroughly in this chapter, the negotiations over the personal domain of students in school contexts provides a major source of both conflict and the potential for student social growth.

Teacher Authority and Domain Appropriate Feedback to Rule Violations

The source of the child's understandings of morality, social convention, and personal issues is the qualitatively differing forms of social interactions associated with each domain. The educational implication of these qualitative differences is that in order for discourse surrounding moral and conventional norms to have maximal impact on students' social and moral growth, it should be concordant with the moral or conventional nature of the social/normative issue under consideration. This means that teacher feedback to students about school norms and norm violations should be different in kind, depending upon whether the norm deals with an issue of morality or convention. As we will see in detail in Chapter 9, curriculum research has shown that domain-concordant instructional methods lead to greater moral and social cognitive growth than methods that are not domain appropriate (Nucci and Weber 1991).

Consistent with those findings are the results of studies that look at students' evaluations of the appropriateness of teacher responses to hypothetical transgressions of school rules. In one such study (Nucci 1984) children in grades 3, 5, 7, and 9 were presented line drawings of children engaging in behaviors that were either moral transgressions or violations of a convention. Following the presentation of each line drawing, the children listened to a tape recording of a teacher providing five possible responses to the student behavior. Each child was asked to rate the teacher's responses on a four-point scale as an excellent, good, fair/so-so, or poor way to respond to what the child had done. The five teacher responses were those that had been shown in observational studies (Nucci and Nucci 1982b; Nucci and Turiel 1978; Nucci, et al. 1982) to be the most prevalent modes of teacher response to classroom transgressions:

1. *Intrinsic features of act statement* indicates that the act is inherently hurtful or unjust. ("John, that really hurt Mike.")
2. *Perspective-taking request* is a request that the transgressor consider how it feels to be the victim of the act. ("Christine, how would you feel if somebody stole from you?")
3. *Rule statement* is a specification of the rule governing the action. ("Jim, you are not allowed to be out of your seat during math.")
4. *Disorder deviation statement* indicates that the behavior is creating disorder or that it is out of place or odd. ("Sally, it's very unladylike to sit with your legs open when you are wearing a skirt.")
5. *Command* is a statement to cease from doing the act without further rationale ("Howie, stop swearing!).

These examples would all be considered domain appropriate. The reader can generate examples of domain-inappropriate responses by simply substituting the form of the responses to items 1 and 2 for the responses given to items 3 and 4 and vice versa. If the reader does this, it should be apparent that moral responses to violations of convention direct the actor to consider a set of intrinsic interpersonal effects that simply are not there (e.g., in response to leaving one's seat during math time: "Darrell, how would you like it if other people got out of their seat during math?" or "Darrell, it upsets people when you leave your seat."). On the other hand, the responses that seem most consonant with violations of conventional norms provide a rather weak basis for evaluating the effects of moral transgressions (e.g., in response to hitting: "John, it's against the rules to hit." or "John, that isn't the way a gentleman should act.").

In the study just described (Nucci 1984) and a subsequent study with preschool-age children (Killen et al. 1994), it was found that children prefer teachers to use domain-concordant methods of intervention (e.g., telling an instigator who doesn't share toys to give some back "because it's not fair to others who do not have any"), rather than domain-inappropriate ones (e.g., telling a child who has hit another child, "You shouldn't do that; it's against the rules to hit." or simply saying, "That's not the way that a student should act.").

In terms of issues of children's evaluations of the legitimacy of teacher authority, we found that children age 10 and older evaluate not only the teachers' responses but also the teachers as respondents (Nucci 1984). Students rated highest those teachers who responded to moral transgressions with statements focusing on the effects of the acts (e.g., "Carlos, that really hurts Mike."). Rated lower were teachers who responded with statements of school rules or normative expectations. Rated lowest were teachers who used simple commands (e.g., "Stop it!" or "Don't hit!").

As one would expect, students rated highest those teachers who responded to breaches of convention with rule statements or with evaluations of acts as deviant, and they rated lower those teachers who responded to such transgressions in terms of their effects on others (e.g., "When you sit like that, it really upsets people.").

In studies examining how teachers spontaneously respond to actual classroom transgressions (Nucci and Nucci 1982b; Nucci and Turiel 1978; Nucci, Turiel, and Encarnacion-Gawrych 1983), we found that teacher responses were not uniform across transgressions but, instead, tended to map differentially onto transgressions as a function of domain (roughly 60% in response to moral transgressions; 47% conventional). These same studies, however, also indicated that about 8% of teacher responses were domain discordant, and another 40% domain-undifferentiated simple commands (e.g., "Stop it!").

During informal conversations, the teachers in these studies indicated that they were unaware that they were responding in such systematically domain-differentiated ways. Their own sense of things was that while they tried on occasion to give reasons for rules or explanations for why a given behavior was wrong, they were mostly giving commands to stop misbehavior or reminding students of how they should behave. This perception of themselves as rule and social-order focused may have been due to the fact that in proportional terms, simple commands made up a substantial proportion of their actual responses. This is interesting in light of the fact that students rated simple commands as low or lower than domain-inappropriate responses to transgression. It would appear, then, that there is room for movement in teachers' current practices toward more domain appropriate patterns of response.

Having looked at some of the general issues associated with domain appropriate practice in relation to school rules and norms, let's turn now to consideration of the sociomoral aspects of schooling at different grade levels. Although there are commonalties across grade levels, there are also important developmental factors and differences in the nature of school structure that need to be taken into account in thinking about schools and classrooms as contexts for sociomoral growth. For example, developmental changes in children's concepts of social convention and the personal impact the ways in which children at different grade levels respond to school norms and authority. As we move through the discussion of educational practices in the rest of this chapter, we will be making connections with the descriptions of development from Part One.

SCHOOL AND CLASSROOM CLIMATE

Early Childhood (Preschool through Grade 2)

A climate of acceptance and warmth toward students is an essential element of moral education at any grade level. However, these elements are expressed differently toward students at different ages. Because young children are in the early phase of integrating affect within their moral and personal schemas, it is important that positive affect be overtly manifest within the school context. As we learned in the Chapter 6 discussion of affect and moral growth, young children are particularly open to displays of warmth by adults and particularly susceptible to the negative effects of adult displays of anger. Thus, in early-childhood contexts, it is important that teachers be even tempered and refrain from emotional outbursts or shouting at children. The desire that young children have for emotionally calm environments accounts for the immense popularity of television such characters as Barney and Mr. Rogers, whose soporific manners bore most adults and older children.

In a broader sense, it is essential that school be perceived as a benign environment in which children are safe from harm and exploitation by others. If we take seriously Arsenio and Lover's (1995) suggestions about the early integration of affect into the child's moral schemas, then we would want to do whatever possible to enable young children to construct a view of the world as benevolent and fair so that they might construct an orientation of "goodwill" toward others. This would be particularly important for young children whose experiences outside of school may be less than benign, and which may contribute to an experience of "ill will" and a consequent tendency to act in terms of self-interest rather than fair reciprocity.

Middle Childhood and Early Adolescence (Grades 3 through 8)

The climate of acceptance and warmth that characterized the good pre-school is also essential at the elementary and middle-school levels. Children at this age range are less dependent on adults, but they still look to them for emotional support and social stability. Because the formal academic curriculum now assumes greater importance, one critical arena in which teachers determine the affective climate is through their approach to academic instruction. A positive climate for social and moral growth is enhanced by academic experiences that foster peer interaction and discussion within a setting that allows for people to make mistakes without the risk of being made to look "dumb." This means that children should be encouraged to ask questions and to risk making mistakes in the process of learning. The key element for the teacher is to convey to students that mistakes are necessary to learning, and that everyone needs to make mistakes if they are to grow. In doing so, the teacher establishes a social context in which differences among people in ability and interest are not used as criteria for inclusion or exclusion from academic activity. In a subtle, experiential way, students are being exposed to a social milieu in which issues of equity and equal treatment are being integrated. While this is an important feature of teaching at all ages, it is especially important for children in middle childhood and early adolescence.

A central issue of middle childhood and early adolescence is how the self appears, relative to the competencies of others (Nicholls 1984, 1989). In a focus group that we conducted this past year with fifth-grade children, we learned that the primary source of conflicts at school was peer exclusion. The instigators of the conflicts were said by both boys and girls to be children who were not well liked because of their lack of social skills (shy, nerdy), their inability to perform well in team sports (kickball), or their tendency to pick fights (bullies). An interesting sidelight of these discussions was the spontaneous tendency of the children to recognize that it was the act of exclusion that was the primary problem, and not just the characteristics of the children who instigated the fights or arguments that followed.

Being made to look dumb in class or being made the outsider on the playground is not simply a problem of peer culture but of the school and its values. Schools can enhance the sense of inclusion through the judicious use of cooperative modes of teaching (Aronson and Patnoe 1997). They can reduce the harmful effects of peer competition and comparison by means of recreational forms of team sports (e.g., American Youth Soccer Organization–style soccer) that focus on participation, skill enhancement, and camaraderie, rather than loss or victory (Shields and Bredemeier 1995). Finally, they can refrain from engaging in practices that magnify peer comparisons, such as posting lists of children who have displayed "good character" (Character Counts Coalition 1993). Such practices do not serve to enhance the values schools wish to promote but, on the contrary, exacerbate tendencies toward invidious social comparison – one of the truly negative features of this developmental period.

Adolescence (High School)

The social climate of the high school should continue to underscore the basic elements of safety and academic and social participation discussed in regard to earlier grade levels. Integrated participation of students is particularly important at the high school level in order to offset the tendencies toward segregation into cliques and crowds that characterize peer relations at this age. While this self-selection serves the purposes of identity formation, it also works toward exacerbating the problems of social exclusion that emerge during earlier developmental periods. While it should not be the goal of schools to interfere with students' friendship networks or associations (elements of the personal domain), school should promote a broader sense of community in which students of diverse interests and abilities interact with one another.

Unfortunately, the sheer size of many American high schools pose special problems for efforts to generate this sense of community and social interaction. The comprehensive high school is a late-nineteenth-century American invention designed to serve the combined educational needs of students in vocational and college-preparatory curricula. This institution was designed to offset the social-class segregation of earlier models in which children of the upper classes attended college preparatory schools, and children of the working classes attended vocational institutes where they learned directly employable skills.

In its present form, the comprehensive high school is a very expensive physical plant, which includes laboratories, computer facilities, technical facilities (wood shops, auto shops, television studios), kitchens, dining halls, theaters, gymnasiums and athletic fields. In order to keep the cost of such facilities within bounds, many communities build high schools that house student populations the size of small community colleges. The advantage of these larger schools with populations in excess of 800 students is that they can offer a much richer curriculum and broader array of extracurricular activities. The disadvantage of these larger schools is that, on a percentage basis, there is actually less student participation in a given activity and less student participation in such things as sports, school newspaper, and theater, overall.

A number of strategies have been devised to offset the social costs of the large comprehensive high school. What these approaches share in common is the goal of breaking down the total population of the school into smaller, socially diverse units within which students can generate a sense of community. In general, these strategies use a common set of courses (e.g., English, history) or a class period (e.g., homeroom) as a way of identifying "houses" or communities within the school. Teachers and students within a given house remain together for at least one academic year and may use specified times throughout the year to address or discuss social issues collectively.

The most well-researched of these school-within-a-school programs are the "Just Community Schools" developed by Lawrence Kohlberg and his colleagues (Power, Higgins, and Kohlberg 1989a). The Just Community School employs weekly whole-group discussion among the 40 to 100 students and teachers who make up the community as a way of resolving moral and social issues that arise among the students. Published reports indicate that this approach is quite effective in reducing student misconduct, and it contributes to students' moral development. A more eclectic use of this school-within-a-school idea is now being attempted on a reasonably large scale within the Chicago public school system through the Small Schools Workshop operated by the University of Illinois at Chicago (Anderson 1998). The latter project is too new to have definitive outcomes. Nonetheless, this project and others, such as the Just Community School, are pointing the way toward practical approaches for reducing the population of the comprehensive high school into human-scale, diverse social communities.

The general affective climate establishes the overall emotional tone within which school rules and norms function. Having discussed some of the basic features of affective climate, we will turn now to a discussion of how domain appropriate practice would structure an educational approach to moral and social-conventional norms.

MORAL RULES AND NORMS

Early Childhood (Preschool through Grade 2)

The great moral achievement accomplished by young children is the construction of an understanding of fair reciprocity. Helping children generate a conception of fairness as requiring the reciprocal coordination of two or more points of view is the central challenge of early-childhood moral education. Because young children generate their initial understandings of morality out of their direct experiences in social interactions, the primary contribution that schools make toward young children's moral development is through the framing of these direct moral experiences. Teachers do this by helping children focus upon the effects of actions and their reciprocal implications. For example, a teacher might respond to moral transgressions in the following way:

"Mike, Matthew needs some clay. Please give him some."

"Veronica, Dawn hasn't had a turn on the swings. Please let her have one."

In both cases, the teacher statements focus upon the needs of the other child, and not simply on the power of the adult. But even these domain-concordant moral statements lack the element of reciprocity. While they do connect up with the young child's conceptions of morality, they do not explicitly direct the child's attention to the reciprocal nature of turn taking or distribution of goods.

There are two ways for a teacher to do this. One is for the teacher to do all of the thinking and lay out the reciprocal implications in statements to the children:

"Mike – how would you like it if Matthew had all of the clay, and you didn't have any? He needs some too. So, please share with him."

This is a reasonably efficient way for a teacher to handle the situation, and it makes sense in contexts where the teacher's time is at a premium. The teacher's response is domain concordant, and it lays out the reciprocal nature of morality and moral justification. However, it does not engage students in active problem solving and is, therefore, not an optimal way for a teacher to make use of this situation. A second, better use of this teachable moment is for the teacher to assist the children in conflict resolution.

The value of engaging children in conflict resolution is that it engages the child in recognizing the contradictions that exist between his own initial way of looking at things and the way in which his own needs and those of another person can be met. This is a slow process that is helped along by the child's inevitable experience of being on more than one side of these prototypical childhood disputes. One day's owner of the clay or the swing is the next day's child on the sidelines. In Piagetian terms, what takes place is the gradual disequilibration of the child's current way of thinking and its gradual replacement by a more adequate reequilibrated form that resolves the contradictions arising from the initial way of looking at things.

From this viewpoint, there is an argument that can be made for allowing the children to solve such problems on their own (Killen 1991; Piaget 1932). Allowing children to solve their own problems has the advantage that the solutions generated are "owned" by the children, and the process contributes to the child's autonomy and social efficacy. In point of fact, teachers cannot enter into every conflict situation that arises among children, and observational studies have indicated that teachers allow a fair number of social conflicts among preschool and early-elementary children to be resolved without adult intervention (Killen 1991; Nucci and Nucci 1982b). In many cases, young children handle these disputes quite well. Approximately 70% of preschool childrens' disputes during free play are resolved by the children themselves, either through reconciliation by the instigator or through compromising and bargaining (Killen 1991).

While these findings are impressive, the value of allowing children to solve their problems on their own can be overstated. Adults have the developmental advantage of being able to see both sides of a moral dispute in ways that young children cannot. Moreover, children look to adults to provide protection from exploitation and harm, and to help them work through social problems (Killen 1991; Nucci and Nucci 1982b; Youniss 1980). As was stated before, adults impede moral growth when they reduce moral situations to ones of convention and adult power. Adults contribute to moral growth when they engage children in moral reflection. With respect to conflict resolution, adults contribute to young children's moral growth by assisting them in identifying the sources of the conflict, by helping them to consider the perspective of the other, and by helping them to arrive at mutual solutions. This approach also provides children with experiences that counter the tendency to conclude that the use of sheer power and intimidation are the only methods by which one can achieve personal goals.

In the swing-set example, the teacher might begin by first asking the children to describe what the problem is and to hear each other's viewpoint and feelings, and then help them work toward a solution. We can imagine the following interchange:

T: Okay, what's the problem?
D: Veronica has been on the swings for a long time, and I haven't had a turn.
T: Veronica, what do you have to say to that?
V: I got on the swing first, and I didn't even get to swing yesterday.
T: Dawn, how do you feel about what Veronica just said?
D: Well, this isn't yesterday, and she is making me really mad.
T: Why is that?
D: It isn't fair. She only gets a turn, and I don't!
T: Well, what do you think we should do?
D: We could share. Veronica could let me swing for a little and then I would let her swing some more.
T: Veronica, Dawn is suggesting that you guys share. Is that something that you can do?
V: Maybe . . . but I should get to have more time than her because I got here first!
T: Well Dawn – how do you feel about that?
D: Okay, but not all day. I need turns too!
T: Okay, why don't you guys give it a try. I bet you can work something out. Call me if you need any help.

This scenario was loosely based on events commonly observed in our classroom observations and on the discourse format of teacher–child conversations in DeVries and Zan (1994). It illustrates how a teacher can provide a scaffold for children to build their own approach to moral problem solving. The key elements are that the children hear each other's point of view, attend to the harm or fairness issues involved, and offer a mutually satisfying resolution. The key roles for the teacher are to act as an honest broker, to assist in thinking about possible solutions, and to offer support for follow-through. This provides a context in which the work is done by the children in an atmosphere of safety and mutual regard.

Naturally, real children do not always engage in cooperative resolutions of conflicts. In such cases, the teacher will need to make a judgment as to whether such harm or injustice is being perpetrated that a direct intervention by the teacher is warranted, or whether the issue is one of rel-atively minor consequence where the children will simply need to deal with the fact that not all situations turn out nicely. For example, if Veron-ica simply is not interested in sharing, but hasn't really been dominating the swing set, the teacher may simply decide to let things stand as they are. She might say to Dawn, "Well, I am sorry to say that Veronica isn't going to share right now. Perhaps you can come back and use the swings later."

One might argue that in doing so, the teacher has rewarded Veronica's "selfishness." This is where a teacher's judgment has to come in. If Veron-ica does not generally behave in a selfish manner, there is little likelihood that an occasional act of self-interest marks a major shift in "character." In Chapter 10 of this book, we will discuss the implications of the multifac-eted nature of human motivation for a realistic approach to character and education. It may well be that Veronica has a special desire to swing that day, or that she doesn't particularly like Dawn and is momentarily acting on that dislike. Unless the teacher is clairvoyant, she will have no way of knowing why Veronica has chosen this moment to act as she has.

In this scenario, Veronica's failure to be "nice" may be irrelevant to her level of morality. As for Dawn, she will live to swing another day. In this case, disappointment would not entail moral tragedy but a practical les-son in human psychology and interpersonal relations. The children's at-tempt at moral discourse would not have resulted in a solution, but it would raise the underlying issues to a level of consciousness from which both children would stand to benefit.

If on the other hand, Veronica has dominated the swing set and is sim-ply unreasonable, the teacher would have a moral obligation to protect the rights of the other children and would step in to ensure that Dawn was given a turn. The teacher might also take disciplinary action toward Veronica. We will also take up the issue of discipline in our discussion of the moral self in Chapter 10. There we will see that discipline is itself a context in which to generate reflection and cognitive change, and not sim-ply a vehicle for punishment.

Middle childhood (Grade 3 through 6)

By the third or fourth grade of elementary school, the morality of children has the element of reciprocity lacking in the preschool child. However, it is a very literal reciprocity in which fairness requires simply that one not come out on the short end of things. On the plus side, children are now much better able to take into account the needs of the other, as well as the self, in making moral decisions. On the down side, this tit-for-tat morality has a basic limitation that elementary school teachers will recognize as being expressed in the kinds of trouble that elementary school children sometimes get themselves into, and in the instances of insensitivity that children of this age sometimes exhibit.

The social exclusion that our focus-group children so readily identified as the primary source of social problems at school is in part sustained by a morality that views fairness in terms of providing rewards in direct proportion to the quality or amount of one's deeds (Damon 1977). From this moral orientation, a child who is not a good kickball player is simply not as entitled to play as someone who is a good player. A child who is shy or not socially skilled is less worthy of invitation to a party than someone who is more socially adept. Excluding these children is, therefore, not unfair. In addition, there is an element of personal choice involved, in that children may view the selection of whom to involve in play or social activity as an aspect of social relations that are a matter of personal prerogative.

Generally, teachers are not involved in helping to resolve these social problems. Unlike the failure to engage in turn taking, which is an overt act of excluding others from common playground equipment, the decision by children not to include a particular child in their games or activities is often viewed by the teachers, as well as the children as a peer matter of choice. On the other hand, children do recognize that teachers have legitimate authority to ensure that school resources (in this case, opportunities to play) are distributed in a fair manner. In addition, children expect teachers to protect not simply their physical safety, but their feelings as well. For a teacher to become involved requires a judgment that a child's exclusion is becoming systematic and, therefore, potentially harmful to the child.

Name calling and fighting are other common examples of moral problems that are compatible with the direct-reciprocity morality of middle childhood. One consequence of a morality based on direct reciprocity is that it can lead to the view that any harm requires a commensurate harmful response. This eye-for-an-eye morality leads to a vicious cycle in which, as Martin Luther King, Jr., put it, all parties end up blind. Virtually every parent and teacher has heard the phrase "He started it!" as an explanation for name calling or fighting. And, as every parent and teacher knows, the tit-for-tat mentality of children makes the efforts to determine "who started it" usually futile.

Domain appropriate responses to social exclusion and fighting are somewhat different, though in both cases the goal is to direct children to consider the intrinsic moral consequences of their actions. Teachers may do this by engaging in the sorts of domain-concordant feedback described with reference to younger children. In applying this to older children, however, the goal is not simply to get each child to consider the other's perspective, but to help them recognize the limitations that result from strict-reciprocity moral reasoning.

Another strategy is to extend the effort at social problem solving, described with reference to preschool children, by bringing in a peer mediator (Deutsch 1993). The advantages of engaging a peer mediator to help with conflicts among elementary and middle-school children are several. First and foremost, the act of peer mediation reduces the tendency for children to see objections to immoral conduct as simply a matter of adult authority. Second, it causes the disputants to see their situation from a third, disinterested vantage point. This third-person perspective moves the issue out of one of direct reciprocity, offering a window into a new way of looking at moral issues. Finally, it is of benefit to the mediator, who is necessarily engaged in moral discourse and reflection. For example, a study examining the impact of peer mediation on second- through fifth-grade students found that students who had served as peer mediators more often resolved their _own_ interpersonal conflicts in ways that took into account the needs of both parties, and they were also less likely to ask for adult intervention than children who had not had this mediator experience (Johnson et al. 1995).

Adolescence (Grades 7 through 12)

The rate at which teachers respond to children's moral transgressions begins to decline by the time children enter the fifth grade. By seventh-grade, teachers and other school personnel are rarely respondents to children's moral transgressions (Nucci and Nucci 1982b). The lack of adult response observed at the seventh-grade level was in part a function of the reduction in rates of moral transgressions that entailed overt acts of aggression and squabbles over such things as playground equipment. Most of the moral transgressions observed at the seventh grade level were in the form of name calling or other forms of psychological harm (Nucci and Nucci 1982b). Teachers provide relatively low response rates to such transgressions at all age levels, including preschool (Killen 1991), leaving such issues up to processes of peer interaction. Commensurate with the observed decline in adult response rate, older children and adolescents tend to seek out adult intervention for moral interactions at much lower rates than do young children (Nucci and Nucci 1982b).

At both the junior and senior high school levels, school authorities appear to respond only to severe breaches of moral conduct, such as fighting and theft. In most schools, this means that teachers and other school personnel have little direct input into the moral interactions of the vast majority of their students. The contributions that traditional junior and senior high schools make to students' moral growth are functions of the degree to which conventional norms are fairly applied, the degree of respect and mutuality that exists between teachers and students, and the degree of openness and interaction that exists in the discourse over academic subject matter. In other words, the contribution of junior and senior high school faculty and administrators to students' moral growth (beyond moral elements of the academic curriculum) is through these general structural features of the school and classroom, rather than any form of direct teacher involvement in student moral interactions.

This state of affairs makes a great deal of sense if one views the primary function of junior and senior high school to be academic instruction, and if one presumes that children should have developed basic moral attitudes prior to adolescence. From this traditional point of view, students may continue to grow in the more subtle aspects of moral life through peer interactions and through engagement in moral discourse and reflection in the context of the academic curriculum.

Objections to this traditional perspective have been raised by those who argue that it is only through direct social experience that one can develop as a moral being, and that academic discourse is insufficient without a direct linkage to students' actual lives (Power 1996). The primary proponents of this point of view are the advocates of democratic education (Lind 1996; Oser 1986) and the Just Community School (Power, Higgins, and Kohlberg 1989a, 1989b). What these approaches share in common are mechanisms by which students come together as a community for open discussions of the moral issues they are confronting within the school context (e.g., thefts, student exclusion or isolation, sexual conduct, racism) in order to arrive at a rational moral consensus (cf. Habermas 1991; Oser 1986) for how such issues should be resolved. Often these resolutions entail the construction of shared moral norms, which are then used to guide the conduct of members of the Just Community (Power et al. 1989a).

In order for these "just communities" to work, schools must give over instructional time on a regular (weekly) basis in order for students to hold these town hall–style meetings. They must also give over to the students and their community advisors the authority to alter, add to, or abolish existing school rules that affect these "quality of life" issues for students. Students are not empowered to change the basic academic framework of the school but, rather, those norms that pertain to problematic areas of their moral interactions. Despite evidence that such just communities result in behavioral and cognitive moral growth, few schools in the United States have adopted this holistic approach.

Moral interactions take place within the conventional normative system of the school. Having discussed issues of morality, we will turn now to a discussion of conventional norms and students' personal domain within school settings.

CONVENTIONAL NORMS AND THE PERSONAL

Early Childhood (Preschool through Grade 2)

Prior to the fourth or fifth grade, children don't generally view the conventions of schools to be their business. Young children rarely, if ever, respond to another child's violation of a conventional school norm (e.g., talking without raising one's hand) (Killen and Smetana 1999; Nucci and Nucci 1982b). This is not to say that young children are unaware of, or disinterested in, social conventions in general. Preschool-age children do respond to violations of general societal norms, such as gender inappropriate dress (Nucci, Turiel, and Encarnacion-Gawrych 1983), violations of conventional roles in the context of fantasy play (Goncu 1993), and transgressions of peer-constructed games (Corsaro 1985). From these findings, it would appear that while young children have a sense of convention and social organization, they have a difficult time making a connection between themselves and the arbitrary conventional norms established by adults. In particular, they seem to maintain a distance between themselves and what they perceive to be the adult-generated rules that run schools as institutions.

One implication of these developmental trends in young children's conceptions in the area of convention is for teachers to accept the fact that children are years away from having any real understanding of schools as social institutions, and to view the establishment of school conventions as a task of responsible adult authority. As mentioned, young children view teachers as having legitimate control over the establishment of school conventions and procedures. It is reasonable then, not only from an adult perspective but also from the point of view of the children for teachers to establish the basic routines, conventions, and customs of the school day.

The distance at which children experience classroom social conventions has been interpreted by some students of early-childhood education as a factor in maintaining a heteronomous or authority-based orientation toward social norms and social hierarchy (DeVries and Zan 1994). Contributing to this concern is the fact that young children tend to view conventional norms in highly prescriptive terms, relative to older children. That is, while they recognize that conventional norms are alterable, they also tend to treat existing conventional regularities as descriptive of an existing empirical order (e.g., men *should* wear shorter hair than women because men generally *do* wear shorter hair than women). This transformation of the typical (is) into the normative (ought) is due in part to a more general effort by young children to seek order and organization in the social and physical world. Few things are as upsetting to young children as chaos and unpredictability. In fact, one aspect of providing children with an environment that they would respond to as benign and supportive is to have a classroom that is orderly and routine and, in the broadest sense, conventional.

These needs of young children for conventional organization and routine should not be confused with a heteronomous moral orientation toward authority and rules. Young children understand that such conventional norms are alterable, but they have little in the way of an understanding as to their social function. This lack of understanding is one reason for teachers to provide-domain concordant social messages to matters of convention in the form of rule statements, statements of order, and social expectation.

Once the teacher has established the basic conventional framework needed to manage a school or classroom, the teacher may engage young children in the construction of conventional norms that affect them directly. This provides young children concrete experience with the collective and negotiated source of these social norms. Doing so also establishes very early on an experiential framework for discussion of social and moral norms that is at the heart of any meaningful social-values curriculum. For example, children may be engaged in forming the conventions that are to guide how the children are to play with the classroom guinea pig (DeVries and Zan 1994, pp. 128–30). The keys to having children construct such rules are to allow children to voice their ideas and to help them negotiate a practical set of shared outcomes. We will discuss these process issues on the values curriculum in more detail in Chapter 9.

Middle Childhood (Grade 3 through 6)

As was described in Chapter 4, the developmental course of concepts of social convention follows an oscillating pattern in which children's affirmations of the purposes of convention are subsequently negated, and these negations then replaced by more comprehensive understandings affirming conventions. Around 7 or 8 years of age (second grade), children start paying attention to the situational inconsistencies in the application of social conventions as evidence that conventions are not describing a "natural order." Such things as being able to call some adults by their first names, rather than titles, are now seen as evidence that conventions don't really matter. As you might expect, there are behavioral correlates of this period of negation, though not as pronounced as what one sees in early adolescence. In our observations of classroom social transgressions, we noted that the rates of conventional transgression are higher in grades 2 and 7 than they are in grade 5 (Nucci and Nucci 1982b). In grade 5, children are about 10 to 11 years old, which corresponds to the modal age for Level 3 affirmation of the functional value of conventions as serving to maintain social order. In contrast, both grades 2 and 7 correspond to modal ages at the front end of phases of negation of convention.

The main tool that teachers possess to help them in constructively dealing with the negation of convention maintained by second- and third-grade children is the general, positive regard that children at these ages have toward teachers. The desire to please adults and to receive their affection is such that young children generally endeavor to comply with adult wishes, even when the child doesn't understand the teacher's purposes. This vulnerability makes it very important that teachers provide fair and consistent feedback for norm violations, and that teacher reprimands focus on conduct and not on attributes of the child. In responding to conventional transgressions by second- and third-grade children, teachers should make use of rule statements and disorder/deviation statements, rather than simple commands, as a way of setting out normative expectations. In so doing, the teacher is helping children to reconstruct their conceptions of convention, both in terms of the shared nature of the behavioral expectation (rule) and in terms of its organizational function (statement of disorder).

With older students, however, teachers should use rule statements infrequently. In our study looking at children's evaluations of the adequacy of teacher responses to transgression, we found that children at third grade and earlier grades evaluated rule statements as an adequate response to conventional transgressions. Older children, however, treated rule statements as no more adequate than domain-inappropriate responses (Nucci 1984). This finding is consistent with observations of children's responses to conventional transgressions indicating that the rate at which they use rule statements in response to peers drops sharply after third grade (Nucci and Nucci 1982a). It would appear that children older than third grade expect their peers to be aware of general social rules. Concordant with that interpretation, it is likely that older students find the teachers' use of rules redundant and noninformative and, hence, an inadequate form of response. So, rather than using a rule statement, such as "Class, let's be quiet. We are not supposed to be talking while we are doing seat work." as a response to disruptive talking, the teacher could provide a statement of disorder, which focuses on the organizational purposes of the norm, such as "It's getting too noisy in here folks. People are trying to work."

In our observations of teachers' actual classroom behavior, we found that the proportion of rule statements provided by teachers remains relatively unchanged (roughly 14% of responses) from grades 2 to 7 (Nucci and Nucci 1982b). If that number is added to the more than 40% of responses to transgression in the form of simple commands, it becomes clear that the form of teacher responses to violations of school conventions is less than optimal. One practical reason for this state of affairs is that teachers are responding to a fairly large number of repeated violations of the same norms.

The vast majority of classroom conventional transgressions committed by elementary school children fall into a few categories: cross-talking, being out of one's seat, talking without raising one's hand, and being out of line (Nucci and Nucci 1982b). Over half of the classroom conventional violations we observed being responded to by teachers were accounted for by a single category: cross-talking (Nucci and Nucci 1982b). In such a situation, the tendency for teachers to short-circuit the process and rely on simple commands is understandable. On the other hand, this situation raises some interesting questions in terms of whether or not a frequently violated conventional norm should be maintained in the first place. Obviously, second- and third-grade children in a negation of convention phase are not the best sources upon which to make such a judgment since their lack of understanding of the purposes of convention contributes to their elevated levels of noncompliance. However, if a norm is violated at a fairly high level across grades, including fifth grade, at which point children are at their most compliant, then there may be reason to reconsider the appropriateness of the convention.

Let's consider the issue of cross-talking for purposes of illustration. Second-grade and fifth-grade children differentiate between disruptive talking, which prevents others from hearing the teacher and doing their work, and merely chatting quietly with a neighbor. During our interviews, children expressed the view that rules against disruptive talking were good ones. In our observations, however, we witnessed teachers responding to children's cross-talking that was neither disruptive to others nor interfering with the overall learning of the children being reprimanded. No one, including second-grade children, is in favor of a chaotic classroom. However, there is a difference between chaos and conversation. Even in the most interactive and well-organized classroom, there is bound to be "down time" in which children will want to simply talk to one another. This is particularly the case when children finish their seat work ahead of their classmates, and during periods of classroom transition from one activity to another. In addition, children (and my university education majors) often find it pleasant to chat occasionally with a neighbor while doing their work. In none of the above examples are educational goals being compromised. Reprimanding children in such situations would seem to add little to their education or their love of schooling. A far better way to make use of the children's desire to socialize is to integrate it into instruction through the uses of discourse and group activity as instructional methods.

A simple suggestion that DeVries and Zan (1994) make with respect to younger children which I would echo here as a general approach, is that teachers and school administrators reduce conventional regulations to those that are actually instrumental to the operation of a school or classroom. In deciding which rules to have, elementary school teachers might consider calling upon the expertise of fifth-grade children. Students at this age are both experienced with the norms and purposes of schooling and are also at a point of affirmation in their concepts of social convention.

During the focus group mentioned earlier in this chapter, we asked fifth-grade children to share with us some of the rules at their schools that they thought weren't especially good ones, or rules that should be modified. Their answers might serve as an illustrative example of how children at this age might be of help to teachers. One school was reported to have a "no passing" rule that forbade anyone from walking past someone else in the hallways. The children readily understood the goal of the rule as helping to reduce the likelihood that someone would run in the halls and either get hurt or knock down a younger student. However, they saw the "no passing" rule as going too far. They pointed out that the "no skip-ping" and "no running in the halls" rules at the school were sufficient to meet those safety goals. These same children also stated objections to the need to raise one's hand in order to say something in class. Again, they expressed an understanding of the organizational purposes of the rule, but they felt that it should only apply to whole-group lessons and should not be enforced in small-group activities. As one girl put it, "We manage to be polite and talk at home without raising our hands, why can't we be expected to do that here?"

Many schools engage fifth- and sixth-grade children in activities, such as student council, and as hall monitors and assistants to school crossing guards. In these ways, schools contribute to the integration of children into the conventional structures of school society. These activities also help to develop children's sense of personal responsibility. What is being suggested here is that schools go beyond the pro forma nature of these in-stitutions and actually engage them, particularly student council, as meaningful forums within which children can contribute to the estab-lishment of the overall set of school conventions. Engaging children in so-cial problem solving in the area of convention would easily mesh with the uses of peer mediation discussed earlier with respect to moral concerns.

Adolescence (Grades 7 through 12)

Early adolescence is a second phase of negation of convention. This is cou-pled with an expansion of what children at this age consider to be per-sonal, rather than under the jurisdiction of adult authority. Although stu-dents generally grant schools the authority to regulate prudential, moral, and conventional issues, they also draw boundaries around teacher au-thority and maintain the view that teachers have no right to regulate ac-tions they consider personal (Smetana and Bitz 1996). Children in ele-mentary school are consistent in claiming personal jurisdiction over such issues as with whom to associate, how to spend lunch money, and choice of hairstyle. In adolescence, students are even less likely than fifth graders to grant legitimacy to teacher authority regarding personal or prudential areas of conduct (Smetana and Bitz 1996).

The developmental double whammy of the early-adolescent negation of convention along with the expansion of the personal is associated with an increase in parent–child conflicts (Smetana 1995b). It also makes teacher–student relations more challenging. School norms that were annoying to fifth graders become highly objectionable to some adolescents in grades 7 through 9. Issues of appearance, manners, tardiness, and talking in class may become a blur of personal choice and arbitrary adult dictate. These adolescent behaviors often give a false impression of self-centeredness, and the resistance to authority is sometimes mistakenly responded to through harsh control.

Through it all, these students are still children in need of affection and structure. Schools are still social institutions that require compliance with certain norms in order to function. The key, then, in terms of positive social climate is to construct a conventional system that allows for personal expression. In many American schools, this is accomplished through generous dress codes that permit oddities, such as green hair, but draw the line at obscene or immodest attire. But open dress codes needn't be the avenue that a given community or school takes. Adolescents are generally able to adjust to the idea that school is a place where behaviors (e.g., public displays of affection, such as kissing) that would be personal matters elsewhere are under legitimate conventional regulation at school (Smetana and Bitz 1996). Students who find it difficult to recognize the school's legitimacy in such areas also tend to show elevated levels of misconduct across a wide range of actions.

A positive approach to this age group is for the teachers to make a distinction between the norms needed to operate the school and to protect student safety and those behaviors that constitute a "minor threat" to the social order. For example, marking a student tardy for being next to his seat, rather than sitting in it, as the bell rings may make the adult feel powerful, but it does little to enhance the student's appreciation of the norm of promptness. Without reducing things to a cliché, this really is a phase that will pass, and some adult patience is called for. Most students who were "good kids" in fifth grade still view teachers as people worthy of fair treatment. For example, a student will call teachers by titles in order not to offend the teacher needlessly, even though the student is clueless as to why using the teacher's first name is offensive. Firm and fair enforcement of rules with a dash of humor will work better than rigid requirements for compliance.

Eventually, junior high school students and high school freshmen reach the point (14–17 years) where they construct an affirmation of convention as basic to the structuring of social systems. As one would expect, this developmental shift is associated with a marked decline in student misconduct (Geiger and Turiel 1983). It is also a period in which students fully comprehend that the array of school conventions structures the high school as a societal system. Even as students move within their own particular crowds and cliques, the larger conventional culture of the high school with its norms, rituals, and traditions provides many students with a sense of belonging.

The risk at this point in development, however, is that students will identify with an alternative social system and remain alienated from the school. This is a well-identified risk among African American male high school students, who in many cases adopt what has been termed a "resistance culture" that stands in opposition to white middle-class values of academic behavior and social convention (Ogbu 1987). This is an ultimately self-defeating perspective motivated by a desire to maintain a distinctive identity in the face of a perceived oppressive, dominant majority. This is not a phenomenon limited to African Americans. Similar orientations have been described among working-class British youth (Willis 1977), and we might describe the adolescent subcultures, such as the "goths," made famous by the tragedy in Littleton, Colorado, as serving analogous identity needs.

Integrating students into the social-conventional structure of high school is aided by processes that give students genuine input into the structure of those conventions. An example of how this can be done within a traditional large high school is provided by the "First Class" program at Deerfield High School in Illinois. First Class originated in 1994 as a result of problems with graffiti, littering, vulgar language, and a basic lack of belonging that was perceived by some students and faculty as characterizing student life at the high school. In response, a committee was formed of students and teachers who set out to establish democratically shared norms of faculty and student conduct, and who agreed upon modes for teachers to address student misbehavior. The result of these efforts was a visible dramatic shift in the overall look of the school, in student behavior, and in the general sense of school community. Unfortunately, the group of students who originated the norms that comprise "First Class" have now all graduated, and the current students feel less ownership for what was accomplished.

The challenge facing Deerfield High School and other schools that might wish to engage in similar sorts of activities is to keep such efforts current and alive. This cannot be done simply by addressing crises and by generating formal codes of conduct. The community discourse needs to become a much more integrative aspect of student life. For this to happen, however, schools will have to recognize that a portion of "instructional time" is going to have to be apportioned for these social developmental purposes.

CONCLUSION

In summary, moral education cannot be divorced from the overall social climate and normative structure of the school and classroom. This unavoidable aspect of schooling means that all teachers are engaged in at least some tacit form of moral and social normative education. The manner in which teachers and schools establish and maintain conventions and moral standards forms a substantial aspect of the schools' contribution to students' sociomoral development. At a basic level, a climate of mutual respect and warmth, with fair and consistent application of rules, forms the elemental conditions for an educationally constructive moral atmosphere. Beyond this general base, what we have seen is that effective practice is enhanced by the coordination of teacher responses with the moral or conventional nature of school norms or student behaviors. Domain appropriate teacher input with regard to moral concerns focuses on the effects that actions have upon the rights and welfare of persons. Teacher contributions regarding social conventions focus on social organization, social expectations, and rules.

We have also seen that the degree and form of teacher involvement with students' moral and conventional behavior shifts as children move from preschool on through high school. The greatest degree of teacher involvement, as well as opportunities for students to solve their own social problems is at the level of the preschool. The level with the least direct teacher involvement with student sociomoral issues, as well as the point of least opportunity for students collectively to resolve or have input into these issues, is the traditional high school. This has much to do with instructional time and the increased emphasis on academics with age.

Social interactions in grades 3 and above are largely constrained by classroom routines. Free social interactional exchanges, during the school day, are confined to recess and lunch periods, which are themselves eliminated as opportunities for social interaction at the high school level. As a consequence, teacher input into students' actual sociomoral interactions becomes increasingly confined to matters of convention. Moral experiences tend to be limited to the fair application of conventional norms and to the fairness of academic practices, such as grades and teacher feedback (Thorkildsen 1989, 2000). The tendency for school social interactions to be focused in the area of convention (Blummenfeld et al. 1987) means that developmental shifts associated with periods of affirmation and negation of convention are felt directly in terms of rates of student transgression. The early adolescent years are a period of particular importance in this regard since it marks a convergence of a period of negation of convention with the increased claims by adolescents to personal discretion in areas that schools and other adults might view as matters for conventional regulation (Smetana and Asquith 1994). Sensitive and creative teacher responses during these periods of transition are important inasmuch as they either foster or subvert adolescent interest in schooling and a sense of respect for legitimate social authority.

Despite the importance attached to this "hidden curriculum" (Jackson et al. 1993), it is rather thin gruel upon which to feed moral growth beyond the elementary school years. The range of conventional and moral issues with which students have direct experience is limited to the particular features of schools as social institutions. In addition, naturally occurring social interactions in traditional school settings do not afford much in the way of time for reflection or discussion. The educative role of schools, however, is not limited to direct social experience. Schools are specialized institutions designed to bring students beyond their own direct encounters with the world to acquire information and to construct understandings that are valued by their culture. This is accomplished through the formal academic curriculum. The curriculum is rife with moral and conventional content, as well as issues of personal choice and identity.

Schools, then, have an opportunity to engage in meaningful moral and social education through an integration of values education with the teaching of regular academic subject matter. This becomes increasingly important from the third grade of elementary school on through high school as students become increasingly capable of reflection, and as the involvement of teachers in the moral lives of students lessens. Employing domain appropriate practice to integrate values education within the academic curriculum is the subject of Chapter 9.

CHAPTER NINE

Integrating Values Education into the Curriculum: A Domain Approach

In this chapter, we will explore some suggestions for incorporating the development of children's conceptions of morality, convention, and personal issues into the existing academic curriculum. The goal is to provide teachers with some guidance for how to engage in domain-appropriate moral education that will complement, rather than compete with, teachers' more general academic aims. The suggestions and examples provided here are not meant to serve as a curriculum per se but, rather, as a template for teachers to use in adapting their course materials and syllabi for moral education.

The purposes of this curricular approach are (1) to stimulate the development of students' moral conceptions of fairness, human welfare, and rights, and (2) to develop their conceptions of societal convention and social organization so that they may (3) participate as constructive citizens and moral beings and (4) develop a critical moral orientation toward their own conduct and the norms and mores of society.

The first three stated purposes of this curricular approach are noncontroversial in that they are resonant with the goals of virtually all traditional forms of values education. In and of themselves, however, those three goals fall short of what is required of a genuinely moral person. In the absence of the capacity to employ one's moral and social judgments in a critical manner, an individual cannot reflect upon the possibility that his or her own moral perspective within certain situations is at odds with what is most fair and right. As we saw in Chapter 5, the dynamics among morality, convention, and informational assumptions are such that they may form a conceptual framework with immoral consequences. The most obvious example from our own social history would be racial segregation. Systems of education that either inculcate students into the existing social normative structure, or that simply focus upon students' construction of moral and conventional understandings within the assumptions and norms of the existing social framework, run the risk of perpetuating the immorality built into the existing social system and its values. For educators to go beyond this, attention needs to be given to developing students' capacities to analyze critically the interrelations among morality, convention, personal claims to choice and privacy, and relevant informational assumptions from a moral point of view. The primary medium that schools have to engage in this process is the academic curriculum.

RESEARCH ON DOMAIN APPROPRIATE CURRICULA

The core assumption of the domain appropriate curriculum is that the forms of educational experience intended for developing students' social values should be coordinated with the domain (i.e., moral, conventional, personal) of the values or issues under consideration. Several years ago, we set out to address whether attention to the domain of social values makes a difference in the development of children's moral and social conventional concepts (Nucci and Weber 1991). The setting for our study was an eighth-grade American history course and a companion course in English composition. Together with the history teacher, we identified a series of issues from American history that were primarily either moral or social conventional in character, as well as events and issues that involved domain overlap. (Examples of the moral issues are slavery and the forced removal of Indians from their lands.) Conventional issues included such things as the adjustments in modes of dress, work conventions (such as time schedules), and dating patterns that resulted from the influx of immigrants and the shift from an agrarian to an industrial society. (Changes in laws permitting women to vote is an example of a mixed-domain issue used in the study.)

Students participated in small-group discussions of these issues once each week for a period of seven weeks. In addition, students were given essay homework assignments based on the issues that they had discussed. These homework assignments were graded by the classroom teacher as a part of his assessment of their learning of history. Finally, students wrote essays on related moral, conventional, or mixed issues in their English composition class.

Students were assigned to one of three forms of instruction. In one condition (Convention), students were directed in their small-group discussions and in their essays to treat all issues as if they were matters of convention. Discussions centered around the norms involved, the function of norms in structuring society, and the impact that altering or violating the norms would have on the social order. In the second condition (Moral), students were directed to treat these same issues as if they were matters of morality. Discussions and essay instructions directed students to consider the justice and welfare implications of the issues under consideration. The third instructional mode fit our definition of Domain Appropriate values education. The focus of discussions and essays was matched with the domain of the particular issue under consideration. In the case of mixed domain issues, students were asked first to consider normative, conventional aspects and then to consider the justice or welfare features of the issue. Finally, students were asked to integrate or coordinate the moral and conventional features of the event. This latter exercise was one that we hoped would increase the capacity of students to respond spontaneously and in a critical way to contradictions between morality and conventions, and to seek moral resolutions of those contradictions in ways that also respected the need for social organization. Examples of the ways in which these discussions were structured will be presented in some detail in the next section of this chapter when we look more closely at how to generate a domain-appropriate curriculum.

Several findings from the study are important for this discussion. First are the outcomes regarding development of morality and convention. Level of moral reasoning was assessed with a group measure – the DIT test (Rest 1979; Rest et al. 1999). The DIT produces an index, the "P" score, indicating the extent to which a person uses principled (justice-based) reasoning to render moral decisions. We assessed students' level of conventional reasoning with the interview procedure developed by Turiel (1978, 1983). All of the subjects in the study were either at Level 4 negation typical of early adolescence, at level 5 affirmation, or at a transitional point between these two levels.

What we found was that subjects in the Moral condition and students in the Domain Appropriate condition had P scores that were very similar and significantly higher than students who had been in the Convention condition. With regard to the development of reasoning about convention, the outcome was the inverse. Students in the Convention and Domain Appropriate conditions had similar levels of conventional reasoning, and both were on average nearly half a stage higher than the conventional levels of students in the Moral condition. These results indicate that attention to domain does matter in terms of efforts to impact on students' social-conceptual development. Students who received instruction focusing in one domain developed in that domain and not the other. Only the students in the Domain Appropriate instructional condition developed in both domains.

A second noteworthy finding of the study had to do with how students dealt with overlapping issues. At the end of the seven-week instructional period, all students were asked to write an essay discussing their views of the social-values issues raised by an event in which morality and convention were in conflict. The matter concerned an actual event in which the king of the Gypsies of the Chicago metropolitan area refused federal money for scholarships to a local public university because it would require him to permit Gypsy women as well as Gypsy men to attend. This actual event pitted the gender-based conventions of Gypsy society against the unfair provision of educational opportunities for one gender and not another. The student essays were scored in terms of whether or not they subordinated the issue to either morality or convention, vacillated between the two domains without coordination, or integrated the moral and conventional elements of the event through domain coordination. Findings were that students who had Domain Appropriate teaching were the only ones to coordinate elements from both domains spontaneously. In contrast, two-thirds of the students in the Moral instructional condition subordinated the issue entirely to its moral elements. Conversely, and as we had expected, a majority of students (including females) in the Convention instructional condition subordinated the issue to its conventional elements.

This last set of findings has particular relevance for our aim to develop students' capacity for critical moral reflection. Obviously, the students in the Convention instructional condition were hampered in their ability to attend to the moral implications of the gender-based conventions of Chicago's Gypsy community. Their prioritization of concerns for social organization was fostered by their recent educational experiences, which heightened the salience of those conventional elements. The social conservatism of their curriculum appeared to foster a similar conservatism in their reading of this real-life social issue.

Conversely, the students in the Moral instructional condition prioritized the moral elements of the situation, guiding the social arguments made in their essays. The prioritization of morality is recognized in philosophy as requisite for ethical judgment and behavior (Baumrind 1998). However, the "idealist" social critics in the Moral condition of our study did not spontaneously consider the social-organizational ramifications of their single-minded attention to morality. In real life, however, there are always organizational costs to any change in the conventional social structure. For example, a single-minded attention to needs for gender equality in careers leaves unanswered any number of practical questions in terms of how one should restructure the conventions of the family. When all is said and done, somebody has to do the dishes, raise the children, and so forth (Harrington, 1999).

The students in the Domain Appropriate instructional condition did prioritize the moral elements of the situation, arguing in their essays against the Gypsy king's decision. However, their arguments also acknowledged the ramifications this decision might have for the conventional organization of Gypsy society, and they offered constructive suggestions for resolving those changes. When we argue for a critical moral perspective as a goal of Domain Appropriate moral education, we are not simply advocating the development of single-minded moral criticism of social-conventional systems but, rather, this more integrative form of social critique.

The results of this study provided the springboard from which we went on to develop domain-based values education at elementary schools, middle schools, and high schools. Our experiences have been primarily with students grades 5 and above. However, the basic principles underlying domain-based values education are applicable at any age level. The general approach, which will be described in this chapter, can easily be integrated into existing developmental approaches to early education, such as those presented by DeVries and Zan (1994) and the Child Development Project (Battistich et al. 1991).

CONSTRUCTING A DOMAIN APPROPRIATE CURRICULUM

Communicative Discourse

A number of media and activities may be employed to generate conceptual change in the social area. Teachers we have worked with have employed diverse activities, from artistic expression through painting, sculpture, and dance to role playing, reading and writing stories, and constructing video presentations as ways to engage students around social and moral issues. Ultimately, however, the construction of more developed social understandings relies on discussion. This is because discussion is the only means we have of allowing one person's ideas to come into direct contact with another's. We see this at an early level in the arguments and negotiations among young children. Without such argumentation, there would be no reason for a child to assume that others do not hold the same position as they do, and certainly no reason to assume that the other person might be in the right (Piaget 1932). At an advanced level, discussion can take place through interactive writing, and we are beginning to see a revolution in that form of communication through the Internet. In whatever form discourse takes, it must result in transformations in the individual's ways of thinking about social issues if it is to have an impact on development.

In early efforts at moral education, it was assumed that discourse had to take place between individuals who were within one developmental stage of each other in terms of their moral reasoning (Blatt and Kohlberg 1975). On the basis of that assumption, teachers were instructed, when leading moral discussions, to provide statements to students one stage above the modal level of the class. Research on this "plus one" assumption proved it to have little use in actual classroom discourse (Berkowitz and Gibbs 1983; Berkowitz, Gibbs, and Broughton 1980). What this research uncovered was that it is very difficult for teachers to generate plus-one statements in the flow of an actual classroom conversation, and they were in fact quite rare in occurrence. More importantly, even when such plus-one statements were provided by experts, their input into the discussion had less of an impact on students' moral reasoning than did the statements of peers.

When the researchers looked at the factors that made for effective discussion, they discovered that the most important variable was whether or not students' statements constituted efforts to actively transform the arguments that they had heard others make. They labeled such statements *transacts*. Transacts are responses that attempt to extend the logic of the speaker's argument, refute the assumptions of the speaker's argument, or provide a point of commonalty between the two conflicting positions. Passive listening and simple efforts to restate or give back the speaker's argument were not associated with conceptual change. This last finding is a rather revealing indictment of simple, direct instruction and regurgitation as an educational method.

The use of transactive discussion in and of itself, however, may not be an optimal vehicle for values education. This is because one can use transactive argumentation in two fundamentally different ways. Here we are going to borrow loosely from the distinction that the philosopher Jurgen Habermas (1991) makes between *strategic* action and *communicative* discourse. When we are engaged in strategic action, our goal is somehow to get the other person to agree with, and go along with, our own point of view and our own goals. A great deal of our conversations are of this strategic kind. The prototype of strategic discourse is debate. In a debate, the goal is to win the argument. It doesn't matter whether or not the position we take is the most defensible, but whether or not we are able to convince the other, or convince the judges, that we have been able to outdo our opponent in presenting our case. When we are engaged in communicative discourse, however, the goal is to arrive at the best, most compelling position regarding the issue. It is the shared recognition of the force of the reasoning and not the power or skill of the debater that is the winner. In a strategic discourse, the outcome is unilateral; someone wins. In a communicative discourse, the outcome is mutual; the argument wins.

The goal of sociomoral discourse is to have the argument win, not an individual student or elite group of students. In our approach to sociomoral education, we attempt to engage students in activities that move toward communicative discourse. In doing this, we are assuming that the overall moral atmosphere of the classroom is compatible with this form of instruction. In effect, the use of communicative discourse contributes to an overall moral climate of mutual respect and cooperation that serves not only social growth but academic achievement as well.

What follows, then, are some suggestions for how to structure communicative discussions, as well as some exercises for how to prepare students to engage in effective sociomoral discussion. Students and teachers find these exercises fun. They should be used early in the term to prepare students for later work. They may be used sporadically thereafter as a way to develop discussion skills, but they shouldn't be overdone. These exercises, constructed with the help of Marvin Berkowitz, make use of the discoveries from his research on transactive discourse, and they borrow from practices that teachers have long used to help students engage in productive discussions. The initial listening exercise may be used at all grade levels. The transactive discourse exercises are intended for use with students in grades 4 and above.

Warm ups: Learning to Listen. In order for students to discuss one another's ideas and points of view, they need to be able to listen to what each other has to say. This first activity is intended simply to address the tendencies among some students to listen to others only in the sense of hearing their voices until they have stopped talking so that the first student may begin. This sort of parallel conversation is common among very young children, but it is an affliction that many older students and adults share as well. The purpose of the game is to get each player to paraphrase the statement of another speaker accurately. It is similar to the game "telephone," except in this case, the goal is accuracy.

Place students in threes. Player (1) tells something brief about himself to player (2). Player (2) restates it as accurately as possible to (3). Player (3) then evaluates whether or not the paraphrase was accurate. Player (2) then tells something brief to player (3) with player (1) as the "checker" until all players have had a turn at each role.

Transactive Discourse: Elaboration Game. One of the simpler transacts is to extend the arguments made by a previous speaker. This game may be used directly after the listening game since it extends the use of paraphrase. In this game, the student must take into account what the previous person said and elaborate on it. Prior to play, the teacher models a simple elaboration of a previous statement. The teacher then gives the class an interesting issue to discuss. Over the past three years we have used the following issues: Should the Chicago Bulls rehire Dennis Rodman? Should the Congress impeach President Clinton? Should the mom have a say in whether or not a person your age cleans up his/her room?

Place students in circles of up to 6 players. Player (1) begins by expressing a point of view. Player (2) paraphrases the statement made by player (1) and elaborates or extends it. Player (3) does the same with the statement made by player (2). This continues until all students have had a turn at extending the argument. With elementary-age children, the teacher should circulate from· group to group to hear whether or not children are accurate in providing elaborations, and helping out when this doesn't occur. With junior and senior high school students, the teacher can assign one member of each group to serve as "checker."

Transactive Discourse: Rebuttal Game. The rebuttal game is an extension of the elaboration game and uses the same procedure, except that each student must paraphrase and offer a refutation of the argument advanced by the previous speaker.

Transactive Discourse: Integrative Resolution. This final version is one that is intended for use with high school sophomores and above, or with very advanced younger students. It requires the students to listen to both an initial argument and its refutation, and then taking both arguments into account, offer an integrative resolution of the two positions. Prior to this exercise, the teacher should model an integrative resolution.

Students are placed in groups of 6. Player (1) states a position, which player (2) then paraphrases and refutes. Player (3) then paraphrases the positions taken by both players (1) and (2) and offers an argument that resolves the differences between the two positions. Player (2) then offers a new position that player (3) refutes and player (4) integrates. This continues until each player has had a turn at offering an integrative resolution.

Employing Communicative Discourse

Once students have developed basic listening and argumentation skills, they are ready to engage in constructive group discussions about social issues. There is no single correct way to go about structuring these discussions. The approach we have taken makes use of work on moral-dilemma discussion (Oser 1986; Power, Higgins, and Kohlberg 1989a), along with the suggestions and guidance of the experienced teachers with whom we have collaborated.

At the outset, it is important to convey the basic norms and goals of communicative discourse. Listing Jurgen Habermas's (1991) formal criteria for communicative discourse is not a particularly good route to take, unless the students are in a university philosophy course. We have found it useful, when presenting the goals of these discussions to students, to compare and contrast winning a debate with the process of talking with friends so as to come up with the best solution to a problem. In order to maximize student participation, and also to allow the teacher to provide some shared experiences with the whole class, the process we have employed uses both small-group and whole-class discussion.

Small groups should contain 5 or 6 students and be diverse in terms of ethnicity, gender, and student academic ability (Aronson and Patnoe 1997). This diversity is in itself a part of the "hidden" values curriculum, and it also maximizes the likelihood that developmental differences important to these discussions will exist among students. The content of the discussions is framed by issues provided by the teacher, which either have been drawn directly from the academic content the students are working on, or is related in some way to an academic goal of the class. The discussions are guided by a series of questions provided by the teacher. One of the students uses this series of questions to direct the course of the conversation. (We will take up the ways in which to construct these materials in the next section of the chapter.)

In our intervention studies, we have tended to divide the class time roughly 60:40 between small-group and whole-class discussion of issues. Whole-class discussion follows the small-group work. It is useful in that it affords an opportunity for students to hear what other positions were taken by class members. It also affords an opportunity for the teacher to direct students to attend to the different arguments that are offered up by class members. In this way, the teacher helps to draw out similarities in strands of thought, and helps students to attend to contradictions in arguments and unresolved positions. The teacher's role here is to serve as a model for how to listen to the flow of an argument and how to bring the pieces of a discussion into focus. The teacher has an opportunity at this juncture of making sure that all of the relevant questions she intended the students to cover have been addressed. The teacher should not short-circuit the students' efforts to construct their own understandings by throwing out the "right" answers. A more useful thing for the teacher to do is to throw out a provocative point for students to ponder further.

In our approach, discussions are used as a tool for academic instruction, not as an added-on activity. Thus, we always link in-class discussions with a written homework assignment in which students are asked to write a brief essay summarizing their position on the issue considered in the class discussion. Language arts teachers naturally use these discussions as a starting-off point for students' written work. This linkage serves several purposes. First, it makes clear to students that the discussion has relevance for their ability to complete their homework or other assignments, and thus increases the likelihood that student discussions will remain on task. Second, the written activity asks the student to think about the issues at a later time and to transform their ideas into another medium. This act of written production, then, serves to deepen the impact of the exercise on the student's thinking. Grading of homework or other academic products is based on standard academic criteria established by the teacher. Grading is never to be based on whether or not the student arrived at the correct "value" or the correct developmental level of social reasoning. (We will take up this issue of assessment in some detail in the final section of the chapter.)

As a final comment before turning to examples of curricular materials, we should keep in mind that any instructional activity can become routine and boring to students if it is overused. We have found it best to limit the use of these discussions to no more than two sessions per week.

GENERATING DOMAIN APPROPRIATE
MATERIALS AND LESSONS

The greatest challenge for a teacher wishing to engage in domain appropriate practice is to identify issues within the regular academic curriculum that will generate discussion and reflection around a particular values domain. Obviously, some academic areas lend themselves more readily to this process than others. Language arts, social studies, and health courses are rife with social and moral values issues. Other courses, such as mathematics, are less amenable to social-values discussion. The natural sciences are somewhere in between.

One of the most effective examples of domain appropriate practice was developed by a high school biology teacher. The unit he developed on reproductive biology and population ecology required that students systematically consider issues of personal choice, societal structure, morality, and the shifting assumptions that discoveries in biogenetics hold for our current view of this set of issues. Among the questions he asked his students to consider was whether parents should be able to select for specific genetic properties in their children, and whether society should be able to require parents to provide gene therapy (i.e., alter the genetic makeup) of a child with a genetic defect, such as Down's syndrome. This teacher's students were, thereby, asked to learn a great deal about biology but were also integrating that knowledge with their moral and social growth.

In constructing domain-related tasks, the teacher uses the criteria for moral, conventional, and personal issues to identify salient value-laden issues in the academic content or assignments for the class. Most issues that are contextualized will have some degree of domain overlap. However, the issue of overlap should only be addressed when elements from more than one domain are highly salient. Once an issue has been identified, the teacher should either present a synopsis or abstract of the issue, or develop a hypothetical situation that illustrates the issue the teacher wants to focus upon. The teacher then prepares a handout that contains a set of questions for students to address. Students are asked via these questions to interpret or resolve the domain-related issues contained in the abstract or scenario.

The issues that the students work with should not be resolvable by looking up information in the textbook. In addition, they should contain some element of controversy, in the sense that students might take different positions in arriving at their conclusions. These two points both are central to generating the cognitive dissonance needed for development and are elements in maintaining student interest and motivation (Nicholls 1984). In traditional developmentally based moral education, issues for discussion are presented in the form of dilemmas. Dilemmas by definition are controversial and are good sources for student discussion. However, not all interesting social issues constitute dilemmas, and reliance on dilemmas as a basis for curricula would be overly restrictive.

Finally, the lesson should be tied to either a homework assignment or some other written product. One way to do this is to ask students to write an essay responding to a short list of the most central questions from the in-class discussion. To get a better idea of how to do this, let's turn to some concrete examples.

Conventional Issues

Examples of social conventions are readily found in literature and stories read by students at all grade levels. Depictions of the routines of family life, manners of dress, or ways of addressing elders have shifted over time, and stories often capture ways of life that bring these conventions into focus for students. In addition, teachers may use the literature from different American ethnic groups to allow students to experience the conventions that differentiate them from one another, as well as the moral commonalties that tie them together.

For example, one of the suburban school districts we work with has begun to intersperse selections from the *Norton Anthology of African American Literature* (Gates and McKay 1997) throughout their junior high and high school American literature courses, rather than focus solely on modern African American writers in the month of February (Black History Month). Among the selections they employ to develop students' concepts of social convention are passages from Gwendolyn Brook's, "Maude Martha" (i.e., "tradition and Maude Martha," "kitchenette folks"), which depict everyday life among African Americans.

History is also a very rich area for social-conventional issues. The following example stems from an event in early American history. The curricular unit was designed for use with eighth-grade students who are moving from the Level 4 negation of social convention to Level 5 affirmation of convention as constitutive of social systems. What follows is the handout that the teacher distributed to his students to generate their full discussion.

King George's Letter to Washington

After the revolutionary war between England and the American colonies, the United states was formed and George Washington was elected first President of the United States. Many problems with England continued, however, because the English government did not recognize the United States as a country. There was no way to exchange ambassadors, have trade agreements, or settle war debts. The king of England wrote a letter to George Washington to start negotiations. He addressed the letter to Mr. George Washington. When Washington received the letter from the king of England, he saw that it was addressed to Mr. George Washington instead of to President George Washington. So, Washington returned the letter without reading it.

Discussion Questions

1. Was Washington right or wrong to return the letter to the king of England because it was addressed to Mr. Washington instead of President Washington? Why?
2. Why do you think Washington returned the letter?
3. In the story we learn that the letter was related to negotiations regarding having England recognize the United States as a country. In what sense might the way that the letter is addressed have something to do with England recognizing the United Sates?
4. What is the significance of titles like president and king for the way a society is structured?
   4a. Who do you think is a more important person, a king or a president?
5. In countries that have kings and queens, people bow or curtsy when they first meet them. Why don't we do that when greeting the president?
6. Suppose that an individual, such as a news reporter, doesn't like or respect a particular president. Would it be all right for that individual to express his or her lack of regard by addressing the president without using a title, such as Mr. President or Madame President?
7. Could we have a society that didn't use different titles for people who are in different positions, such as doctors or presidents?
   7a. How might that change society?
8. How about at school? Why do we use titles here for teachers (Mr. and Mrs.) but not for students?
   8a. What do those titles tell us about the way our society at school is structured?
9. Suppose we did away with using titles like Mr. and Mrs. for teachers. What do you think of that?

This issue works well with this age group (grades 7–9) because it captures students at a point in developmental transition, and it forms a natural point in which students will disagree over Washington's conduct, based on their interpretation of the structural function of conventions. The teacher has placed hints, here and there, of the relationship between convention and social structure (i.e., question 3) both to draw out these understandings from the developmentally advanced students and to provide a scaffold for the students who have no idea as to why Washington would return the letter. In fact, the structural nature of development does not permit immediate transformations in students' thinking, and students who are solidly in Level 4 provide explanations for Washington's conduct as based on personal conceit and as functionally irresponsible; "After all, what's more important, his title or getting things going with England?" In his use of the whole-class follow-up discussion, the teacher directed the class to address the main positions taken by the students. For example, he asked the class, "Some people seem to be arguing that Washington's actions were due to his own personal conceit. What do you think of that?"

As we indicated earlier in the chapter, this type of exercise, conducted over several months, does lead to conceptual shifts in students' understandings of convention. We have also discovered that development in the conventional domain has ramifications for students' abilities to comprehend certain aspects of the academic curriculum. As an offshoot of our work with teachers of history, we explored whether or not students' conceptions of social convention were related to their academic success in the course itself (Nucci and Charlier 1983). The medium for the study was a freshman-year world history course. World history concerns many issues, but a central element in making sense of the myriad dates, places, and names is to see history as interactions and transformations among societies. For example, students in world history classes are presented with the customs and traditions of various cultures at different points in time and are asked to relate them to current conditions.

The question that we addressed in our study was whether or not students' levels of understanding about convention would be related to how well they did on various components of their history tests. We were also interested in knowing whether success on history exams was due to the level of conventional reasoning or to general cognitive growth. We assessed general cognitive growth with a Piagetian measure of formal operations, which had been theorized as the level of cognitive reasoning needed to understand societies as social systems.

The instructional unit that was the focus of the study dealt with early China. The unit exam had two parts, a multiple-choice section, which asked students to identify the names of particular historical figures, dates, and places on a map of China, and an essay portion, which asked students to interpret elements of the content of their chapter. The content of the essay exam was drawn directly from the questions presented at the end of the chapter. It included questions such as the following: "Confucius said, 'Let the ruler be a ruler, and the subject a subject; let the father be a father, and a son a son.' What did Confucius mean by this? How does this relate to how Confucius thought Chinese society should be organized?"; "How was the view of society described by Confucianism related to Chinese religion and the organization of the family in early China?"; "How is Taoism different from Confucianism? Which of these two views is most like American society?" The multiple-choice portion of the exam was machine scored, and the essay portion was graded by another experienced teacher who was not a faculty member at the students' high school.

What we discovered was that general cognitive development (whether a student was a concrete or formal operational thinker) had no relationship to students' level of reasoning in the social-conventional domain, and it had no predictive value on the students' essays. Piagetian level was correlated with their scores on the multiple-choice part of the exam. Level of reasoning about societal convention, however, positively contributed to the students' scores on both the multiple-choice and essay parts of the test. Societal-domain level alone accounted for 54% of the variation in students' essay scores. In fact, by combining a student's multiple-choice score and his or her level of conventional domain reasoning, we were able to account for 97% of the variations in the grades students received on their essays. What we also found in this study was that the students who were participating in an experimental section, which integrated domain appropriate values education into their history course, scored higher on a schoolwide final exam than did students in the other sections, which employed traditional instruction.

Moral Issues

A number of moral issues cut across age groups and come up in the academic curriculum. One of these issues is what constitutes a fair or just response to harm that was done to you. The eye-for-an-eye reasoning we brought up in Chapter 8 has variations that reappear in different contexts in literature and history. With younger children, these issues are often presented through stories about animals in order to reduce the anxiety they might produce. One story, called "Bimbo the Bully," that was used by a second-grade teacher we work with tells of an aquarium that decided to introduce a young whale into the dolphin area. The whale was so boisterous that he continually injured the dolphins. So the aquarium keepers reduced the water level until it beached the whale but allowed the dolphins to continue swimming. As a a result, the whale was very upset and began crying out in distress. The dolphins, who were free to swim around, did not ignore the whale but instead came up close to him and comforted him. Afterwards the aquarium keepers raised the water level and allowed the whale to swim freely again. But now the whale swam carefully so as not to hurt his dolphin friends.

This teacher reported to us that her students all respond to this story, but that it is especially useful for her class "bullies" who often identify with the whale. In discussing the story, the teacher takes advantage of this identification to help the "bully" see why the dolphins were afraid of him, and to help the other children see that the "bully" might also need their friendship and comfort. In her discussions, she asks the children whether or not the dolphins would have been justified in hitting the whale back, when the water level was low, in order to teach him a "lesson." She also asks the children to explain why they thought that the dolphins acted as they did. If, in her view, she feels that the "bully" is feeling safe in the conversation, she connects the story to the children's own experiences by asking them to describe similar incidents on the playground. She uses this "teachable moment" not to preach about what the children should do or to label the virtues brought out in the story, such as kindness or forgiveness, but rather to engage the students in their own process of problem solving.

The theme of justice versus retribution is also captured in the following incident in American history, which several teachers have used with junior and senior high school students. It concerns John Brown's raid. What follows is an example of these units taken from the same curriculum as the George Washington example.

John Brown's Raid

In May, 1856, a border raid from Missouri devastated the antislavery town of Lawrence, Kansas. Within a few days, John Brown, who was strongly opposed to slavery, together with his sons and a few companions retaliated by attacking a settlement at Pottawatomie Creek, Missouri. The raid killed five settlers. John Brown had hoped that his actions would spark a slave rebellion, but that did not occur.

Discussion Questions

1. Was John Brown justified in leading a retaliatory raid against the proslavery settlement?
2. How far should a person go in retaliation? Is it right to hurt others as much as they have hurt you or the people you care about?
   2a. Is there a difference between vengeance and justice?
3. Brown had hoped that his actions would set off a slave rebellion. If that had taken place, would it have justified the raid?

Some of the teachers using this unit extend the discussion by having students discuss the following quotations from Martin Luther King, Jr., and Malcolm X, which the teacher first saw at the end of the Spike Lee movie *Do the Right Thing*.

> Violence as a way of achieving racial justice is both impractical and immoral. It is impractical because it is a descending spiral ending in destruction for all. The old law of an eye for an eye leaves everybody blind. It is immoral because it seeks to humiliate the opponent rather than win his understanding; it seeks to annihilate rather than to convert. Violence is immoral because it thrives on hatred rather than love. It destroys community and makes brotherhood impossible. It leaves society in monologue rather than dialogue. Violence ends by defeating itself. It creates bitterness in the survivors and brutality in the destroyers.
>
> Martin Luther King, Jr.

> I think there are plenty of good people in America, but there are also plenty of bad people in America and the bad ones are the ones who seem to have all the power and be in these positions to block things that you and I need. Because this is the situation, you and I have to preserve the right to do what is necessary to bring an end to the situation, and it doesn't mean that I advocate violence, but at the same time I am not against using violence in self-defense. I don't even call it violence when it's self-defense, I call it intelligence.
>
> Malcolm X

Discussion Questions

1. Which of these positions do you favor? Why?
2. Can you integrate these two positions? How would you do it?

For their homework assignment, the teacher asks the students to write an essay in which they compare and contrast and also attempt to integrate the views presented in these quotations. This exercise can be taken a step further by extending the discussion to include two class periods on the death penalty. I mention this because it is an excellent example of how a teacher may integrate informational assumptions into a values lesson. What students learn from the following exercise is to recognize that their moral positions may rest on incomplete or faulty informational assumptions.

During the first class period, the teacher simply presents the following proposition to her students and asks them to engage in communicative discourse and arrive at a shared position:

"It is resolved that the state of Illinois shall not have a death penalty."

During the last ten minutes of the class period, the teacher lists the unresolved differences among the students. These differences stem primarily from factual disagreements over the cost of incarceration, the rate of error in conviction and execution, the tendency for convicts with life sentences to be released and commit additional crimes, the need for victims' families to receive retribution, and the social class and racial discrepancies in the use of the death penalty. The teacher then divides the class up into research teams charged with obtaining as much information as they can about each of these unresolved factual matters. She then distributes copies of the reports to the class and reconvenes the discussion for a second class period.

Mixed-Domain Issues

There are multiple ways in which moral, conventional, and personal elements may overlap in social situations. What follows are examples of curricular units dealing with (1) second-order moral concerns, (2) structural contradictions between convention and morality, and (3) interactions among convention, morality, and personal choice.

This first example illustrates second-order moral/conventional overlap. It is an extension of the discussion on the use of forms of address developed in the unit on King George's letter to Washington. The extension illustrates how the unfair application of a convention can have immoral consequences. However, in order for the student to see this in the present example, he would have to understand the role of forms of address in signifying a person's social position. This was the central element of the king's letter unit. The extension comes from American literature. It is a passage from Maya Angelou's *I Know Why the Caged Bird Sings*. The passage describes an incident in which a local judge mistakenly refers to Angelou's grandmother by the title Mrs. This was a mistake because the conventions of the period were that whites, but not blacks, were referred to by titles. In the situation Angelou describes, her grandmother was subpoenaed to give testimony before the judge. What follows is the passage and the stimulus questions students use to guide their discussion:

The judge asked that Mrs. Henderson be subpoenaed, and when Momma arrived and said she was Mrs. Henderson, the judge, the bailiff and other whites in the audience laughed. The judge had really made a gaffe, calling a Negro woman Mrs., but then he was from Pine Bluff and couldn't have expected that a woman who owned a store in that village would also turn out to be colored. The whites tickled their funny bones with the incident for a long time, and the Negroes thought it proved the worth and majesty of my grandmother. (Angelou, p. 39)

Discussion Questions

1. What was the source of humor for the white people described in the passage?
2. What did the title "Mrs." signify? Why did it matter so much?
   2a. How is this use of the title "Mrs." similar to the use of the title "Mr." in the George Washington situation we discussed earlier?
3. How did the use of titles for grown-ups reflect American society at that time?
4. What issues of fairness do you see in this passage?
5. How do they relate to the use of titles?
   5a. Is it always unfair to call an adult by their first name rather than by their title? If not, then why would it matter here?

The next example illustrates how an existing norm, in this case the conventional treatment of older children as having more privileges than younger ones, is in conflict with the moral requirements of equality. The example unit is used in fourth- and fifth-grade language arts. It makes use of role play. The academic component asks students to write a "polemic" essay addressing the issue of age discrimination.

Children's Wages (Role Play and Discussion)

Three children (3 girls) select roles and scripts. One girl is an adult, the other two girls sisters.

Teacher: In this scene we have a girl who is 11 (use student's name), her sister (use student's name) who is 16, and a woman (use Mrs. with student's last name) who needs to hire a baby-sitter. Her regular baby-sitter is the younger sister. However, she is busy and can't do it. So, Mrs. X asks her older sister to baby-sit for her.

Older sister: [Talking with younger sister] Hi (sister's name). Guess what. I agreed to baby-sit for Mrs. (name) this weekend. So, you don't have to worry about it.

Younger Sister: That's great! How much is she paying you?

Older sister: $5

Younger Sister: What! She only pays me $3!

Older sister: Well, I am in high school, you know. I guess she figures that she should pay me more because I am older after all.

Younger sister: This stinks. I'm gonna call Mrs. (name) and see what gives.

Younger sister: [On phone] Hi, Mrs. (name), my sister (name) told me that you pay her $5 to baby-sit, but you only offered me $3.

Mrs. (Name): [On phone] Well, (name) your sister is five years older than you. I think that $3 is a good wage for an 11-year-old.

Younger sister: But, I am doing exactly the same job, and I baby-sit more for you than she ever does.

Mrs. (name): Yes, but you are only 11 and your sister is in high school. I am offering you $3, take it or leave it.

Group Discussion

Teacher opens the discussion to the class:

1. Well, what do you think (younger sister) should do, accept the baby-sitting job at the wage Mrs. X is offering or not? How come?

The teacher then turns to the girls who enacted the role play and asks: "Girls – answer the question of what she should do as the person whose role you are playing." Once each girl has spoken from the perspective of her role, the teacher returns to class discussion.

1. Is it okay for Mrs. X to offer the younger sister less than her older sister?
2. Do you think older teenagers generally get paid more than younger kids? How come?
3. What reasons can you think of for why older teenagers might get paid more for the same job than younger kids?
4. What do you think of those reasons?
5. Suppose that all of the adults in the neighborhood did the same thing and paid teenagers more than kids your age for doing the same the job? That was the norm. Would that be all right?
6. Taking everyone into account, what would be the best thing for Mrs. X to do in this situation? Why is that the best thing?
7. Okay, one last thing. We talked about what the younger sister should do, and what Mrs. X should do. But suppose Mrs. X stays with her original offer to the younger sister, should the older sister do anything in that case?
8. Is this really something the older sister should get involved in, or is this just something between the younger sister and Mrs. X?

The last portion of the discussion in this example is directed at having children consider whether a person in a position of relative advantage is obligated or should come to the aid of someone less advantaged. The following example, which illustrates the use of domain overlap, brings up the issue of personal responsibility along with other elements of personal choice. It also comes from our work with American history teachers. It concerns child labor laws and the shifts in conventions governing children and adults in the workplace as the country moved from an agrarian to an industrial society. The teacher who developed the original version of this unit provided the quotations used in its introduction, as well as the scenario used to guide discussion. Subsequent teachers have modified it to include the action-oriented segments concerning current child labor practices in producing the goods that U.S. children purchase. To help the reader follow the logic of the questions, I have inserted the letters M, C, or P next to questions to indicate which domains of thinking (moral, conventional, personal) the teacher is attempting to stimulate.

Glassborough Story
(Mixed-Domain Issue, Primarily Moral)

What follows are some quotations to get you to start thinking:

1. "The most beautiful sight we see is the child at labor; as early as he may get to labor, the more beautiful, the more useful does his life become."
   Asa Chandler (founder of Coca Cola)

2. "In Lawrence, Massachusetts, half the textile workers in the mills were girls between the ages of fourteen and eighteen."

3. "A considerable number of boys and girls die within the first two or three years of beginning work. Thirty-six of every one hundred of all the men and women who work in the mill die by the time they are twenty-five years old. The life span of the average mill worker in Lawrence is twenty-two years shorter than that of the owner."

The late 1800s was a period of rapid industrial growth in the United States. Competition among businesses was fierce as companies competed against one another for customers. In order to cut costs some businesses hired children under the age of 15 since they would work for lower wages than adults. This placed companies which did not hire children at a disadvantage. One business caught in this situation was the Glassborough bottle factory.

The owner of the Glassborough bottle factory, Mr. Galle, did not wish to hire children since his factory was dangerous and the children would have to work long hours after school. On the other hand, if he didn't hire children he would not be able to sell his bottles for a competitive price, and he would risk going out of business. In the end, Mr. Galle decided to hire children to work in his factory.

Discussion Questions

1. Was Mr. Galle right or wrong to have hired children to work in his factory? Why/Why not?
2. In Glassborough it was customary for children to work alongside adults on the farms and in the factories. How should that affect what Mr. Galle should do? (C)
3. What impact do child labor laws have on the way society is structured? (C)
4. Why might a society want to have children work alongside adults in factories? (C)
5. Did Mr. Galle have a right to hire children in order to remain competitive? Was it fair for him to have done that? (M)
6. In hiring children to work in his factory, Mr. Galle is placing them in a situation of considerable personal danger. What are Mr. Galle's obligations, given those conditions? (M)
7. Should children under the age of 15 have a right to work in a dangerous factory such as Mr. Galle's if they wish to? (P)
8. Taking everything into account, what would have been the right thing for Mr. Galle to have done in this situation? (M, C)

The following questions were designed for use with high school students:

9. Today, many products manufactured by American companies are produced in countries that allow young children to work in factories. Can you name any of those products?
10. Is it okay for individual Americans to buy those products? (M, P)
11. Should Americans take any actions to change the policies of the governments which allow child labor? (M, P)
12. Do members of one society have a right to intervene in the social practices of another society? (M, C)
13. On what moral basis, if any, can one society judge the customs and conventions of another society to be morally wrong?

In this last example, we see the questions developed by the high school teacher taking her students head-on into issues of moral and cultural relativism, tolerance, and moral chauvinism. These are questions that are important for helping students to begin taking moral stands and to recognize the relationships those moral positions have to social structure and culture. By having the students parse the moral and conventional aspects of the problem, she has provided them with an opportunity to develop a set of analytic tools for engaging in principled reflection on one of the thorniest issues of our ever-shrinking world. She has also given them a window into the process of moral self-reflection.

Issues of Assessment

A final question that might arise concerning the use of domain appropriate curricula is how one would go about conducting measurement or evaluation. From our perspective there are two levels to this question. At one level is determining whether or not a given programmatic use of domain appropriate practice results in sociomoral growth. A district, for example, may wish to determine the effectiveness of its values-education programs, or a university researcher may wish to determine if a particular application of domain apppropriate practice results in an increase in students' generation of domain coordinations. These are research questions that can be addressed most definitively by university researchers or professional evaluators employing interview methods (Turiel, 1983) or other tools available to the research community.

A second aspect of measurement and evaluation is at the level of the classroom. Here, the formal assessment tools used for programmatic evaluation are neither useful nor ethically justified. The scores generated by formal measurement instruments have little utility for a classroom teacher. What would it mean, for example, to learn that a group of students moved up half a stage in conventional reasoning over the course of the academic year? How does this translate into goals that a teacher can use to evaluate his or her effectiveness? How would a teacher translate such scores into meaningful evaluation of individual student progress? If John's conventional reasoning score moved up half a level, and Mark's score moved up one quarter of a level, does John deserve a higher grade? Is John a better person?

We have taken the position that assessment of all domain-based values units should be done solely in terms of the regular academic criteria of the class. These would include tests of knowledge of a subject area, integrative writing, flow of argument, or other traditional means of academic assessment. Students' moral and social reasoning can be included within such an assessment, but not as something separate from an evaluation of the assignment as a whole. For example, a language arts teacher may provide feedback to a seventh-grade student on the success or shortcomings of his efforts to take into account the moral and conventional elements of a multifaceted social issue. This would be similar to providing feedback on an essay in terms of the student's more general attention to basic elements of an argument. In such a case, the teacher is not grading the student as a sociomoral being but is providing standard academic feedback appropriate to the purposes of the course.

A teacher wishing to evaluate her own effectiveness as a sociomoral educator can use the arguments from classroom discussion and in written products to look for general shifts in the sociomoral reasoning of her students consistent with their developmental level. Table 4.1 in Chapter 4 provides some guidance in terms of age-typical levels of sociomoral reasoning. A third-grade teacher, for example, might look for movement among her students toward efforts to engage in moral reciprocity, rather than in egocentric resolutions of moral problems. At later grades a teacher would be looking for efforts by students to generate integrative moral positions that display attempts to find positions that would be most fair for all concerned. From fifth grade and above, these shifts in general level of thought should be coupled with evidence that children are developing a critical moral perspective (as described in this chapter) when dealing with multifaceted social issues. This approach to assessment is global in nature and does not ask that the teacher either grade her students on moral-development criteria or shift her focus from the academic purposes of her classroom. What is being proposed is a way for teachers to have a sense of their own efficacy in an often neglected area without adding yet another domain in which education becomes a matter of "teaching to the test."

DOMAIN APPROPRIATE CURRICULUM: SUMMARY AND NEW DIRECTIONS

The examples in this chapter are intended to provide a sense of the ways in which teachers may incorporate attention to domains of social reasoning in their everyday academic instruction. What these examples serve to illustrate is how one can use the curriculum to stimulate thought within a given domain and also bring children's social knowledge to bear in critically examining multifaceted social issues. The purpose of this book is to stimulate a new direction in teachers' thinking about how to go about integrating moral and social-values education into their everyday teaching. There are undoubtedly many other creative ways to address morality, convention, and personal issues within the curriculum, other than the methods just illustrated. There are also other areas of application to be developed.

Among the applications to be explored are how best to address personal conduct in such areas as substance use and abuse and sexuality. These are problematic behaviors dealt with in the general curriculum as specialty topics within health or other courses in response to the perceived failure of other institutions (e.g., the family) to address them adequately. A part of the difficulty in dealing with these topics successfully is that their multifaceted nature is often reduced by interested parties to one or another domain, rather than being dealt with in its entirety.

Drug use, for example, is treated by most adolescents as primarily a matter of prudence and personal choice (Berkowitz, Guerra, and Nucci 1991; Berndt and Park 1986; Killen, Leviton and Cahill 1989; Nucci, Guerra, and Lee 1989; Tisak and Tisak 1990). One study (Nucci et al. 1989) found that less than 20% of non–drug-using adolescents viewed regular use of cocaine as wrong because of the harm it might cause to others. This does not mean that most adolescents take a laissez-faire attitude toward drug use but, rather, that the decision of whether or not to do so is generally determined by their reading of the potential benefits and negative costs associated with drug consumption. For most adolescents, the perceived personal costs keep them from engaging in substance abuse. Adolescents can be directed to consider the social costs of their conduct to others (e.g., harm to family members, contributions to criminal activity) and to view it as wrong to engage in such conduct if it has consequences for other people (Killen et al. 1989). On the other hand, few adolescents prior to college age spontaneously consider such moral ramifications of the consumption of drugs or alcohol.

The example of drug use illustrates that we cannot simply reduce our concerns regarding all serious forms of children's and adolescents' behavior to issues of morality and moral education. In some instances, as in the case of sexual conduct, issues are so complex that they draw from a number of areas of social understanding. As we saw in Chapter 3 in our interviews with devout Christian and Jewish children, even a behavior as heavily condemned as premarital intercourse was not treated as an inherently moral issue. The moral aspect of sexuality, as in any other area of interpersonal conduct, has to do with issues of fairness, caring, and human welfare (Okin 1996). To the extent that moral education may be integrated into sex education, it would be in these often overlooked aspects of intimate conduct, which go beyond questions of whether or not to engage in sexual intercourse to include more basic questions of male–female relations.

A serious effort to engage adolescents in considering such multifaceted issues of personal conduct would require going beyond their cursory treatment in a mandatory health course to a more intensive and frank set of discussions extended over the time that students are in junior and senior high school. Such discussions would be structured around the principles of communicative discourse and domain appropriate practice that have guided our approach to the curriculum.

For example, discussions around sexual relations might include face-to-face conversations with groups of male and female students in which they would share their views of how they would like to be treated in a given situation. This would allow males and females to get beyond their own gender-based experiences to learn to interpret one another's intentions and aspirations. Such understandings would make use of universal moral motivations, but they would also allow males and females to begin to decode and adjust the conventions that are causing misunderstandings and inequities in male–female interactions. This is something quite different from preaching to boys about how to treat girls properly, and preaching to girls about how to act as women. It is also more than giving students strategies for how to resist peer pressure, and how to say "no" in response to requests to engage in improper or unwanted conduct. It is, instead, a process by which adolescent boys and girls would work through their own misperceptions about one another to arrive at a shared set of understandings about how to treat each other with mutual respect and grace.

As we saw in Chapter 8, such discussions could take place through domain appropriate adaptations of the "just community" model, recognizing that many of these issues have as much to do with restructuring convention and personal choice as they do with morality. There is also a considerable element of fact finding that would need to go into these discussions, and an important function of the teacher/advisor would be to direct students toward resources to help them get information that would inform their perspectives. There is, therefore, no reason not to use these discussions over social issues as a way to enhance students' more general academic skills and appreciation for their utility in resolving real-life concerns. Unfortunately, most traditional high schools now relegate student discussion around such issues to special after-school programs (such as "snowball") that attract a minority of students. In the future, a more effective approach will require some structural accommodation in school scheduling to permit discourse by all students around these central issues of social life.

We have now covered both the social climate and curricular aspects of domain appropriate sociomoral education. These two complementary elements comprise the essence of values education. What remains to be discussed is how schools may contribute to the integration of the students' sociomoral knowledge in their motivational system. It is this third leg of the triangle that we will address in Chapter 10.

CHAPTER TEN

Fostering the Moral Self

The purpose of moral education is to increase the likelihood that students will develop into people who engage in moral conduct and who work to improve the moral structure of society. An integral part of that purpose is accomplished through the development of students' moral knowledge. It is sociomoral understanding that provides the capacity to evaluate the moral elements of social situations and the normative structure of society. Knowing the good, however, is not always sufficient to motivate someone to do the good. For moral action to take place the individual must also want to do what is moral, rather than to engage in actions that lead to other goals.

There are two basic ways in which individuals are motivated to do something. One is to respond to external incentives in the form of punishments and rewards. The second is to engage in actions because of their perceived value to the individual (Deci 1995). It is obviously much easier for teachers and schools to manipulate external rewards and punishments than it is to somehow connect up with or influence students' intrinsic reasons for doing something. Yet it is the connection with intrinsic, non-pragmatic motivation (Subbotsky 1995) that is the most effective and enduring way in which to link up moral reasoning with action. As we saw in Chapter 7, this means building up the linkages among children's moral affect, their moral understandings, and their construction of personal identity. The integration of these three elements of affect, reasoning and identity form the "moral self."

CHILDHOOD ANTECEDENTS OF THE MORAL SELF
AND CLASSROOM PRACTICES

The connections between moral identity and behavior do not have much force until middle childhood and adolescence. However, the foundation for moral identity is formed in early childhood. There are three related aspects of the process by which young children link their conduct to their sense of self. The first is the generation of a general world view and the corresponding placement of self in relation to that world view. The second aspect is the construction of self-regulation or self-discipline that enables the child to engage in actions concordant with his or her moral identity. The third aspect is the assignment of meaning to the labels associated with the various components of children's social and personal identities, such as gender, race, age, and whether they are "good" or "bad" children. We will take up this last element of early childhood identity later in this section.

Teachers and schools can help to establish the child's moral world view by means of the components of moral atmosphere discussed in Chapter 8. A climate of predictability, trust, emotional warmth, and reciprocity are the key elements to establishing a pattern of "goodwill" (Arsenio and Lover 1995) conducive to the emergence of the moral self (Noam 1993). As we discussed in Chapter 6, the child's sentiment of goodwill is critical to the child's willingness to forgo actions that might serve his or her own self-interest in situations where those actions would cause harm or injustice to someone else. By the same token, if the child concludes that the world is a dangerous, unloving, or arbitrary place then there is the possibility that the child will self-define as an outcast, or potential victim, and be more likely to feel justified in acting from self-interest in social situations where such actions would result in negative moral consequences for others.

With a positive moral atmosphere as a backdrop, schools can further contribute to the young child's construction of moral self-regulation through methods of classroom discipline that support and sustain the child's intrinsic reasons for acting in accord with what is morally right and socially appropriate (Deci 1995). For most developmentalist moral educators, approaches to classroom discipline that emphasize children's intrinsic motivation and moral autonomy are considered an integral part of what they would consider to be a positive moral classroom atmosphere (Battistich et al. 1991; DeVries and Zan 1994). However, an atmosphere of warmth, predictability, and fair treatment can also form the backdrop for more traditional, consequentialist approaches to classroom discipline and parenting (Smetana 1995b, 1996). Therefore, we will treat methods of classroom discipline as a separate element of children's socialization. Borrowing from the Child Development Project, I refer to these newer constructivist models by the term "developmental discipline."

Developmental Discipline

In recent years there has been a convergence around methods of class-room discipline with young children (Battistich et al. 1991; DeVries and Zan 1994; Dreikurs 1968; Dreikurs, Grunwald, and Pepper 1982) that are compatible with constructivist views of children's motivation (Deci 1995; Harter 1992; Nicholls 1984, 1989), and sociomoral development. The core idea behind each of these developmental approaches, and the position be-ing advocated here, is a conception of classroom discipline as supporting acts of self-regulation that are consonant with the person's autonomously determined sociomoral goals. The key to these approaches is to get peo-ple to adopt what is socially desirable for their own reasons, rather than exerting external control over them. In Deci's (1995) terms, the goal is to have children construct integrated, rather than introjected, modes of self-regulation. The latter are imposed from outside, whereas the former are autonomously adopted/constructed as consistent with one's own beliefs and, in later years, one's true identity. The following classroom sugges-tions are derived from the shared tenets of these approaches.

Supporting Positive Behavior. One way to avoid discipline problems in the classroom is to provide feedback that supports children's positive behavior. This feedback can come in the form of tangible rewards, but most often comes in the form of adult praise. While the use of positive feedback and rewards can help sustain and guide a child's developing morality, an overreliance on rewards and positive adult feedback can backfire and actually undermine the child's moral motivation (Deci 1995). Although this is a relatively new position within American psychology, hints of this point of view were already being suggested in the 1950s by B. F. Skinner (1948, 1953), who argued that intrinsic reinforcement was more effective than external reinforcement in stimulating and maintain-ing human behavior.

The limitations of external reinforcement are most readily apparent with the case of offering children tangible rewards for their good behav-ior. There is a substantial research literature indicating that providing ex-ternal rewards to children, such as gold stars or stickers, reduces their tendency to engage in the rewarded behavior spontaneously. In other words, children shift from engaging in the behaviors for their own in-trinsic reasons toward doing things simply for the "money." This is not to say that rewards should never be given, but that the use of rewards should serve to *validate* what the child is already motivated to do, rather than as a means of "shaping" the child's behavior to conform to the wishes of adults (Deci 1995). For example, a child who has consistently treated classmates with kindness and generosity might well respond to a "citizenship" award as reflecting social validation for her actions, rather than as an effort to shape her behavior. On the other hand, the routine awarding of pins or other emblems, and the weekly public listing of the names of children who have displayed "virtue" or "character" as advocated by some neotraditionalist programs (cf., Character Counts), exemplify how *not* to support children's positive behavior (Kohn 1997). In such cases, the rewards become overt sources of competition and commodities in and of themselves. While they may temporarily serve to mold and shape children's conduct, they also undermine the very motives such programs seek to instill.

Similarly, in providing praise to a child, we need to differentiate between positive statements that validate the child and encourage his or her efforts at moral action from "controlling praise" that serves the adult's desire to "mold and shape" the child. Controlling praise focuses attention upon the child, rather than the child's actions, is nonspecific in content, and often employs terms that are superlative in nature. Examples of such praise are "Allison, you are such a good girl." "Jack, you are the nicest child I have had in class in years." The effect of controlling praise is to give the child a momentary boost in self-esteem, but at the cost of setting the bar at an unrealistically high level. Is it realistic to assume that Allison and Jack are always going to be so superlatively well behaved? In addition, the feedback to the child says little about what it is that warranted being labeled "such a good boy" or "the nicest child in years." Any reasons that the children might have had for doing the behaviors that won them their accolades are lost in the focus upon the evaluations of the children themselves. Thus, one risk associated with controlling praise is that it moves the desire to engage in a behavior from intrinsic valuing of the action to an ego-oriented focus upon one's own perceived social status (Nicholls 1989). The moral self that is constructed on this basis may be superficially oriented toward behaving morally, but not for moral reasons. The child who needs to always be "such a good boy" in order to fit social expectations is not operating out of moral motivation but in order to sustain external approval.

In contrast, praise that takes the form of encouragement uses moderate language and focuses on the specifics of the action. Such praise lets the child know that his or her actions are appreciated, and also indicates that it is the actions that are being evaluated, and not the child himself. Examples of validating praise would be "Tatiana, that was a kind thing that you just did. I am sure that Marcy appreciated the time you spent with her when she wasn't feeling well." "Mike, thanks for helping clean up the room. It makes everything better for everyone. I really appreciate it." Encouraging praise is especially effective as a response to what we might refer to as "everyday acts of character." In the "encouraging praise" example, Mike might have been one of the children who never helped with cleanup time. For him to have done so might well have taken considerable personal effort. Acknowledgment from the teacher in the form of thanks would let him know that his efforts were recognized and his contribution validated. The teacher might even add a word of encouragement to "keep up the good work." Of course, a behaviorist might justifiably argue that such positive feedback is serving to shape Mike's positive social behavior. There is no reason to quibble over this point. The key elements are whether the teacher acts out of a genuine sense of appreciation, and whether Mike interprets the statement as validating his own efforts. In any case, praise should be used in moderation and directed at specific acts, rather than at the characteristics of children.

Responding to Misbehavior. An essential aspect of all learning is the making of mistakes. It would be nice to believe that moral education is a matter of guiding children down the "right" path, but the fiction of "error-free" learning has even less to do with morality than other aspects of education. While children are rarely, if ever, motivated to make purposeful mistakes in academic areas, the very nature of sociomoral misconduct is that it often involves actions that are counter to what the child knows to be the "right" thing to do. Correcting errors in the sociomoral area is not simply a matter of pointing out mistakes but also helping the child to choose to act in ways that are not always concordant with the child's immediate desires. Piaget's (1962) "conflict of will" is what is at stake, and not simply the epistemic question of the "objectively" right thing to do.

Helping the child choose to want to do the right thing is in part a function of teachers' disciplinary responses to children's misbehavior. In Chapter 8 we discussed the importance of providing domain-concordant messages as a way of connecting up with and furthering the child's moral and conventional understandings. Here we are dealing with the role of teacher-imposed sanctions. The complement to the developmentalist position regarding the use of rewards for appropriate behavior is that sanctions provided to young children in response to their misbehavior should not take the form of expiatory punishments designed solely to inflict discomfort or cost to the child (DeVries and Zan 1994). Expiatory punishments are to be avoided since they do not provide the child with any reason beyond the pragmatic goals of punishment avoidance or generation of teacher favor as a motivation for action. Since students associate expiatory punishments with the person meting them out, rather than with their own misconduct, such punishments invite revenge and provide students with a sense that they have the right to retaliate (Dreikurs and Cassel 1972). In other words, the morality of the situation becomes turned on its head as the student, guilty of misconduct, now becomes in his or her own mind the aggrieved party. Through the use of expiatory punishment, the teacher transforms the affective climate of the classroom into an environment of "ill will" that supports students' self-protective and "selfish" motivations.

Instead, sanctions should take the form of logical consequences connected in a meaningful way with the nature of the transgression (DeVries and Zan 1994; Dreikurs 1968; Dreikurs et al. 1982). Logical consequences include such things as restitution, depriving the transgressor of the thing misused, and exclusion. Because of the nonarbitrary, reciprocal nature of morality, it is somewhat easier to envision logical consequences for moral transgressions than for violations of social conventions. For example, if a child takes something away from another child, a logical consequence would be for the child to have to replace it. However, even conventions, once in place, have a logic associated with their function. A student who talks disruptively during story time might be asked by the teacher to leave the story area until he or she is able to rejoin the group and sit quietly. If this sanction is coupled with a domain appropriate statement of the rule or social-organizational function of the norm, the student is likely to see the connection between the sanction and the misbehavior. An indefinite or extended expulsion from the story area, however, would shift the consequence away from the behavior and become an arbitrary, expiative punishment, rather than a logical consequence (Dreikurs and Cassel 1972).

Teachers can increase the likelihood that children will accept the logical consequences of misbehavior by engaging them in group discussions about patterns of misbehavior occurring in the classroom, and by seeking their advice on how to avoid or reduce such problems in the future (Battistich et al. 1991; DeVries and Zan 1994). In Chapter 8 we offered the use of group discussions as a way of engaging children in the consideration of rules that should be in place to regulate or help guide children's conduct. In this case, the discussion concerns what to do about behaviors that the children agree are problematic. Through group discussion, the teacher can guide children to generate ideas about what would constitute appropriate logical consequences. Part of the teacher's role is to help the children focus on prevention of misbehavior. Another part is to help children moderate their tendency to come up with overly harsh consequences. Young children, because of their limited conceptions of fair reciprocity, are especially prone to mete out punishments that exceed what are reciprocal and fair consequences. By engaging children in such discourse, teachers move the consequences of misconduct from a top-down, adult-imposed act of power to autonomously constructed, objectified, logical outcomes reflecting values shared by the children.

Finally, an ethical response to children's misconduct must allow for the child's reentry and acceptance into the social group. Once the logical consequence has been met, the child must have the opportunity to move forward as a class member. Otherwise, the logical consequence is transformed into expiatory punishment with all of the negative ramifications already discussed. This is a fairly easy requirement to meet when it comes to typical transgressions of social convention. It is not always so easy when the transgression involves moral consequences to other classmates. While the teacher may be willing to move forward, the children may be unwilling to risk interactions with someone who had caused them pain or injustice. In such cases, as with an aggressive child, the teacher needs to help the transgressor understand the connections between aggressive conduct and the responses of his or her classmates. The teacher must also help the other children to decenter enough to recognize that they would not want to be permanently excluded either. This requires patience and persistence on the teacher's part, and is helped or hindered by the overall moral and affective climate of the school and classroom.

Summary

In sum, developmental discipline affords an approach to classroom management that is consistent with the processes by which children construct their sociomoral knowledge. By integrating developmental discipline with domain appropriate forms of teacher feedback (discussed in Chapter 8), teachers can contribute to children's construction of autonomously adopted, integrated reasons for wanting to act in moral and socially appropriate ways. Because these early patterns of action and moral motivation are concordant with the child's own perceptions and choices, they are coherent with the child's own emergent sense of personal identity. It is for this reason that such early experience provides a precursor for the construction of moral character – what we have referred to as the moral self.

In the context of a stable, emotionally warm and fair moral environment, children not only are likely to construct a sense of goodwill toward the social world but are also likely to adopt sociomoral self-labels of being a "good" or "nice" boy or girl. In early childhood, these moral self-labels are quite global in nature, and fleshing them out is a gradual and continuous lifelong process of integrating one's own personal narrative with one's developing sociomoral understandings within a cultural framework and worldview. Because of their generality, these aspects of self-concept do not serve as an important source of moral motivation for the young child. Instead, it is the sociomoral action schemata that children generate out of their social interactions, including their experiences with social sanctions, that guide sociomoral conduct in early childhood. Early-childhood educators contribute to children's moral development primarily through the ways in which actual classroom experiences impact upon children's sociomoral constructions.

However, early-childhood educators also impact upon the development of young children's construction of the moral self by means of the information they provide symbolically through their actions as role models and by the provision of cultural narratives contained in fairy tales, stories, and other media. These sources of symbolic interaction, which engage the child's imagination and feelings, provide young children with models against which to compare their own conduct, and with worlds against which to compare their own social experiences. As children develop, they begin to differentiate and to integrate this cultural information with their own personal experience to form more particular and psychologically potent notions of themselves as sociomoral beings.

EDUCATION AND FORMATION OF THE MORAL SELF
IN MIDDLE CHILDHOOD AND ADOLESCENCE

Elementary and secondary teachers can contribute to the child's formation of the moral self through continuation of the basic approach to discipline just outlined for young children, and by engaging students' burgeoning interest in constructing their sense of personal identity. Around 8 to 10 years of age, children begin assigning comparative values to the various aspects of their personal competencies and behavioral tendencies (Broughton 1978; Harter 1983; Nicholls and Miller 1984; Nucci 1977). It is at about this time that the "moral self" begins to take on motivational force. Children are now capable of, and interested in, comparing their actions against their self-conceptions (Power and Khmelkov 1998). The sociomoral worldview and action schemes established in early childhood provide the core content for the middle-childhood construction of a moral aspect of self. In adolescence, the process of identity formation becomes accelerated as the notion of self shifts from simple behavioral descriptions to a conception of self in terms of internal thoughts, feelings, beliefs, and values.

Throughout this process of identity formation, the moral self does not emerge in a vacuum but is constructed alongside of the child's notions of other aspects of themselves, such as boy or girl, student, athlete, and family member. In addition, the self that is emerging, while reflecting idiosyncratic preferences and choices, is also integrating cultural values, mannerisms, and predispositions toward reading social events in particular ways. This multifaceted and contextualized construction of self means that the relative salience of morality, and its role in defining the person as a whole, is neither simple nor straightforward.

Educators influence this process of moral self-construction by using the curricular practices outlined in Chapter 9 and by the direct treatment of students through the classroom moral atmosphere and disciplinary practices. These aspects of schooling provide students with opportunities to generate moral understandings and to connect them up with their own conduct. In addition, educators can affect the construction of the moral self through practices that engage students in self-reflection and provide students with information both from symbolic sources and direct experience that may heighten the salience of morality in students' lives.

In thinking about these practices, the educator is confronted with the same ethical issues that arise in the context of the social-values curriculum. Among the issues to recognize is that one cannot limit the notion of "good" children to conformity to the status quo and, at the same time, engage in the curricular and classroom discipline practices advocated in this book. The notion that moral education entails enabling students to employ their moral understandings to evaluate the conventional practices of their own culture is meaningful only if we also view moral education as fostering a moral identity in which the person self-defines as someone who is open to the possibility that morality may require changes in the ways in which society operates. This critical moral perspective would also hold for one's own point of view, and would necessitate a sense of humility and openness, rather than moral rectitude. Thus, while hopefully raising the salience of morality as an element of students' self-definition, the multifaceted view of social knowledge and social existence that emerges from domain theory also directs us as educators away from a monolithic view of human character, and toward the selection of educational experiences that foster a range of self-definitions consistent with moral autonomy.

Responding Constructively to Resistance. For many young people, the road toward defining a moral identity involves detours and explorations of forbidden territory. The reasons for this are probably several, including the relative costs and benefits of acting in ways that are immoral or unconventional. More important, however, than any straightforward cost–benefits analysis is the fundamental motivation to establish agency, autonomy, and a unique personal identity. As we discussed in Chapter 3, children and adolescents express the need for uniqueness through claims to an area of personal prerogative, privacy, and choice. A sense of agency, however, also operates in any domain in which the person perceives him- or herself as initiating decisions and actions (Deci 1995).

As children begin to understand that being "good" is not only about your actions but about your self-definition, there arises an existential problem not evident in the personal domain. If you act morally or in accordance with convention, then at the level of action, you are "being good" in a way that is common to all members of a social group. There is nothing personally unique in such actions, since they have universal or consensual origins. In order for you to act morally or in accord with conventional standards, and still maintain your sense of agency, then you need to be sure that you are "being good" for your own reasons.

In large part, this sense that one is being good for one's own reasons is implicit in the justifications children provide for moral judgments beginning in early childhood. A child who argues that hitting is wrong because it hurts is not saying this simply in order to conform to social expectations. However, establishing one's moral positions as issues become more contextualized and tied up with adult expectations may entail a certain degree of playfulness and perhaps contrarian conduct.

In the ensuing discussion, I am not attempting to account for children who have become so alienated that their conduct is seriously harmful or criminal, but rather for the typical child or adolescent with "contrarian" conduct. Examples of what I have in mind here are the well-known phenomena of adolescent petty crime, such as shoplifting, and adolescent engagement in so-called status offenses (e.g., underage drinking). I recently polled my undergraduate students, all of whom are planning to become classroom teachers, and found that nearly all had engaged in petty theft as adolescents, had cheated on tests in high school, and had engaged in various status offenses, ranging from drinking to attending unauthorized parties or breaking community curfews. Not a person with good character in the bunch, it would appear. Ditto for my doctoral students in an advanced seminar on social development.

In traditional psychoanalytic accounts, such behavior is seen as the result of a weakening of the structures of morality (A. Freud 1969) associated with the resurgence of sexual impulses at puberty. More behaviorally oriented traditionalists see such adolescent conduct as evidence of social decay and poor social support for youth (Wynne 1989). What I am suggesting is that the ubiquitousness of such conduct has other sources that educators and parents can respond to in positive and constructive ways. If the motivation for such contrarian conduct is tied up with efforts at establishing personal autonomy, then neither should we be surprised that it happens nor should we overreact with punitive measures. Instead, we should begin to view such events as "teachable moments" rife with opportunities in which to engage the young person in taking personal responsibility for his or her actions and the logical consequences that follow, employing the same principles of developmental discipline used with young children.

We should also not be surprised when youths see through our contrivances for building character, such as enrolling them in the boy scouts or requiring them to engage in service activities. As part of a study of the impact of service learning on adolescent character, Jim Leming (1999) interviewed participants regarding their views of such programs. One thing that stood out in his interviews was that students across the United States stated that they resented what they perceived to be attempts by the school systems to make them into certain kinds of people. In effect, they told Leming in their interviews, "We know who we are already, and we already know how we want to act. We don't need this." Leming interprets these young people as saying that they already have a moral identity and resent efforts to tamper with it (Leming, personal communication, October 1999).

The educational suggestions that follow are intended to increase the likelihood that students will construct a sense of self in which morality plays an integral part. They are also intended to engage students' efforts to maintain personal autonomy and agency.

Symbolic Sources of Self: Fictional and Historical Figures in Literature

Advocates of social-learning theory (Bandura 1977) and traditional character education (Wynne 1989) have long extolled the educative power of role models. As we have learned from cognitive psychology (Kohlberg 1966, 1984), children do not passively adopt the behaviors exhibited by role models but, instead, evaluate them in relation to their perceived relevance and informational value. Individuals whom children accept as role models serve as sources of information for how to act socially and how to define themselves in the social world. Parents, teachers, siblings, and media figures are potential role models. Whether a child will view someone as a role model will be a function of the child's age and interests. Thus, we cannot know that any particular role model will engage a given child. What we can do as teachers, however, is to expose children to potential role models who exhibit the sorts of decisions and actions that we hope children will also incorporate into their self-definitions. Obviously, the place to begin is with the teacher him- or herself. A teacher who establishes the sort of moral atmosphere described in Chapter 8, and who employs the disciplinary practices described in this chapter, will likely evidence many of the personal qualities consistent with what one would hope to engender in students.

In addition to encounters with actual persons, school offers opportunities for students to broaden their exposure to potential role models through literature and history. A student's personal narrative can become enriched by engagement in reflective activities that would link up the student with the person being read about. There are two main advantages of such symbolic encounters, from an educational point of view. First, they allow the teacher to select the sort of person toward whom to direct student attention. Second, they allow the teacher an opportunity to structure assignments that will actively engage students in evaluating the personal qualities of someone with whom the student does not subsequently have to interact. In this way, the student can assume a critical stance toward the model without fear of alienating the person.

The following are some suggestions for using historical or fictional characters for moral education:

1. *Use characters who are related to the academic unit being taught.* This is essentially the same suggestion made regarding other aspects of sociomoral educational activities. The more integrated the activities are with regular classroom academic practices, the more natural they will be for students, and the more readily teachers can use them. In practice, this means selecting historical figures from the period being studied, or fictional characters from the assigned literature.
2. *Allow students choice in the characters they are to focus upon, or in the as-*

signment they are to work on. Providing students with choice increases the probability of student intrinsic interest, and the likelihood that they will allow themselves to connect up with the model. It also decreases the likelihood that they will view the assignment as forcing them to agree with a predetermined adult point of view.

3. *Provide accessible characters.* Historical figures, such as Martin Luther King, Jr., Madame Curie, or Abraham Lincoln provide models of greatness, and having children learn about them has value. However, the sheer magnitude of their historical accomplishments often renders these personages so distant as to be inaccessible or unrealistic as models from the point of view of students. Who can match such people? There are several ways to deal with this difficulty. One is to provide other figures or personages to look at who are less well known, yet worthy of emulation. The second is to take a "warts and all" view of figures, such as Jefferson or Lincoln, and have students assess them as total people. In both cases, student assignments can involve library research, as well as evaluative discussions and student writing. The third is to employ characters who are similar in age as the students themselves. This can include biographies of youths from historical periods or characters from fiction.

4. *Provide exposure to models whose moral actions "go against the grain" of contemporary conventions.* People of character evidence their moral steel when they act contrary to popular sentiment or the status quo. In addition, such models emulate a moral orientation that takes a critical stance toward received mores. This is, in part, what one hopes students will adopt as part of their sense of moral identity. Such an ethical stance is the essence of what is entailed in responding morally to instances of domain overlap, wherein the existing conventions of society or social systems (e.g., one's own family) are counter to fairness and human welfare.

Martin Luther King is a prototype for this sort of moral personage. So also were some leaders of the suffragettes and the more-recent women's movement. Such models don't need to come from history; they can also be depicted in fictional accounts in which a young person stands up for what is right in opposition to peer pressure or convention.

5. *Provide exposure to models who struggle with what is the right thing to do.* Huckleberry Finn is a well-known example of a flawed character whose moral strength is tested to the fullest. Flawed characters provide students with ways to connect with the internal struggle that accompanies moral conflict.

6. *Expose adolescents to antiheroes.* One of the most enduring and popular figures in American fiction is Holden Caulfield in *The Catcher in the Rye.* This character's appeal is, to a large extent, due to his vulnerability, moral sweetness, and superficial vulgarity. He is the quintessential adolescent searching for meaning in a morally confusing universe.

Less appealing to adults, but no less powerful to adolescents trying to find a moral world, are characters who search for what is right in the midst of pathological or immoral worlds, such as urban gang life. Good examples are the characters in Jess Mowry's (1993) *Way Past Cool,* which describes youth dealing with gangs and drug dealers in urban California. The power of such models is that they allow young people to measure themselves against others whose choices may not always be moral ones, but whose struggles reflect the process of coming to terms with oneself as a moral being.

Summary. Effective educational use of historical or fictional characters depends on the engagement of students in reflective activities. Merely asking students to prepare a biography or to summarize the main attributes of a particular fictional character may serve certain academic aims but will contribute very little to students' character formation. In order for such activities to benefit students' moral development, they should include oral or written analysis and reflection. These reflections should focus upon the connections between the moral or normative issues at stake and the main character's approach to dealing with them. This first task would ask the student to identify the moral and conventional elements of the situation, as well as any personal or prudential factors at work. With middle-school and older students, this aspect of the reflective exercise would also include asking the student to identify explicitly relevant factual assumptions operating in the main character's decisions. Second, these reflections should engage the student in making an evaluative assessment of the figure in terms of what they saw as positive in the person's actions and why, and what limitations, if any, they saw in the figure's approach.

Finally, the student may be asked to make a connection between the figure and the student's own personal qualities. This latter activity risks exposure of some aspects of the student's private life, and it should be done in a way that permits the student options. For example, the students may be given the choice of writing or discussing (1) what they saw in the person that was either similar to or different from themselves, (2) how they dealt with a similar situation, (3) what they might have done if they were in the person's position, or (4) what advice they would have given to the person if he or she was a close friend. In sum, the purpose of symbolic models is to engage students in value-driven reflection, and to make connections between the decisions and personal attributes of such figures and their own sense of moral self.

Direct Self-Reflection

This last set of activities entails a shift away from simply evaluating a model to conducting some degree of self-evaluation. The most direct method of engaging a person in considering his or her own moral qualities is self-reflection. Virtually all religious systems employ some sort of self-review as an element of spiritual and moral renewal. The experiential wisdom behind these traditional practices is that the process of self-reflection can have a meaningful impact on a person's self-definition and connection to a particular value system. Employing self-reflection within a public school setting has obvious differences from the religious context, but the main purpose of such an exercise is similar. It is to draw a comparison between one's own behavior with a goal or ideal.

Persons who are on a diet or exercise program often establish measurable goals against which to determine their rate of success. Although setting specific behavioral goals can help students develop self-control over their own conduct (Bandura 1986; Schunk 1989), moral self-reflection, as discussed here, does not generally have this sort of quantitative element. Instead, the purpose of such reflection is to determine in a global sense whether one is measuring up to one's own internal moral standard. There is, then, an interdependence between a person's conceptions of morality and his or her moral standard. The mere exercise of engaging in such reflection perforce causes the person to raise, if only momentarily, the relative salience of the moral aspect of self. Thus, meaningful moral self-reflection has potential for moral growth on several levels. It causes one to pay attention to the moral aspects of self, thus making morality more salient. It causes one to measure oneself against a personal standard, thus having the potential for motivating moral growth and behavioral change. Finally, it causes one to reflect on one's own moral position, thus providing a potential motivating source for conceptual moral growth.

While engaging students in moral self-reflection has potential benefits, it is no simple task. For one thing, it runs the obvious risk of inviting student resistance. Such resistance comes from the desire to maintain personal privacy, and teachers would be wise to respect students' privacy needs. Resistance also comes from students who view school-based assignments that require self-reflection as a way for teachers to manipulate the students' own sense of self. This latter form of resistance is similar to that of students who resent mandatory school-based public-service activities.

One way to overcome some of these obstacles and to engage students in moral self-reflection is through the use of private journals. We recently employed this approach with middle-school students as part of a more general values-education program. We directed sixth-grade students to write, on separate pages of a privately kept personal journal, descriptions of themselves as they are now, the self they would like most to become, and the person they would least like to become. We also asked them to draw a picture of each of these self-descriptions as a way to engage those children who use visual imagery as a primary mode of expression. We then asked the children to consider the ideal person that they had described and to think about what sort of person they could realistically become in the next two months if they really worked at it. After they had completed this exercise, we engaged the children in a group brainstorming session to generate strategies that they would use to actualize their personal goals and become the sorts of people that they would want to be in two months. In the context of this open discussion, children often revealed their goals as they laid out their strategies. However, no one was required to discuss their own approach, and the children in our program readily volunteered their suggestions. Students thoroughly enjoyed this reflective activity and rated it as one of the best parts of the program. The strength of the exercise is that it is intrinsically interesting to the children and does not violate their privacy. The limitation of the approach is that it is not directly connected to regular school activity, and thus does not lend itself to teacher evaluation.

As children enter adolescence, they become even more resistant to public expressions of their private goals, including the use of journals for school purposes. However, literature and writing courses offer natural avenues for moral self-reflection concordant with traditional academic aims. American literature, for example, introduces students to Henry David Thoreau and the transcendentalists with their concerns about individual liberty and community. In the context of teaching this academic unit, a Chicago-area high school teacher has her students write an essay on the theme "The Time I Defied Authority." The instructions for the theme required the student to provide a personal context for the event and a clear moral justification for going beyond authority's commands. Students who find Thoreau a big yawn are transfixed by this assignment, which draws them into the very concerns of transcendentalist literature while opening them up to their inner moral selves. In this one assignment, this very creative teacher transforms adolescent resistance into a vehicle for moral self-exploration, as well as a gateway into American literature.

Finally, students can be engaged in self-reflection through processes of creative writing or artistic expression that ask them to create characters who deal with moral conundrums common to adolescent life. Here again, the teacher can offer a selection of issues to deal with can and allow students to take whatever perspective they may find most interesting. In most cases, students will end up projecting their own issues into their characters. By working things through in this fictional mode, young people are drawn into a process of reflection, working through their own personal moral issues and the place that morality holds within their own self-systems.

Given such an assignment, some students will elect to write about contrarian personalities whose choices are immoral. In most cases, these contrarian depictions represent efforts by students to play with moral identity and to explore selves that they would not feel comfortable acting out. This permits the students a chance to compare their own moral perspective with other possible selves, and to claim ownership of their own moral identity as an autonomous choice, rather than the product of social conformity. In other cases, these contrarian representations may alert the teacher to students who are suffering serious struggles with their moral selves (Noam 1993), and they provide a window for the teacher to engage the student in counseling or therapy.

Summary. Through direct reflection on the moral aspect of self, students integrate their moral knowledge with their moral identity. Teachers can engage students in these processes of self-reflection through activities that are concordant with their academic goals. This permits teachers to evaluate students on academic criteria, such as the flow of their writing, paragraph development, sentence construction, or depth of analysis of themes within literature. It does not entail evaluating students in terms of their character.

Opportunities for Engagement in Moral Action: Service Learning

The last issue we will discuss is the provision of opportunities for students to engage in prosocial or moral activities. The purpose behind such activities is to bring students into the realm of action and, thereby, afford opportunities for young people to make direct connections between themselves and their capacity to engage in helpful behavior. The assumption is that the formation of moral identity is made easier if children and adolescents can explore forms of moral action, if they are supported in these explorations of moral conduct by relationships with people they trust and admire, and if they feel that their actions genuinely contribute to the welfare of others (Hart 1992). A final element required for such activities to have meaning for the young person is that they be voluntary or have a significant element of choice (Barker and Eccles 1997; Hart 1992; Hart and Fegley 1995; Hart, et al., 1995; Hart, Atkins, and Ford 1998; Hart et al. 1999).

Research examining service-learning programs has reported that students who have been involved in voluntary participation in a variety of extracurricular activities, including service as a referee or coach for youth sports, help with a community food-distribution program, tutoring, and so forth, were less likely than other adolescents to be involved in any of the following problem behaviors: theft of $50 or more, assault, breaking and entering, or student misconduct requiring that a parent be brought to school (Hart, Atkins, and Ford 1998). Other studies have reported that early engagement in social organizations is associated with long-term engagement in social activities (Yates and Youniss 1998). Perhaps most impressive is that such community-service activities can have a positive impact on inner-city youth whose daily lives do not provide environmental support for the construction or enactment of positive moral identities (Hart and Fegley 1995; Hart, Atkins, and Ford 1998).

The collective impact of these studies is that children and adolescents benefit from opportunities to engage in community-service activities if they are provided a range of options for how they might serve, such that their involvement is concordant with their own sense of personal autonomy, as well as their burgeoning moral identities. Examples of such an approach are elementary school districts that require service hours for graduation from the eighth grade but allow students a large menu of options through which to meet such community service.

Service learning need not be limited to extracurricular activities but may take place as a regular part of school life. The Developmental Studies Project, for example, includes a "buddy system" in which upper-grade students serve as tutors for lower-grade students (Battistich et al. 1991). Less effective are programs that mandate students to perform particular services, especially when such community service is thought by the students to be pointless. An example of the latter are wealthy high school districts that, out of a well-intentioned desire to engage their students in community service and to provide them with some direct connection with children of poverty, require students to participate in service activities in inner-city neighborhoods or public-housing projects. This sort of program results in the alienation Leming (1999) reported among adolescents who saw through what they perceived to be blatant attempts by the schools to make them into particular sorts of people.

SUMMARY AND CONCLUSION

The educative process fosters the moral self through the establishment of a positive moral atmosphere, the use of developmental discipline, opportunities for personal self-evaluation and reflection, and the enactment of moral responsibility. These processes increase the likelihood that students will integrate the construction of moral and social-normative understandings as salient components of their personal identities.

Each of the educational components described in this discussion of the moral self is consistent with, and can occur together with, the curricular and classroom structural suggestions laid out in Chapters 8 and 9. In fact, a comprehensive approach to moral education would necessitate their integration. This is because the rhythm of social development establishes a reciprocal to-and-fro between the construction of sociomoral conceptual frameworks and the formation of personal identity. Development in one system ordinarily affects the structure and function of the other. When self and sociomoral knowledge become disconnected, the result is stunted growth and a loss of human potential.

Engaging students in that educative process is something quite different, however, from any formulaic attempt to "raise good children" or to "create people of character." This is because the moral self that emerges is one part of the complex totality of any real person. That totality includes the cultural biases and informational assumptions that have been incorporated into the individual's social constructions. It also includes the idiosyncratic aspirations and social interpretations that enter into any real person's reading of contextualized social situations. Moral education can influence the development of a person's sociomoral understandings, and it can affect the degree to which morality matters as an aspect of a person's sense of self. But moral education cannot determine how any given person is going to interpret particular real-life social situations. Domain theory teaches us how to understand what goes into a person's moral decisions and actions, and how to influence the development of those systems of meaning. In the end, however, it is the person who determines the moral meaning of events in his or her own life.

Conclusion: Keeping Things in Perspective

The Art Institute of Chicago is home to one of the world's great collections of impressionist and postimpressionist paintings. Perhaps the most popular piece in their collection is Georges Seurat's *A Sunday Afternoon on the Island of la Grande Jatte*. This magnificent painting takes up an entire wall of one main gallery. As you enter the gallery, you are immediately drawn into a fanciful park scene with couples in formal wear strolling with umbrellas in a wooded area by a shimmering lake. On the lake, sailboats, steamers, and a scull boat with crew glide by. Once you adjust to the sheer size of the painting, you begin to pay attention to smaller details. A young girl is skipping through the lawn. One of the women is walking a monkey on a leash. The experience of seeing this painting is breathtaking. It is made even more remarkable if you move from looking at the painting from a distance to looking at it from a few inches from the canvas. Standing close up you can see that the subtle effects of light and shadow, the shimmering of the sun on the water, and the shapes of the figures are achieved with tiny dots of basic color spaced closely together.

The nuances of visual experience captured by Seurat's use of basic color form a metaphor for the ways in which basic domains of social knowledge interact to account for the subtleties and complexities of social life in context. Each domain is a discrete and distinct system corresponding to qualitatively different aspects of social interaction. Each, so to speak, is a basic color corresponding to the personal, social organizational, and moral aspects of social life. As in Seurat's paintings, these basic colors are rarely seen in isolation but tend instead to co-occur in relationship to one another. The visual effect of Seurat's technique rests not in the dots of paint but in the coordinations imposed upon them by our cognitive system of perception. In like manner, the interpretations we give to sociomoral events reflect the ways in which we coordinate their domain-salient features.

In this book I have presented evidence that the domain of morality is constructed early in life out of the child's experiences with universal and unavoidable aspects of interactions with other people. Young children construct intuitions about issues of harm and welfare, fairness and rights, that develop into later moral conceptions of justice, equity, and compassion. These core elements of morality transcend culture and are independent of the person's religious affiliation. It is this universal, transcendent core of morality, available to persons at all ages, that permits moral reflection upon the social lives that we lead as individuals, and upon the structure and norms of the society that we inherit. With development, our moral and societal concepts allow us to better comprehend our social world, and they provide us with more powerful tools for guiding our moral conduct.

As educators, we enable our students to discern the basic elements that go into their understandings of the social world. We also enrich their lives by providing them with the capacity to understand how the moral, societal, and personal aspects of social life interact in the course of everyday social events. In order to do this, we need to become familiar with the nature of social development and its implications for the curriculum, classroom climate, and modes of student discipline. This book presented some suggestions for how teachers can do those things. Those suggestions are intended as a starting point in what will necessarily be an extended conversation.

The ethics of our profession demand that we do more than teach children how to recapitulate an inherited picture of the social world. Instead, moral education involves helping young people to understand and manipulate the moral canvas of their own lives and the social worlds they inherit. This allows for personal renewal and moral reexamination. It also provides the possibility for the moral growth of society as a whole.

Additional Resources

Readers may continue the dialogue opened up in this book and remain current with issues in the area of moral development and education by exploring the web site operated by the author for the Office for Studies in Moral Development and Education of the University of Illinois at Chicago, College of Education. The site URL is: http://MoralEd.org

The site provides access to recent articles on moral development, character formation, and education. It also provides information about books on the topic, classroom practices, assessment, and links to related sites. The site sponsors an international e-mail listserver for persons interested in participating in dialogue around issues of moral development and education.

References

Abu-Lughod, L. 1993. *Writing women's worlds: Bedouin stories.* Berkeley: University of California.

Anderson, V. May, 1998. School reform: What matters most – smaller is better. *Catalyst,* 1–3.

Angelou, M. 1971. *I know why the caged bird sings.* New York: Bantam Books.

Aristotle. 1985. *Nicomachean ethics.* Trans. T. Irwin Trans. Indianapolis, IN: Hackett.

Aronson, E., and S. Patnoe. 1997. *The jigsaw classroom: Building cooperation in the classroom.* New York: Longman.

Arsenio, W. 1984. *The affective atmosphere of the classroom: Children's conceptions of teachers and social rules.* Paper presented at the annual meeting of the American Educational Research Association, New Orleans.

——— 1988. Children's conceptions of the situational affective consequences of sociomoral events. *Child Development* 59, 1611–22.

Arsenio, W., and R. Kramer. 1992. Victimizers and their victims: Children's conceptions of the mixed emotional consequences of victimization. *Child Development* 63, 915–27.

Arsenio, W., and A. Lover. 1995. Children's conceptions of socio-moral affect: Happy victimizers, mixed emotions, and other expectancies. In M. Killen and D. Hart, eds., *Morality in everyday life,* pp. 87–130. New York: Cambridge University Press.

Astor, R. A. 1994. Children's moral reasoning about family and peer violence: The role of provocation and retribution. *Child Development* 65, 1054–67.

Augustine. 401/1963. *The confessions of St. Augustine.* Trans. R. Warner. New York: The New American Library.

Baldwin, J. M. 1897. *Social and ethical interpretations in mental development.* New York: Macmillan.

——— 1906. *Thought and things.* Vol. 1. London: Swan Sonnenschen.

Bandura, A. 1977. *Social learning theory.* Englewood Cliffs, NJ: Prentice-Hall.

——— 1986. *Social foundations of thought and action: A social cognitive theory.* Upper Saddle River, NJ: Prentice Hall.

——— 1991. Social cognitive theory of moral thought and action. In W. Kurtines and

J. Gewirtz, eds., *Handbook of moral behavior and development*. Vol. 1, *Theory* pp. 45–104. Hillsdale, NJ: Erlbaum.

Barden, R., F. Zelko, S. Duncan, and J. Masters. 1980. Children's consensual knowledge about the experiential determinants of emotion. *Journal of Personality and Social Psychology* 39, 968–76.

Barker, B., and J. Eccles. April, 1997. *Student coucil volunteering, basketball, or marching band: What kind of extracurricular involvement matters?* Symposium: Adolescent Involvement in Community. Biennial meeting of the Society for Research in Child Development. Washington, DC.

Barnard, C. 1963. *The functions of the executive*. Cambridge, MA: Harvard University Press.

Bartz, K. W., and E. S. Levine. 1978. Child rearing by Black parents: A description and comparison to Anglo and Chicano parents. *Journal of Marriage and the Family* 40, 709–19.

Battistich, V., M. Watson, D. Solomon, S. Schaps, and J. Solomon. 1991. The child development project: A comprehensive program for the development of prosocial character. In W. Kurtines and J. Gewirtz, eds., *Handbook of moral behavior and development*. Vol. 3, *Applications*, pp. 1–34. Hillsdale, NJ: Erlbaum.

Baumrind, D. 1971. Current patterns of parental authority. *Developmental Psychology Monographs* 4 (1), pt. 2.

    1972. An exploratory study of socialization effects on Black children: Some Black–White comparisons. *Child Development* 43, 261–7.

    1973. The development of instrumental competence through socialization. In A. D. Pick, ed., *Minnesota Symposium on Child Psychology*. Vol. 7. Minneapolis: University of Minnesota Press.

    1998. From ought to is: A neo-Marxist perspective on the use and misuse of the culture construct. *Human Development* 41, 145–65.

Bearison, D., and H. Zimiles. 1986. Developmental perspectives of thought and emotion: An introduction. In D. Bearison and H. Zimiles, eds., *Thought and emotion: Developmental perspectives*, pp. 1–10. Hillsdale, NJ: Erlbaum.

Bellah, R., R. Madsen, W. M. Sullivan, A. Swidler, and S. Tipton. 1985. *Habits of the heart: Individualism and commitment in American life*. New York: Harper & Row.

Bennett, W. 1992. *The de-valuing of America: The fight for our culture and our children*. New York: Simon & Schuster.

    1993. *The book of virtues: A treasury of great moral stories*. New York: Simon & Schuster.

Benninga, J. 1991. *Moral, character, and civic education in the elementary school*. New York: Teachers College Press.

Berkowitz, M., and J. Gibbs. 1983. Measuring the developmental features of moral discussions. *Merrill-Palmer Quarterly* 24, 399–410.

Berkowitz, M., J. Gibbs, and J. Broughton. 1980. The relation of moral judgment stage to developmental effects of peer dialogues. *Merrill-Palmer Quarterly* 26, 341–57.

Berkowitz, M., N. Guerra, and L. Nucci. 1991. Sociomoral development and drug and alcohol abuse. In W. Kurtines and J. Gewirtz, eds., *Handbook of moral behavior and development.* Vol. 3, *Applications,* pp. 35–54. Hillsdale, NJ: Erlbaum.

Berndt, T., and K. Park. 1986. *Children's reasoning about morality, convention, personal issues, & drug use.* Unpublished manuscript, Purdue University, Lafayette, IN.

Blasi, G. 1983. Moral cognition and moral action: A theoretical perspective. *Developmental Review* 3, 178–210.

———. 1984. Moral identity: Its role in moral functioning. In J. Gewirtz and W. Kurtines, eds., *Morality, moral behavior, and moral development,* pp. 128–39. New York: Wiley.

———. 1993. The development of identity: Some implications for moral functioning. In G. Noam and T. Wren, eds., *The moral self,* pp. 99–122. Cambridge, MA: MIT Press.

Blasi, G., and K. Glodis. 1995. The development of identity: A critical analysis from the perspective of the self as subject. *Developmental Review* 15, 404–33.

Blatt, M., and L. Kohlberg. 1975. The effects of classroom moral discussion upon children's level of moral judgment. *Journal of Moral Education,* 4, 129–61.

Blumenfeld, P. C., P. R. Pintrich, and V. L. Hamilton. 1987. Teacher talk and students' reasoning about morals, conventions, and achievement. *Child Development* 58, 1389–1401.

Borowitz, E. 1968. *A new Jewish theology in the making.* Philadelphia: Westminster.

Brehm, S. S., and J. W. Brehm. 1981. *Psychologcal reaction: A theory of freedom and control.* New York: Academic Press.

Brontë, C. 1847/1977. *Jane Eyre.* New York: New York University Press.

Broughton, J. 1978. The development of concepts of self, mind, reality, and knowledge. In W. Damon, ed., *Social cognition.* San Francisco: Jossey-Bass.

Brown, T. 1996. Affective dimensions of meaning. In E. Reed, E. Turiel, and T. Brown, eds., *Values and knowledge,* pp. 167–90. Hillsdale, NJ: Lawrence Erlbaum.

Brown, T., and L. Weiss. 1987. Structures, procedures, heuristics, and affectivity. *Archives de Psychologie* 55, 59–94.

Buss, D. M. 1994. *The evolution of desire.* New York: Basic Books.

Byrne, B. 1984. The general/academic self-concept nomological network: A review of construct validation research. *Review of Educational Research* 54, 427–56.

Campos, J., and K. Barrett. 1983. Toward a new understanding of emotions and their development. In C. Izard, J. Kagan, and R. Zajonc, eds., *Emotions, cognition, and, behavior.* Cambridge: Cambridge University Press.

Chao, R. K. March, 1993. *Clarification of the authoritarian parenting style and parental control: Cultural concepts of Chinese child rearing.* Paper presented at the 60th anniversary meeting of the Society for Research in Child Development, New Orleans.

Character Counts Coalition. May/June, 1993. *Ethics in action.* Marina del Rey, CA: Joseph and Edna Josephson Institute of Ethics.

Colby, A., and W. Damon. 1992. *Some do care: Contemporary lives of moral commitment.* New York: Free Press.

Colby, A., and L. Kohlberg. 1987. *The measurement of moral judgment.* Vol. 1,

Theoretical foundations and research validation; Vol. 2, *Standard issue scoring manual.* New York: Cambridge University Press.

Colby, A., and L. Kohlberg, J. Gibbs, and M. Lieberman. 1983. A longitudinal study of moral judgment. *Monographs of the Society for Research in Child Development* 48 (Serial No. 200).

Coopersmith, S. 1967. *The antecedents of self-esteem.* San Francisco: W. H. Freeman.

Corsaro, W. 1985. *Peer culture in the early years.* Norwood, NJ: Ablex.

Crittenden, P. 1990. *Learning to be moral.* London: Humanities Press International.

Crockenberg, S., and C. Litman. 1990. Autonomy as competence in 2-year olds: Maternal correlates of child defiance, compliance, and self-assertion. *Developmental Psychology* 26, 961–71.

Cushman, P. 1991. Ideology obscured: Political uses of the self in Daniel Stern's infant. *American Psychologist* 46, 206–20.

Damon, W. 1975. Early conceptions of positive justice as related to the development of concrete operations. *Child Development* 46, 301–12.

——— 1977. *The social world of the child.* San Francisco: Jossey-Bass.

——— 1984. Self-understanding and moral development in childhood and adolescence. In J. Gewirtz and W. Kurtines, eds., *Morality, moral behavior, and moral development.* New York: Wiley.

Damon, W., and W. Hart. 1988. *Self-understanding in childhood and adolescence.* Cambridge: Cambridge University Press.

Danon, H. 1972. *To be a Jew.* New York: Basic Books.

Darwin, C. 1872/1965. *The expression of the emotions in man and animals.* Chicago: University of Chicago Press.

Davidson, P., E. Turiel, and A. Black. 1983. The effect of stimulus familiarity on the use of criteria and justifications in children's social reasoning. *British Journal of Developmental Psychology* 1, 46–65.

Deci, E. 1995. *Why we do what we do: The dynamics of personal autonomy.* New York: G. P. Putnam.

Deutsch, M. 1993. Educating for a peaceful world. *American Psychologist* 48, 510–17.

DeVries, R., and B. Zan. 1994. *Moral classrooms, moral children: Creating a constructivist atmosphere for early education.* New York: Teachers College Press.

Dodsworth-Rugani, K. 1982. *The development of concepts of social structure and their relationship to school rules and authority.* Unpublished Ph.D. diss., University of California, Berkeley.

Dreikurs, R. 1968. *Psychology in the classroom: A manual for teachers.* 2d ed. New York: Harper and Row.

Dreikurs, R., and P. Cassel. 1972. *Discipline without tears.* New York: Hawthorne Books.

Dreikurs, R., B. B. Grunwald, and F. C. Pepper, 1982. *Maintaining sanity in the classroom: Classroom management techniques.* 2d ed. New York: Harper & Row.

Dunn, J., and P. Munn. 1985. Becoming a family member: Family conflict and the development of social understanding in the second year. *Child Develop-ment* 56, 480–92.

1987. The development of justifications in disputes. *Developmental Psychology,* 23, 781–98.

Dunn, J., and C. Slomkowski. 1992. Conflict and the development of social un-derstanding. In C. U. Shantz and W. Hartup, eds., *Conflict in child and ado-lescent development,* pp. 70–92). Cambridge: Cambridge University Press.

Durkheim, E. 1925/1961. *Moral education.* Glencoe, IL: The Free Press.

Dworkin, R. 1977. *Taking rights seriously.* Cambridge, MA: Harvard University Press.

Eckman, P. 1993. Facial expressions and emotion. *American Psychologist* 48, 384–92.

Eibl-Eibesfeld, I. 1970. *Ethology: The biology of behavior.* New York: Holt, Rinehart, and Winston.

Eisenberg, N. 1986. *Altruistic emotion, cognition and behavior.* Hillsdale, NJ: Erl-baum.

Emde, R., Z. Birigen, R. Clyman, and D. Openheim. 1991. The moral self of in-fancy: Affective core and procedural knowledge. *Developmental Review* 11, 251–70.

Entwisle, D. R., K. L. Alexander, A. M. Pallas, and D. Cadigan. 1987. The emer-gent academic self-image of first graders. *Child Development* 19, 846–55.

Erikson, E. 1963. *Childhood and society.* New York: Norton.

1968. *Identity, youth, and crisis.* New York: W. W. Norton.

Etzioni, A. 1993. *The spirit of community: The reinvention of American society.* New York: Touchstone.

Ferguson, T. J., H. Stegge, and I. Damhuis. 1991. Children's understandings of guilt and shame. *Child Development* 62, 827–39.

Fivush, R. 1993. Emotional content of parent–child conversations about the past. In C. A. Nelson, ed., *Memory and affect in development. The Minnesota Sym-posium on Child psychology,* pp. 39–77. Hillsdale, NJ: Erlbaum.

Frankena, W. K. 1978. *Ethics.* Englewood Cliffs, NJ: Prentice-Hall.

Freud, A. 1969. Adolescence as a developmental disturbance. In G. Caplan and S. Lebici, eds., *Adolescence: psychological perspectives,* pp. 5–10. New York: Basic Books.

Freud, S. 1923/1960. *The ego and the id.* New York: Norton.

1930/1961. *Civilization and its discontents.* New York: Norton.

Gates, H. L. Jr., and N. Y. Mckay. eds. 1997. *The Norton anthology of African Amer-ican literature.* New York: Norton.

Geertz, C. 1984. From the natives' point of view: On the nature of anthropolog-ical understanding. In R. A. Shweder and R. Levine, eds., *Culture theory,* pp. 123–36. Cambridge: Cambridge University Press.

Geiger, K., and E. Turiel. 1983. Disruptive school behavior and concepts of so-cial convention in early adolsecence. *Journal of Educational Psychology* 75, 677–85.

Gesell, A. 1928. *Infancy and human growth.* New York: Macmillan.

Gewirth, A. 1978. *Reason and morality.* Chicago: University of Chicago Press.

1982. *Human rights: Essays on justification and application.* Chicago: University of Chicago Press.

Gilligan, C. 1982. *In a different voice: Psychological theory and women's development.* Cambridge, MA: Harvard University Press.

Gilligan, C., and G. Wiggins. 1987. The orgins of morality in early childhood relationships. In J. Kagan and S. Lamb, eds., *The emergence of morality in young children*, pp. 277–305. Chicago: University of Chicago Press.

Goncu, A. 1993. Development of intersubjectivity in social pretend play. *Human Development* 36, 185–98.

Gralinski, H., and C. Kopp. 1993. Everyday rules for behavior: Mothers' requests to young children. *Developmental Psychology* 29, 573–84.

Greenfield, P. M., and R. R. Cocking. eds., 1994. *Cross-cultural roots of minority child development.* Hilldale, NJ: Erlbaum.

Habermas, J. 1991. *Moral consciousness and communicative action.* Cambridge, MA: MIT Press.

1996. *Between facts and norms: Contributions to a discourse theory of law and democracy.* Cambridge, MA: MIT Press.

Haidt, J., S. H. Koller, and M. G. Dias. 1994. Affect, culture, and the morality of harmless offenses. *Journal of Personality and Social Psychology* 65, 613–29.

Hansen, D. T. 1996. Teaching and the moral life of classrooms. *Journal for a Just and Caring Education* 2, 59–74.

Harrington, M. 1999. *Care and equality: Inventing a new family politics.* New York: Knopf.

Hart, D. 1992. *Becoming men: The development of aspirations, values, and adaptational styles.* New York: Plenum.

Hart, D., R. Atkins, and D. Ford. 1998. Urban America as a context for the development of moral identity in adolescence. *Journal of Social Issues* 54, 513–30.

Hart, D., and S. Fegley. 1995. Prosocial behavior and caring in adolescence: Relations to self-understanding and social judgment. *Child Development* 66, 1346–59.

Hart, D., M. Yates, S. Fegley, and G. Wilson. 1995. Moral commitment in inner-city adolescents. In M. Killen and D. Hart, eds. *Morality in everyday life: Developmental perspectives.* New York: Cambridge University Press.

Harter, S. 1983. Developmental perspectives on the self-system. In P. H. Mussen, ed., *Handbook of child psychology.* Vol. 4, *Socialization, personality, and social development*, pp. 275–85. New York: Wiley.

1985. *The self-perception profile for children: Revision of the perceived competence scale for children.* Unpublished manuscript, University of Denver, Denver, CO.

1986. *The self-perception profile for adolescents.* Unpublished manuscript, University of Denver, Denver, CO.

1992. *Visions of self: Beyond the me in the mirror.* In J. Jacobs ed., *Nebraska Symposium on Motivation.* Vol. 40. Lincoln: University of Nebraska Press.

Harter, S. and Buddin, N. (1987). Children's understanding of the simultaneity of two emotions: A five-stage developmental acquisition sequence. *Developmental Psychology, 23,* 388–399.

Hartshorne, H., and M. A. May. 1928. *Studies in the nature of character.* Vol. 1, *Studies in deceit.* New York: Macmillan.

1929. *Studies in the nature of character.* Vol. 2. *Studies in service and self control.* New York: Macmillan.

1930. *Studies in the nature of character.* Vol. 3, *Studies in organization of character.* New York: Macmillan.

Helwig, C., M. Tisak, and E. Turiel. 1990. Children's social reasoning in context: Reply to Gabbenesch. *Child Development* 61, 2068–78.

Hermans, H., Kempen, H., and van Loon, R. 1992. The dialogical self: Beyond individualism and rationalism. *American Psychologist* 47, 23–34.

Hoffman, M. L. 1981. Is altruism part of human nature? *Journal of Personality and Social Psychology* 40, 121–37.

1983. Affective and cognitive processes in moral internalization. In E. Higgins, A. Ruble, and W. Hartup, eds., *Social cognition and social development: A sociocultural perspective,* pp. 236–74. Cambridge: Cambridge University Press.

Hollos, M., P. Leis, and E. Turiel. 1986. Social reasoning in Ijo children and adolescents in Nigerian communities. *Journal of Cross-Cultural Psychology* 17, 352–76.

Illich, I. 1971. *Deschooling society.* New York: Harper & Row.

Izard, C. 1983. Emotion-cognition relationships and human development. In C. Izard, J. Kagan, and R. Zajonc, eds., *Emotions, cognition, and, behavior,* pp. 17–37. Cambridge: Cambridge University Press.

1986. Approaches to developmental research on emotion-cognition relationships. In D. Bearison and H. Zimiles, eds., *Thought and emotion: Developmental perspectives,* pp. 21–38. Hillsdale, NJ: Erlbaum.

Jackson, P. W., R. Boostrom, and D. T. Hansen. 1993. *The moral life of schools.* San Francisco: Jossey-Bass.

James, W. (1899. *The principles of psychology.* London: Macmillan.

Johnson, D. W., R. Johnson, B. Dudley, M. Ward, and D. Magnuson. 1995. The impact of peer mediation training on the management of school and home conflicts. *American Educational Research Journal,* 32, 829–44.

Jung, M. K., and E. Turiel. 1994. *Korean children's concepts of adult and peer authority.* Unpublished manuscript, Graduate School of Education, University of California, Berkeley.

Kant, I. 1785/1959. *Foundations of the metaphysics of morals.* Trans. L. W. Beck. Indianapolis, IN: Bobbs-Merrill.

Katz, L. F., and J. M. Gottman. 1991. Marital discord and child outcomes: A social psychophysiological approach. In J. Garber and K. Dodge, eds., *The development of emotion regulation and dysregulation,* pp. 129–53. New York: Cambridge University Press.

Kernberg, O. F. 1975. *Borderline conditions and pathological narcissism.* New York: J. Aronson.

Killen, M. 1989. Context, conflict and coordination in early social development. In L. T. Wnegar, ed., *Social interaction and the development of children's understanding,* pp. 114–36. Norwood, NJ: Ablex.

1991. Social and moral development in early childhood. In W. Kurtines and J.

Gewirtz, eds., *Handbook of moral behavior and development*. Vol. 2, *Research*, pp. 115–38). Hillsdale, NJ: Erlbaum.

Killen, M., and J. Smetana. 1999. Social interactions in preschool classroooms and the development of young children's conceptions of the personal. *Child development* 70, 486–501.

Killen, M., and E. Turiel. 1991. Conflict resolution in preschool social interactions. *Early Education and Development* 2, 240–55.

Killen, M., S. Breton, H. Ferguson, and K. Handler. 1994. Preschoolers' evaluations of teacher methods of intervention in social transgressions. *Merrill-Palmer Quarterly* 40, 399–416.

Killen, M., M. Leviton, and J. Cahill, 1991. Adolescent reasoning about drug use. *Journal of Adolescent Research*. 6, 336–356.

Kirkpatrick, W. 1992. *Why Johnny can't tell right from wrong*. New York: Simon and Schuster.

Kochanska, K. 1993. Toward a synthesis of parental socialization and child temperment in early development of conscience. *Child Development* 64, 325–47.

Kohlberg, L. 1958. *The development of modes of moral thinking and choice in the years ten to sixteen*. Unpublished Ph.D. diss., University of Chicago.

———. 1963. The development of children's orientations toward a moral order. *Vita Humana* 6, 11–33.

———. 1966. A cognitive-developmental analysis of children's sex role concepts and attitudes. In E. Maccoby, ed. *The development of sex differences*. Stanford, CA: Stanford University Press.

———. 1984. *Essays on moral development*. Vol 2, *The psychology of moral development*. San Francisco: Harper & Row.

Kohn, A. February, 1997. How not to teach values. *Phi Delta Kappan*, 429–39.

Kohut, H. 1978. *The search for the self: Selected writings 1950–1978*. New York: International University Press.

Kuczinski, L., G. Kochanska, M. Radke-Yarrow, and O. Girnius Brown. 1987. A developmental interpretation of young children's non-compliance. *Developmental Psychology* 23, 799–806.

Lapsley, D. 1982. *The development of retributive justice in children*. Unpublished Ph.D. diss., University of Wisconsin, Madison.

———. 1996. *Moral psychology*. Boulder, CO: Westview.

Lau, S., and C. C. Ping. 1987. Relations between Chinese adolescents' perceptions of parental control and organization and their perception of parental warmth. *Developmental Psychology* 23, 726–29.

Laupa, M., and E. Turiel. 1986. Children's conceptions of adult and peer authority. *Child Development* 57, 405–12.

———. 1993. Children's conceptions of authority and social context. *Journal of Educational Psychology* 85, 191–7.

Lee, P. C., C. Statuto, and G. Vedar-Voivodas. 1983. Elementary school children's perceptions of their actual and ideal school experience: A developmental study. *Journal of Educational Psychology* 75, 838–47.

Leming, J. 1999. *The impact of integrating a structured ethical reflection program into high school service-learning experiences of students' sociomoral development*. Unpublished manuscript, Southern Illinois University, Carbondale, IL.

Levy, R. I. 1984. Emotion, knowing, and culture. In R. Shweder and R. A. Levine, eds., *Culture theory: Essays on mind, self, and emotion*, pp. 214–37. Cambridge: Cambridge University Press.

Lickona, T. 1991. *Educating for character: How our schools can teach respect and responsibility.* New York: Bantam Books.

Lincoln, A. 1989. First Innaugural Address, March 4, 1861. In Don E. Fehrenbacker, ed., *Abraham Lincoln: Speeches and Writings 1859–1865*, pp. 215–24. New York: Library of America.

Lind, G. April, 1996. *Which educational environment promotes self-sustaining democratic development?* Paper presented at the annual meeting of the American Educational Research Association, New York.

Lind, G., Hartman, H., and R. Wakenhut. (1985). *Moral development and the social environment.* Chicago: Precedent Press.

Lopez, B. H. 1978. *Of wolves and men.* New York: Scribner's Publishing.

Lorenz, K. 1960. *So kam der mensch auf den hund.* Vienna: Borotha-Schoeler.

Ludemann, P. 1991. Generalized discrimination of positive facial expressions by 7-month old infants. *Child Development* 62, 55–67.

Lyman, I. 1998. *Home schooling. Back to the future?* (Policy Analysis no. 294). Washington, DC: Cato Institute.

MacIntyre, A. 1984. *After virtue.* 2d. ed. Notre Dame, IN: University of Notre Dame Press.

Madden, T. 1992. *Cultural factors and assumptions in social reasoning in India.* Unpublished Ph.D. diss., University of California, Berkeley.

Mahler, M. S. 1979. *The selected papers of Margaret S. Mahler.* Vols. 1 and 2. New York: J. Aronson.

Mancuso, J., and T. Sarbin. 1998. The narrative construction of emotional life: Developmental aspects. In M. Mascolo and S. Griffin, eds., *What develops in emotional life?*, pp. 297–316. New York: Plenum.

Marsh, H. W., I. D. Smith, and J. Barnes. 1985. Multidimensional self-concepts: Relation with sex and academic achievement. *Journal of Educational Psychology* 77, 581–96.

Martin, G. B., and R. D. Clark. 1982. Distress crying in newborns: Species and peer specificity. *Developmental Psychology* 18, 3–9.

Masterson, J. 1981. *The narcissistic and borderline disorders.* New York: Brunner/Mazel.

Metz, M. H. March, 1978. *Clashes in the classroom: The importance of norms for authority.* Paper presented at the annual meeting of the American Educational Research Association, Toronto.

Milgram, S. 1963. Behavioral study of obedience. *Journal of Abnormal and Social Psychology* 67, 371–8.

Miller, J., and D. M. Bersoff. 1992. Culture and moral judgment: How are conflicts between justice and interpersonal responsibilities resolved? *Journal of Personality and Social Psychology*, 62, 541–54.

Mischel, W. 1973. Toward a cognitive social-learning reconceptualization of personality. *Psychological Review* 80, 250–83.

——— 1990. Personality dispositions revisted and revised: A view after three decades. In L. A. Pervin, ed. *Handbook of personality theory and research*, pp. 11–134. New York: Guilford.

Moore, G. E. 1903. *Principia ethica.* Cambridge: Cambridge University Press.

Morris, D. 1969. *The naked ape.* New York: Dell.

——. 1994. *The human animal: A personal view of the human species.* New York: Crown.

Mowrey, J. 1993. *Way past cool.* New York: HarperCollins.

Much, N., and R. A. Shweder. 1978. Speaking of rules: The analysis of culture in breach. In W. Damon, ed., *New directions for child development.* Vol. 2, *Moral development.* San Francisco: Jossey-Bass.

Mullener, N., and J. D. Laird. 1971. Some developmental changes in the organization of self evaluation. *Developmental Psychology* 5, 233–6.

Nelson, C. 1987. The recognition of facial expressions in the first two years of life: Mechanisms of development. *Child Development* 58, 889–909.

Nicholls, J. 1984. Achievement motivation: Conceptions of ability, subjective experience, task choice, and performance. *Psychological Review* 9, 328–46.

——. 1989. *The competitive ethos and democratic education.* Cambridge, MA: Harvard University Press.

Nicholls, J., and J. Miller, 1984. Reasoning about the ability of self and others: A developmental study. *Child Development* 55, 1990–9.

Nicholls, J., and T. Thorkildsen. 1988. Children's distinctions among matters of intellectual convention, logic, and fact. *Child Development* 59, 939–49.

Nielsen, K. 1973. *Ethics without God.* Buffalo, NY: Prometheus.

Nisan, M. 1987. Moral norms and social conventions: A cross-cultural comparison. *Developmental Psychology* 23, 719–25.

Noam, G. 1993. "Normative vulnerabilities" of self and their transformations in moral action. In G. Noam eds., *The moral self,* pp. 209–38. Cambridge, MA: MIT Press.

Nucci, L. 1977. *Social development: Personal, conventional, and moral concepts.* Ph.D. diss., University of California, Santa Cruz.

——. 1981. Conceptions of personal issues: A domain distinct from moral or societal concepts. *Child Development* 52, 114–21.

——. 1982. Conceptual development in the moral and coventional domains: Implications for values education. *Reveiew of Educational Research* 52, 93–123.

——. 1984. Evaluating teachers as social agents: Students' ratings of domain appropriate and domain-inappropriate teacher responses to transgressions. *American Educational Research Journal* 21, 367–78.

——. 1985. Children's conceptions of morality, societal convention, and religious prescription. In C. Harding, ed., *Moral dilemmas: Philosophical and psychological issues in the development of moral reasoning,* pp. 115–36. Chicago: Precedent Press.

——. 1989. Knowledge of the learner: The development of children's concepts of self, morality, and societal convention. In M. Reynolds, ed., *Knowledge base for beginning teachers,* pp. 117–27. Oxford: Pergamon Press.

——. 1996. Morality and the personal sphere of actions. In E. Reed, E. Turiel, and T. Brown, eds., *Values and knowledge,* pp. 41–60. Hillsdale, NJ: Lawrence Erlbaum.

——. 2000. Kultur, kontext unddie psychologischen quellen des begrifs der menschenrechte (Culture, context, and the psychological sources of human rights concepts). In W. Edelstein and G. Nunner-Winkler, eds., *Moral im sozialen kontext* (Morality in social context), pp. 442–80. Frankfurt am Main: Suhrkamp.

Nucci, L., and P. Charlier. April, 1983. *Cognitive development in the societal domain and comprehension of social studies content.* Paper presented at the annual meeting of the American Educational Research Association, Montreal.

Nucci, L. C. Camino, and C. Sapiro. 1996. Social class effects on northeastern Brazilian children's conceptions of areas of personal choice and social regulation. *Child Development* 67, 1223–42.

Nucci, L. and J. Y. Lee. 1993. Morality and personal autonomy. In G. Noam and T. Wren, eds. *The moral self*, pp. 123–48. Cambridge, MA: MIT press.

Nucci, L., and C. Milnitsky Sapiro. 1995. *The impact of region and social class on Brazilian mothers' conceptions of children's areas of personal choice.* Unpublished manuscript, University of Illinois at Chicago.

Nucci, L., and M. S. Nucci. 1982a. Children's responses to moral and social-conventional transgressions in free-play settings. *Child Development* 53, 1337–42.

——— 1982b. Children's social interactions in the context of moral and conventional transgressions. *Child Development* 53, 403–12.

Nucci, L., and J. Smetana. 1996. Mothers' concepts of young children's areas of personal freedom. *Child Development* 67, 1870–86.

Nucci, L., and E. Turiel. 1978. Social interactions and the development of social concepts in pre-school children. *Child Development* 49, 400–7.

——— 1993. God's word, religious rules, and their relation to Christian and Jewish children's concepts of morality. *Child Development* 64, 1475–91.

Nucci, L. and E. Weber. 1991. Research on classroom applications of the domain approach to values education. In W. Kurtines and J. Gewirtz, eds., *Handbook of moral behavior and development*. Vol. 3, *Applications*, pp. 251–266. Hillsdale, NJ: Erlbaum.

——— 1995. Social interactions in the home and the development of young children's conceptions within the personal domain. *Child Development* 66, 1438–52.

Nucci, L., N. Guerra, and J. Y. Lee. 1991. Adolescent judgments of the personal, prudential, and normative aspects of drug usage. *Developmental Psychology* 27, 841–8.

Nucci, L., Y. Hasebe, and M. Nucci. April, 1999. *Parental intrusion into the personal domain and adolescent psychopathology: A cross-national study [in] the U.S. and Japan.* Paper presented at the biennial meeting of the Society for Research in Child Development, Albuquerque, NM.

Nucci, L., E. Turiel, and G. Encarnacion-Gawrych. 1983. Children's social interactions and social concepts in the Virgin Islands. *Journal of Cross-Cultural Psychology* 14, 469–87.

Nunner-Winkler, G. 1984. Two moralities? A critical discussion of an ethic of care and responsibility versus an ethic of rights and justice. In W. M. Kurtines and J. Gewirtz, eds., *Morality, moral behavior, and development*, pp. 348–64. New York: Wiley.

Nunner-Winkler, G., and B. Sodian. 1988. Children's understanding of moral emotions. *Child Development* 59, 1323–38.

Nussbaum, M. 2000. Emotions and social norms. In L. Nucci, G. Saxe, and E. Turiel, eds., *Culture, thought, and development.* Mahwah, NJ: Erlbaum.

Ogbu, J. 1987. Variability in minority school performance: A problem in search of an explanation. *Anthropology and Education Quarterly* 18, 312–34.

Okin, S. 1996. The gendered family and the development of a sense of justice. In E. Reed, E. Turiel, and T. Brown, eds., *Values and knowledge* pp. 61–74. Hillsdale, NJ.: Lawrence Erlbaum.

Oser, F. 1986. Moral education and values education: The discourse perspective. In M. C. Wittrock, ed., *Handbook of research on teaching.* 3d ed. New York: Macmillan.

Piaget, J. 1932. *The moral judgment of the child.* New York: Free Press.

1962. Will and action. *Bulletin of the Menninger Clinic* 26, 138–45.

1980. *Adaptation and intelligence.* Chicago: University of Chicago Press.

1981. *Intelligence and affectivity: Their relationship during child development.* Trans. and ed. T. Brown and C. Kaegi. Palo Alto, CA: Annual Reviews Monographs.

1985. *The equilibration of cognitive structures.* Chicago: University of Chicago Press.

Plato 1956. *Great dialogues of Plato.* Trans. W. H. D. Rouse. New York: The New American Library.

Plutchik, R. 1987. Evolutionary bases of empathy. In N. Eisenberg and J. Strayer, eds., *Empathy and its development,* pp. 38–46. Cambridge: Cambridge University Press.

Power, C., and V. T. Khmelkov. 1998. *Character development and self-esteem: Psychological foundations and educational implications.* Unpublished manuscript, Liberal Studies, University of Notre Dame, Notre Dame, IN.

Power, C., A. Higgins, and L. Kohlberg. 1989a. *Lawrence Kohlberg's approach to moral education.* New York: Columbia University Press.

1989b. The habit of the common life: Building character through democratic community schools. In L. Nucci, ed. *Moral development and character education: A dialogue,* pp. 125–44. Berkeley, CA: McCutchan.

Pugh, G. E. 1977. *The biological origin of human values.* New York: Basic Books.

Rest, J. 1979. *Revised manual for the Defining Issues Test.* Minneapolis: Moral Research Projects.

Rest, J., D. Narvaez, M. Bebeau, and S. Thoma. 1999. *Postconventional moral thinking: A neo-Kohlbergian approach.* Mahwah: NJ, Erlbaum.

Rohner, R. P., and S. M. Pettengill. 1985. Perceived parental acceptance and rejection and parental control among Korean adolescents. *Child Development* 56, 524–8.

Rosenberg, M. 1965. Society and the adolescent self-image. Princeton, NJ: Princeton University Press.

Ross, H. 1996. Negotiating principles of entitlement in sibling property disputes. *Developmental Psychology* 32, 90–101.

Ross, L., and R. M. Nisbett. 1991. *The person and the situation: Perspectives on social psychology.* Philadelphia: Temple University Press.

Ryan, K. 1989. In defense of character education. In L. Nucci, ed., *Moral development and character education: A dialogue,* pp. 3–17. Berkeley, CA: McCutchan.

1996. Character education in the United States: A status report. *Journal for a Just and Caring Education* 2, 75–84.

Ryan, K., and T. Lickona. 1992. *Character development in schools and beyond.* 2d ed. Washington, DC: InterUniversity Council.

Ryan, K., and G. F. McLean. eds. 1987. *Character development in schools and beyond.* New York: Praeger.

Sampson, E. E. 1977. Psychology and the American ideal. *Journal of Personality and Social Psychology* 35, 767–82.

1985. The decentralization of identity: Toward a revised concept of personal and social order. *American Psychologist* 40, 1203–12.

Sarbin, T. 1986. *Narrative psychology: The storied nature of human conduct.* New York: Praeger.

1995. Emotional life, rhetoric, and roles. *Journal of Narrative and Personal History* 5, 213–20.

Sarbin, T., and V. L. Allen. 1968. Role theory. In G. Lindsey and E. Aronson, eds., *Handboook of social psychology.* Vol. 1, pp. 590–660. Boston: Addison Wesley.

Schlegel, A., and H. Barry. 1991. *Adolescence: An anthropological inquiry.* New York: Free Press.

Schunk, D. 1989. Social cognitive theory and self-regulated learning. In B. J. Zimmerman and D. H. Schunk, eds. *Self-regulated learning and academic achievement: Theory, research and practice.* New York: Springer-Verlag.

Searle, J. R. 1969. *Speech acts.* London: Cambridge University Press.

Sedlak, A., and M. D. Walton. 1982. Sequencing in social repair: A Markov grammar of children's discourse about transgressions. *Developmental Review* 2, 305–29.

Selman, R. 1980. *The growth of interpersonal understanding: Developmental and clinical analyses.* New York: Academic Press.

Shields, D. L., and B. J. Bredemeier. 1995. *Character development and physical activity.* Champaign, IL: Human Kinetics.

Shweder, R. A. 1979a. Rethinking culture and personality theory. Part 1. A critical examination of two classical postulates. *Ethos* 7, 255–78.

1979b. Rethinking culture and personality theory. Part 2: A critical examination of two classical postulates. *Ethos* 7, 279–311.

1990. In defense of moral realism: Reply to Gabennesch. *Child Development* 61, 2060–7.

Shweder, R. A., and E. J. Bourne. 1984. Does the concept of the person vary cross-culturally? In R. A. Shweder and R. A. Levine, eds., *Culture Theory: Essays on mind, self, and emotion,* pp. 158–99. New York: Cambridge University Press.

Shweder, R. A., and R. Levine. eds. 1984. *Culture theory: Essays on mind, self, and emotion.* Cambridge: Cambridge University Press.

Shweder, R, M. Mahapatra, and J. Miller. 1987. Culture and moral development. In J. Kagan and S. Lamb eds., *The emergence of morality in young children.* pp. 1–82. Chicago: University of Chicago Press.

Shweder, R. A., E. Turiel, and N. Much. 1981. The moral intutions of the child: In J. H. Flavell and L. Ross, eds., *Social cognitive development: Frontiers and possible futures,* pp. 288–305. New York: Cambridge University Press.

Simon, S., L. Howe, and H. Kirschenbaum. 1972. *Values clarification*. New York: Hart.

Skinner, B. F. 1948. *Walden two*. New York: Macmillan.

——— 1953. *Science and human behavior*. New York: Macmillan.

——— 1971. *Beyond freedom and dignity*. New York: Knopf.

Smetana, J. 1982. *Concepts of self and morality: Women's reasoning about abortion*. New York: Praeger.

——— 1989a. Toddler's social interactions in the context of moral and conventional transgressions in the home. *Developmental Psychology* 25, 499–508.

——— 1989b. Adolescents' and parents' reasoning about actual family conflict. *Child Development* 60, 1052–67.

——— 1995a. Morality in context: Abstractions, ambiguities, and applications. In *Annals of Child Development* Vol. 10, pp. 83–130.

——— 1995b. Conflict and coordination in adolescent-parent relationships. In S. Shulman, ed., *Close relationships and socioemotional development*, pp.155–84). Norwood, NJ: Ablex.

——— 1996. Adolescent–parent conflict: Implications for adaptive and maladaptive development. In D. Cicchetti and S. L. Toth, eds., *Rochester Symposium on Developmental Psychopathology*. Vol. 7, *Adolescence opportunities and challenges*, pp. 1–46. Rochester NY: University of Rochester Press.

Smetana, J., and P. Asquith. 1994. Adolescents' and parents' conceptions of parental and adolescent autonomy. *Child Development* 65, 1147–62.

Smetana, J., and B. Bitz. 1996. Adolescents' conceptions of teachers' authority and their relations to rule violations in school. *Child Development* 67, 1153–72.

Smetana, J., J. L. Braeges, and J. Yau. 1991. Doing what you say and saying what you do: Reasoning about adolescent–parent conflict in inteviews and interactions. *Journal of Adolescent Research* 6, 276–95.

Smetana, J., D. Bridgeman, and E. Turiel. 1983. Differentiation of domains and prosocial behavior. In D. Bridgeman, ed., *The nature of prosocial development: Interdisciplinary theories and strategies*, pp. 163–83. New York: Academic Press.

Smetana, J., M. Killen, and E. Turiel. 1991. Children's reasoning about interpersonal and moral conflicts. *Child Development* 62, 629–44.

Smetana, J., J. Yau, A. Restropo, and J. Breages. 1991. Adolescent–parent conflict in married and divorced families. *Developmental Psychology* 27, 1000–10.

Snarey, J. 1985. Cross-cultural universality of social-moral development: A critical review of Kohlbergian research. *Psychological Bulletin* 97, 202–32.

Solomon, R. C. 1984. Getting angry: The Jamesian theory of emotion in anthropology. In R. Shweder, and R. A. Levine, eds., *Culture theory: Essays on mind, self, and emotion*, pp. 238–56. Cambridge: Cambridge University Press.

Song, M. J., J. Smetana, and S. Y. Kim. 1987. Korean children's conceptions of moral and conventional transgressions. *Developmental Psychology* 23, 577–82.

Spiro, M. 1993. Is the Western conception of the self "peculiar" within the context of the world's cultures? *Ethos* 21, 107–53.

Staub, E. 1971. Helping a person in distress: The influence of implicit and explicit "rules" of conduct on children and adults. *Journal of Personality and Social Psychology* 17, 137–44.

Stern, D. 1985. *The interpersonal world of the infant: A view from psychoanalysis and developmental psychology*. New York: Basic Books.

Sternberg, C., J. Campos, and R. Emde. 1983. The facial expression of anger in seven month old infants. *Child Development* 54, 178–84.

Stipek, D., J. H. Gralinski, and C. B. Kopp. 1990. Self-concept development in the toddler years. *Developmental Psychology* 26, 972–7.

Subbotsky, E. V. 1995. The development of pragmatic and non-pragmatic motivation. *Human Development* 38, 217–34.

Thorkildsen, T. A. 1989. Justice in the classroom: The student's view. *Child Development* 60, 323–34.

———. 2000. The way tests teach: Children's theories of how much testing is fair in school. In M. Leicester, C. Modgil, and S. Modgil, eds., Education, culture and values volume III: Classroom issues: Practice, pedagogy and curriculum, pp. 61–79. London: Falmer Press.

Tisak, M. 1986. Child's conception of parental authority. *Child Development* 57, 166–76.

———. 1995. Domains of social reasoning and beyond. *Annals of Child Development* 11, 95–130.

Tisak, M., and J. Tisak. 1990. Children's conceptions of parental authority, friendship, and sibling relations. *Merrill-Palmer Quarterly* 36, 347–67.

Tisak, M., and E. Turiel. 1984. Children's conceptions of moral and prudential rules. *Child Development* 55, 1030–9.

———. 1988. Variations in seriousness of transgressions and children's moral and conventional concepts. *Developmental Psychology* 24, 352–7.

Triandis, H., R. Bontempo, M. Villareal, M. Asai, and N. Lucca. 1988. Individualism and collectivism: Cross cultural perspectives on self-ingroup relationships. *Journal of Personality and Social Psychology* 59, 1006–20.

Triandis, H. C. 1988. Collectivism vs. individualism: A reconceptualization of a basic concept in cross-cultural social psychology. In C. Bagley and G. K. Verma, eds., *Personality cognition and values: Cross-cultural perspectives of childhood and adolescence*. London: Macmillan.

———. 1989. Cross-cultural studies of individualism and collectivism. *Nebraska Symposium on Motivation* 37, 41–133.

Tugendhat, E. 1993. The role of identity in the constitution of morality. In G. Noam and T. Wren, eds., *The moral self*, pp. 3–15. Cambridge, MA: MIT Press.

Turiel, E. 1975. The development of social concepts: Mores, customs, and conventions. In D. J. DePalma and J. M. Foley, eds., *Moral development: Current theory and research*, pp. 7–38. Hillsdale, NJ: Erlbaum.

———. 1978. The development of concepts of social structure: Social convention. In Joseph Glick and K. Alison Clarke-Stewart, eds., *The development of social understanding*, pp. 25–108. New York: Gardner Press.

———. 1983. *The development of social knowledge: Morality and convention*. Cambridge: Cambridge University Press.

———. 1994. Morality, authoritarianism, and personal agency in cultural contexts. In

R. J. Sternberg and P. Ruzgis, eds., *Intelligence and personality*, pp. 271–99. Cambridge: Cambridge University Press.

1996. Equality and hierarchy: Conflict in values. In E. Reed, E. Turiel, and T. Brown, eds., *Values and knowledge*, pp. 41–60. Hillsdale, NJ.: Lawrence Erlbaum.

1998a. The development of morality. In W. Damon, ed., *Handbook of child psychology.* 5th ed., Vol. 3. N. Eisenberg, ed., *Social, emotional, and personality development*, pp. 863–932. New York: Academic Press.

1998b. Notes from the underground: Culture, conflict and subversion. In J. Langer and M. Killen, eds., *Piaget, evolution, and development*, pp. 271–96. Mahwah, NJ: Lawrence Erlbaum.

2000. Unbehagen und behagen bei kulturellen praktiken: Es hangt alles davon ab, auf welcher seite man steht (Cultural practices as "funny things." It depends on where you sit). In W. Edelstein and G. Nunner-Winkler, eds., *Moral im sozialen kontext* (Morality in social context), pp. 261–98. Frankfurt am Main: Suhrkamp.

Turiel, E. and P. Davidson. 1986. Heterogeneity, inconsistency, and asynchrony in the development of cognitive structures. In Iris Levin, ed., *Stage and structure: Reopening the debate*, pp. 106–43. Norwood, NJ: Ablex.

Turiel, E., C. Hildebrandt, and C. Wainryb. 1991. Judging social issues: Difficulties, inconsistencies and consistencies. *Monographs for the Society for Research in Child Development* 56 (Serial no. 224).

Turiel, E., M. Killen, and C. Helwig. 1987. Morality: Its structure, functions, and vagaries. In Jerome Kagan and Sharon Lamb, eds., *The emergence of morality in young children*, pp. 155–243. Chicago: University of Chicago Press.

Turiel, E., and J. Smetana. 1984. Social knowledge and social action. The coordination of domains. In W. M. Kurtines and J. L. Gewirtz, eds., *Morality, moral behavior, and moral development: Basic issues in theory and research*, pp. 261–82. New York: Wiley.

Veldman, D., and R. Peck. 1963. Student–teacher characteristics from the pupil's viewpoint. *Journal of Educational Psychology* 54, 346–55.

Waal, F. B. M., de. 1996. *Good natured: The origins of right and wrong in humans and other animals*. Cambridge, MA: Harvard University Press.

Wainryb, C. 1991. Understanding differences in moral judgments: The role of informational assumptions. *Child Development* 62, 840–51.

Wainryb, C. and E. Turiel. 1994. Dominance, subordination, and concepts of personal entitlements in cultural contexts. *Child Development* 65, 1701–1722.

Walker, L. October, 1998. *The perceived personality of moral exemplars*. Paper presented at the annual meeting of the Association for Moral Education, Dartmouth College, Hanover, NH.

Weston, D., and E. Turiel. 1980. Act–rule relations: Children's concepts of soial rules. *Developmental Psychology* 16, 417–24.

Willis, P. 1977. *Learning to labor*. Lexington, MA: D. C. Heath.

Wilson, J. Q. 1993. *The moral sense*. New York: The Free Press.

Wright, R. 1994. *The moral animal: The new science of evolutionary psychology*. New York: Pantheon.

Wynne, E. 1986. The great tradition in education: Transmitting moral values. *Educational Leadership* 43, 4–9.

1989. Transmitting traditional values in contemporary schools. In L. Nucci, ed., *Moral development and character education: A dialogue,* pp. 19–36. Berkeley, CA: McCutchan.

Wynne, E., and K. Ryan. 1993. *Reclaiming our schools: A handbook on teaching character, academics, and discipline.* New York: Macmillan Publishing Company.

Yates, M., and J. Youniss. 1998. Community service and political identity development in adolescence. *Journal of Social Issues* 54, 495–512.

Yau, J., and J. G. Smetana. 1995. *Adolescent–parent conflict among Chinese adolescents in Hong Kong.* Unpublished manuscript, University of Hong Kong.

Youniss, J. 1980. *Parents and peers in social development.* Chicago: University of Chicago Press.

Zahn-Waxler, C., and K. Kochanska. 1990. The origins of guilt. In R. Thompson, ed., *Nebraska Symposium on Motivation, 1988.* Vol. 36, *Socioemotional development,* pp. 183–258. Lincoln: University of Nebraska Press.

Zahn-Waxler, C., M. Radke-Yarrow, and R. King. 1979. Child rearing and children's prosocial initiations toward victims of distress. *Child Development* 50, 319–30.

Zajonc, R. 1984. On the primacy of affect. *American Psychologist* 39.

Index of Names

Abu-Lughod, L. 98, 99
Allen, V. L. 126
Anderson,V. 151
Angelou, M. 186, 187
Aristotle. 127
Aronson, E. 150, 177
Arsenio, W. 112–114, 118, 119, 136, 143,
   145, 148, 197
Asquith, P. 68–70
Astor, R. 122, 213
Atkins, R. 122, 213
Augustine 52

Baldwin, J. M. 54
Bandura, A. 81, 206, 210
Barden, R. 117
Barker, B. 213
Barnard, C. 143
Barnes, J. 130
Barrett, K. 111
Barry, H. 70
Bartz, K. W. 62
Battistich, V. 127, 173, 197, 198, 201, 213
Baumrind, D. 57, 62, 63, 172
Bearison, D. 108
Bellah, R. 53
Bennett, W. 53, 74
Benninga, J. 174
Berkowitz, M. 174, 175, 193
Berndt, T. 193
Bersoff, D. 53
Bitz, B. 164, 165
Black, A. 11, 86
Blasi, G. 128, 129, 131–133
Blatt, M. 174
Blumenfeld, P. C. 144, 167
Boostrom, R. 142
Borowitz, E. 28
Bourne, E. J. 55
Breages, J. 11, 68, 69

Bredemeier, B. J. 150
Bridgeman, D. 54
Brehm, J. W. 57, 60
Brehm, S. S. 57, 60
Bronte, C. 20
Broughton, J. 129, 174, 203
Brown, T. 108, 109
Buddin, N. 118
Buss, D. M. 110
Byrne, B. 130

Cahill, J. 193
Camino, C. 64
Campos, J. 111
Cassel, P. 201
Chao, R. K. 62
Character Counts Coalition 150
Charlier, P. 182
Clark, R. D. 110, 111
Cocking, R. R. 55
Colby, A. 80, 81, 90, 92, 93, 128
Coopersmith, S. 130
Corsaro, W. 18, 159
Crittenden, P. 21
Crockenberg, S. 57
Cushman, P. 55

Damhuis, I. 115
Damon, W. 17, 54, 73, 87, 88, 91, 128, 129,
   134, 156
Danon, H. 32
Darwin, C. 110
Davidson, P. 11, 86, 87
Deci, E. 196–199, 205
Deutsch, M. 157
DeVries, R. 81, 154, 160, 163, 173, 197, 198,
   200, 201
Dias, M. G. 12
Dodsworth-Rugani, K. 144
Dunn, J. 16

237

Dreikurs, R. 198, 201
Durkheim, E. 74, 142
Dworkin, R. 6, 73

Eccles, J. 213
Eckman, P. 111
Eibl-Eibesfeld, I. 111
Eisenberg, N. 87, 115, 119
Emde, R. 111, 116
Encarnacion-Gawrych, G. 8, 16, 18, 147, 159
Entwisle, D. R. 130
Erikson, E. 54, 56
Etzioni, A. 53

Fegley, S. 134, 135, 213
Ferguson, T. J. 115
Fivush, R. 121
Ford, D. 213
Frankena, W. K. 6
Freud, A. 206
Freud, S. 52

Gates Jr., H. L. 180
Geertz, C. 98, 100
Geiger, K. 165
Gesell, A. 56
Gewirth, A. 6, 73
Gibbs, J. 174
Gilligan, C. 6, 121, 122
Glodis, K. 128, 131, 132
Goncu, A. 159
Gottman, J. M. 116
Gralinski, H. 16, 18, 57
Greenfield, P. M. 55
Grunwald, B. 198
Guerra, N. 54, 70, 120, 193

Habermas, J. 6, 93, 95, 158, 174, 177
Haidt, J. 12, 115
Hamilton, V. L. 144
Hansen, D. T. 142
Harrington, M. 173
Hart, D. 54, 73, 118, 129, 134, 135, 213
Harter, S. 118, 129, 130, 198, 203
Hartman, H. 93
Hartshorne, H. 125–127
Hasebe, Y. 71
Helwig, C. 8
Hermans, H. 55
Higgins, A. 81, 125, 151, 158, 177
Hildebrandt, C. 104
Hoffman, M. L. 115, 116, 136
Hollos, M. 12, 95
Howe, L. 20

Illich, I. 74
Izard, C. 111

Jackson, P. W. 142, 143, 168
James, W. 54
Johnson, D. W. 157
Johnson, R. 157
Jung, M. K. 63

Kant, I. 52
Katz, L. F. 116
Kempen, H. 55
Kernberg, O. F. 55
Killen, M. 18, 68, 146, 153, 157, 159, 193
King, R. 116
Kirkpatrick, W. 53
Kirschenbaum, H. 20
Khmelkov, V. T. 127, 128, 131, 133–135, 203
Kochanska, K. 116, 136
Kohlberg, L. 8, 78, 79, 81, 82, 86–93, 125, 127, 151, 158, 174, 177, 207
Kohn, A. 124, 127, 199
Kohut, H. 54, 55
Koller, S. H. 12
Kopp, C. 16, 18, 57
Kramer, R. 118
Kuczinski, L. 60

Laird, J. D. 130
Lapsley, D. 78, 89, 91, 93, 126
Lau, S. 63
Laupa, M. 143
Lee, J. Y. 54, 70, 134, 193
Lee, P. C. 143
Leming, J. 206, 214
Levine, E. S. 62
Leviton, M. 193
Levy, R. I. 121
Lickona, T. 125, 127
Lincoln, A. 119
Lind, G. 93, 158
Litman, C. 57
Lopez, B. H. 110
Lorenz, K. 110
Lover, A. 112, 118, 119, 136, 148, 197
Ludemann, P. 111
Lyman, I. 21

MacIntyre, A. 120
Madden, T. 11
Mahapatra, M. 53
Mahler, M. S. 54–56
Mancuso, J. 121
Marsh, H. W . 130
Martin, G. B. 111
Masterson, J. 55
May, M. A. 125–127
Mckay, N. Y. 180
Metz, M. H. 143
Milgram, S. 96
Miller, J. 53, 203

Milnitsky Sapiro, C 65, 67.
Mischel, W. 126
Moore, G. E.. 120
Morris, D. 110
Mowrey, J. 209
Much, N. 14, 16
Mullener, N. 130
Munn, P. 16

Nelson, C. 111
Nicholls, J. 144, 149, 179, 198, 199, 203
Nielsen, K. 43
Nisan, M. 13, 95
Nisbett, R. M. 126
Noam, G. 135–137, 197, 212
Nucci, L. 8, 11, 13, 14, 16–18, 21, 26, 55, 57, 59, 61, 64, 65, 67, 70–72, 79, 80, 93, 95, 114, 130, 134, 135, 142, 145–147, 153, 157–159, 161, 162, 170, 182, 193, 203
Nucci, M. S. 14, 17, 18, 71, 147, 153, 157–159, 161, 162
Nunner-Winkler, G. 117, 118, 122
Nussbaum, M. 117, 120, 121

Ogbu, J. 166
Okin, S. 77, 98, 99, 193
Oser, F. 158, 177

Park, K. 193
Patnoe, S. 150, 177
Peck, R. 143
Pepper, F. C. 198
Pettengill, S. M. 62, 63
Piaget, J. 8, 17, 52, 72–74, 76, 82, 87, 108, 109, 119, 153, 174, 200
Ping, C. C. 63
Pintrich, P. R. 144
Plutchik, R. 111
Power, C. 81, 125, 128, 131, 133, 134, 151, 158, 177, 203
Pugh, G. E. 108, 109

Radke-Yarrow, M. 116
Rest, J. 81, 171
Rohner, R. P. 62, 63
Rosenberg, M. 130
Ross, H. 16
Ross, L. 126
Ryan, K. 6, 8, 74, 125, 127, 128

Sampson, E. E. 53, 55
Sapiro, C. 64
Sarbin, T R. 64
Schlegel, A. 70
Schunk, D. 210
Sedlak, A. 14
Searle, J. R. 7
Selman, R. 54

Shields, D. L. 150
Shweder, R. A. 11, 12, 14, 16, 53, 95, 98, 100, 102, 105, 114
Simon, S. 20
Skinner, B. F. 5, 198
Slomkowski, C. 16
Smetana, J. G. 8, 11, 16, 17, 60, 61, 63, 67–71, 77, 159, 164, 165
Smith, I. D. 130
Snarey, J. 93, 95, 96
Sodian, B. 117, 118
Solomon, D. 121
Solomon, R. C. 121
Song, M. J. 12
Spiro, M. 55
Statuto, C. 143
Staub, E. 87
Stegge, H. 115
Stern, D. 55, 56
Sternberg, C. 111
Stipek, D. 57
Subbotsky, E. V. 196

Thorkildsen, T. A. 144, 167
Tisak, J. 193
Tisak, M. 8, 23, 69, 193
Triandis, H. C. 64, 98
Tugendhat, E. 115
Turiel, E. 87–92, 97, 99, 100, 104, 143–147, 165, 171, 191

van Loon, R. 55
Vedar-Voivodas, G. 143
Veldman, D. 143

Wainryb, C. 53, 67, 99, 100, 103, 104, 144
Waal, de F. B. M. 110
Wakenhut, R. 93
Walker, L. 93
Walton, M. D. 14
Weber, E. 16, 57, 59, 61, 79, 93, 145, 170
Weiss, L. 108
Weston, D. 143, 144
Wiggins, G. 121, 122
Willis, P. 166
Wilson, J. Q. 13, 136
Wright, R. 110
Wynne, E. 8, 53, 74, 125, 127, 142, 206

Yates, M. 213
Yau, J. 63, 68, 99
Youniss, J. 153, 213

Zahn-Waxler, C. 116
Zajonc, R. 111
Zan, B. 154, 160, 163, 173, 197, 198, 200, 201
Zimiles, H. 108

Index of Subjects

adolescent-parent conflict 68–72; and culture 70; and family patterns 70–71
aggression: in childhood 119, 120; among urban adolescents 122
anger expressed by parents and teachers: effects on young children 116, 148
Aristotle and virtue, habit, and justice 127
autonomy 52; and the individual 54

Bush, George Sr. 52, 68

character: defined 124; limitations of traditional conceptualization of 125–128
Character Counts Coalition 150; program 199
character education: bandwagon 128; generalists 127; limits of traditional approach to 129
Child Development Project 173, 197, 213
collectivism-individualism dichotomy 52, 53, 64, 72
communicative discourse 174–175, 177
comprehensive high school 150–151
conventions in schools and classrooms: and adolescent students 164–167; and early childhood students 159–160; and middle-childhood students 164
culture: conflicts within 98; and emotion 120–122; gender and rights and duties in relation to 99–101; and morality and convention 94–96; and the personal domain 54, 64–67

Defining Issues Test (DIT) 171
deontic and aretaic judgments 124
developmental discipline: and logical consequences to misbehavior 201; and praise, validating versus controlling 198–200, 203; and responses to positive behaviors 198–200; in support of moral

autonomy 197, 198; and uses of group discussion 201–202
domain appropriate curriculum: and assessment issues 191–192; and controversial issues, approaches to 193–194; and conventions, focusing upon 180–183; constructing lessons within 178–179; core assumptions of 170; and mixed domain issues, focusing upon 186–191; and moral issues, focusing upon 183–186; purposes of 169–170
domain interactions: as domain mixture 77; forms of response to 77–78; as second order moral events 77
drug use and social judgments 70
Druze Arabs and gender in relation to rights and duties among 98–100
Dutch Reform Calvinists 43, 44

emotion: and culture 120–122; and cognition 107–109; displays of in infancy 110–111; evolution of and morality 110–112; and gender 121, 122; as heuristic guide to action 108–109; and moral habits 116; and moral judgment 120; morality and convention in relation to 112–116; and motivation 108
emotional development and morality 118–120
emotivism 120
empathy 111–115
expiatory punishment 200–201
eudaimonia 133
Euthyphro dialogue 43
external rewards and moral motivation 196, 198

factual assumptions and moral judgments 101–104

240

fairness of academic practices, student perceptions of 167
First Class program 166
formalist ethics 6

happy victimizer phenomenon 113, 117–119; and aggressive children 119; and emotional development 119
Hartshorne and May studies of character 125
Hegel 28

Judaism: the enlightenment and 28; and laws of man and laws of God distinction 39; and the orthodox-reform schism 28
Just Community School 151, 158, 194

Kohlberg stages of moral development: A and B types of 81, 90; limitations of 80–82; reconceptualized 82–93

Malcolm X 185
Martin Luther King Jr. 156, 185, 208
Mennonites/Amish 26–27
Meno, The 138
Milgram studies of obedience; and domain overlap 96–97; and moral judgment 96
moral conflict resolution in schools: in adolescence 157–159; in early childhood 152–154; in middle childhood 155–157
moral development, levels of: in adolescence and adulthood 91–93; in early childhood 86–87; in middle-childhood 87–88; in pre-adolescence 89–91
Moral domain: defined 7; and formalist ethics 6
moral education: inherent controversy of 104–105; teacher's role in 105–106
moral self 128, 131–133; in adolescence 134–136; and behavior 134–135; and early childhood classroom practices 197; early childhood antecedents of 133–134; ideal and dreaded forms of 134; resistance to being "good" and formation of 205–206; summary of the development of 137–138
moral self reflection: limitations of 210–211; through classroom activities 211–212; through use of personal journals 211
morality: of care 121; and God's word 42, 46–49; innate sense of 13; and judgment 2–5; and personal freedom 52, 53, 72; traditional view of 8

morality-convention distinction: criteria for 9–10; and culture 11–13; and formalist ethics 9; and social class 13; social interaction origins of 13–18; at young ages 11

NBC News Poll of beliefs of Catholics 23

parenting styles 62; and culture 62–63
personal domain: and adolescent-parent conflict 68–72; and adolescent pathology 71; and culture 54, 64–67; defined 54; and identity and individuality 54; mother-child interactions and 56–61; psychological need for 55, 72, 74; and rights concepts 72–74; and social class 64–67, 70, 71
personality traits, contemporary view of 126
Pope John Paul II 77
prudential issues 69, 70

religion: and the First amendment 20; and home schooling 21; and public schools 20, 21, 51; and separation of church and state 20
religious norms and morality: among Catholics 21–26; among Christians 29–33; among Jews 29–33; and judgments of alterability 30, 31; and judgments of God's word contingency 33; and judgments of universality 31–33
role models: classroom uses for fostering the moral self 207–210; limitations of 207; in literature 207–298

school climate: and competition 150; in early childhood 148–149; in middle childhood 149–150; and size of American high schools 150–151
school rules: and domain appropriate practice 143–148; and the hidden curriculum 142; and the personal domain 164–165; and school culture 141–142; and teacher authority 143–145
self: and culture 55; and the personal domain 55
self concepts: development of 129; and school achievement 130
service learning: features of successful programs 213–214; impact on behavior 213; negative reactions to 206
Seurat, G. 215
Small Schools Workshop 151
social convention: defined 6; and morality 14–17
social hierarchy and morality 97–101

sociomoral discussion: in classrooms 177–178; educational value of 173; exercises for 175–177; and the plus-one assumption 174; transactive form of 174

Socrates 138

Spinoza 28

terrible twos 56

transgressions, moral and conventional: in adolescence 18; and domain appropriate feedback 146–147; in early childhood 16; at home 16; in middle childhood 14, 15, 17; responses by adults 16–18; responses by children 14–16; at school 16, 161–166; in toddlers 16

values clarification 20

will, the "problem of": and disciplinary practices 200; and moral action 119

William James 54